CU00406384

Film Remakes

'In this groundbreaking study, Constantine Verevis explores an aspect of commercial film production interesting to the scholar and movie enthusiast alike: remaking. *Film Remakes* can be profitably viewed from a number of perspectives, and this book provides an intriguing and revealing anatomy of the phenomenon. Verevis writes with verve and insight; an important feature of *Film Remakes* is the series of individual analyses that sparkle with revealing and intelligent comment as they clarify general points about remaking. Though theoretically informed, this book is wonderfully accessible to the general reader.'

R. Barton Palmer,
Calhoun Lemon Professor of Literature at Clemson University

Film Remakes

Constantine Verevis

Edinburgh University Press

© Constantine Verevis, 2006

Edinburgh University Press Ltd
22 George Square, Edinburgh

Typeset in 11/13 Ehrhardt
by Servis Filmsetting Ltd, Manchester, and
printed and bound in Great Britain by
MPG Books Ltd, Bodmin, Cornwall

A CIP record for this book is available from the British Library

ISBN 0 7486 2186 5 (hardback)
ISBN 0 7486 2187 3 (paperback)

The right of Constantine Verevis
to be identified as author of this work
has been asserted in accordance with
the Copyright, Designs and Patents Act 1988.

Contents

Preface

I see an endless film with sequences signed by various authors in a
complex game of quotations, influences, remakes, variations and references.
(Bernardo Bertolucci, in Ungari, 1987)

This book seeks to provide a broad and systematic approach to the phenomenon of cinematic remaking. Drawing upon recent theories of genre
and intertextuality, *Film Remakes* describes remaking as both an elastic
concept and a complex situation, one enabled and limited by the interre-
lated roles and practices of industry, critics and audiences. This approach
to remaking, outlined in the book's introduction, is developed across its
three parts. The first of these, *Remaking as Industrial Category*, deals with
issues of production, including commerce and authors; the second,
Remaking as Textual Category, considers genre, plots and structures; and
the third, *Remaking as Critical Category*, investigates issues of reception,
including audiences and institutions. The film remake emerges from this
discussion as a particular case of repetition, a function of cinematic and
discursive fields that is maintained by historically specific practices, such
as copyright law and authorship, canon formation and media literacy, film
criticism and re-viewing. That is, while *cinematic remaking* belongs to the
entire history of cinema and can refer to any number of technological,
textual and cultural practices, this book contributes to an understanding of
how the *film remake* is maintained as a separate yet connected phenomenon.

Film Remakes seeks to address some of the central critical issues around
the concept of remaking, striving to deliver a broad theoretical approach to
provide both an understanding of the phenomenon of cinematic remaking
and of individual film remakes. This book takes an interest primarily in the
industrial and institutional conditions of remaking in contemporary
Hollywood cinema, and acknowledges that more and different work needs

to be undertaken through comparative studies that reach across other historical moments, national cultures and cross-cultural transactions. Additionally, this book seeks to introduce a wide readership to the concept of cinematic remaking and to the various issues – industrial, textual and critical – attending it. Accordingly, it works to provide an overview of existing approaches, to simplify theoretical concerns and to make its arguments through well-known and readily available film examples. Finally, the ideas presented in *Film Remakes* have been developed in a number of places and with the assistance and support of many people. In particular I would like to thank: Paul Coughlin, Sarah Edwards, John Frow, Matt Holden, Sonya Jeffery, Jane Landman, Julie Palmer, Barton Palmer, Lesley Stern and Deane Williams.

Acknowledgements

Material contributing to this book appeared in earlier versions in the following publications and is reprinted here with the permission of the editors.

1. 'Through the Past Darkly: Noir Remakes of the 1980s', in Alain Silver and James Ursini (eds), *Film Noir Reader 4*. New York: Limelight, 2004, pp. 307–22.
2. 'Remaking Film', *Film Studies*, no. 4 (2004), pp. 87–103.
3. 'Television Features: A Survey', *Metro*, no. 123 (2000), pp. 34–41.
4. 'Re-Viewing Remakes', *Film Criticism*, vol. 21, no. 3 (1997), pp. 1–19.

For Julie, Zoi and Mia
And in memory of Emmanuel and Irene Verevis

Introduction: Remaking Film

This book provides a broad introduction to some of the issues and concerns arising from the concept of film remaking. Although the cinema has been repeating and replaying its own narratives and genres from its very beginnings, film remaking has received little critical attention in the field of cinema studies. What is film remaking? Which films are remakes of other films? How does film remaking differ from other types of repetition, such as quotation, allusion and adaptation? What is the relationship between remakes and other commercial forms such as sequels, cycles and series? How is film remaking different from the cinema's more general ability to repeat and replay the same film over and again through reissue and redistribution? And how does remaking differ from the way every film is 'remade' – dispersed and transformed – in its every new context or *re*-viewing? These are questions that have seldom been asked, let alone satisfactorily answered, in cinema studies.

Recent accounts of cinematic remaking have variously defined film remakes as 'films based on an earlier screenplay',[1] as 'new versions of existing films'[2] and as 'films that to one degree or another *announce* to us that they embrace one or more previous movies'.[3] Although there may be sufficient cultural agreement on the existence and nature of film remakes to allow for a clear understanding – especially in the case of those remakes which carry a pre-sold title *and* repeat readily recognisable narrative units – when considered alongside the broader concept of intertextuality, film remaking can refer to 'the infinite and open-ended possibilities generated by all the discursive practices of a [film] culture'.[4] As David Wills points out, 'what distinguishes the remake is not the fact of its being a repetition, [but] rather the fact of its being a precise institutional form of the structure of repetition, . . . the citationality or iterability, that exists in and for every film'.[5]

As in the case of film genre, a fundamental problem for film remaking has arisen from 'the ever-present desire for a stable and easily identifiable [set of] objects of analysis', and a related attempt to reduce film remaking to a '*corpus* of texts' or set of textual *structures*.[6] Such approaches often succumb to the problems of taxonomism and associated difficulties, such as the exclusion of marginal examples and canonisation of favourites. In addition, these textual accounts of remaking risk essentialism, in many instances privileging the 'original' over the remake or measuring the success of the remake according to its ability to realise what are taken to be the essential elements of a source text – the property – from which both the original and its remake are derived.[7] While there is often sufficient semantic and syntactic evidence to suggest that remakes are particular textual structures, film remakes (like genres) 'exist always *in excess* of a corpus of works'.[8] Film remaking depends, too, 'on the existence of audience activity', not only prior knowledge of previous texts and intertextual relationships, but an understanding of broader generic structures and categories.[9] In addition to this, film remaking is both enabled and limited by a series of historically specific institutional factors, such as copyright law, canon formation and film reviewing which are essential to the existence and maintenance – to the discursivisation – of the film remake.[10] In these ways, film remaking is not simply a quality of texts or viewers, but a 'by-product' or the secondary result of broader discursive activity.[11]

This chapter refers to several books and essays dealing directly with 'film remakes' and (more broadly) the concept of 'remaking film', from Michael B. Druxman's early survey of film remakes, *Make It Again, Sam* (1975), through to more recent theorisations of remaking in anthologies such as Andrew Horton and Stuart Y. McDougal's *Play It Again, Sam* (1998) and Jennifer Forrest and Leonard R. Koos's *Dead Ringers* (2002). A number of key points developed here have been made (differently) by John Frow and Lesley Stern in their work on intertextuality[12] and remaking[13] respectively, and also in their reviews of the Horton and McDougal anthology.[14] In addition, this account of remaking draws upon Rick Altman's *Film/Genre* (1999), developing from that book the idea that, although film remakes (like genres) are often 'located' in either authors *or* texts *or* audiences, they are in fact not located in any single place but depend upon a network of historically variable relationships.[15] Accordingly, this chapter falls into three broad (though not unrelated) sections: the first, *remaking as industrial category*, deals with issues of production, including industry (commerce) and authors (intention); the second, *remaking as textual category*, considers texts (plots and structures) and taxonomies; and the third, *remaking as critical category*, deals with issues of reception, including audiences (recognition) and institutions (discourse).

Remaking as industrial category

As in some approaches to film genre, remakes can be understood as *industrial products*, located in 'the material conditions of commercial filmmaking, where plots are copied and formulas forever reiterated'.[16] For film producers, remakes are consistently thought to provide suitable models, and something of a financial guarantee, for the development of studio-based projects. In a commercial context, remakes are 'pre-sold' to their audience because viewers are assumed to have some prior experience, or at least possess a 'narrative image',[17] of the original story – an earlier film, literary or other property – before engaging in its particular retelling.[18] Remakes of cult movies such as *King Kong* (Merian C. Cooper and Ernest B. Schoedsack, 1933; John Guillermin, 1976; Peter Jackson, 2005), *Godzilla* (Ishiro Honda, 1954; Roland Emmerich, 1998) and *Planet of the Apes* (Franklin J. Schaffner, 1968; Tim Burton, 2001) are revived through massive production budgets as cultural juggernauts, with strong marketing campaigns and merchandising tie-ins. For instance, in the mid-1970s *King Kong* was seen as a 'natural' for remaking, not only because of the success of the original, its pioneering special effects and cult status, but for the opportunities it provided for promotional tie-ins, from Jim Beam King Kong cocktails to 7–11 store slurpy drinks in special Kong cups.[19] In the case of recent cross-cultural remakes, such as *Vanilla Sky* (Cameron Crowe, 2001; *Abre Los Ojos*, Alejandro Amenábar, 1997), *The Ring* (Gore Verbinski, 2002; *Ringu*, Hideo Nakata, 1998) and *Insomnia* (Christopher Nolan, 2002; Erik Skjoldbjaerg, 1997), foreign films are dispossessed of 'local detail' and 'political content' to exploit new (English-language) markets.[20] In these examples, remaking is not only evidence of Hollywood being an 'aesthetic copy-cat', but (worse) of 'cultural imperialism' and 'terroristic marketing practices' designed to block an original's competition in the US market.[21]

A number of commentators[22] have observed that the remake, along with the sequel and series, has become typical of the defensive production and marketing strategies of a contemporary, or 'post-*Jaws*', Hollywood.[23] For instance, Jim Hoberman says that:

> The trickle of remakes that began . . . with *Farewell, My Lovely* in 1975 became a flood of recycled Jazz Singing Scarfaced King Kong 'landmarks', Roman numeral'd replays of old and recent mega-hits, and retired mixed-media figures [Flash Gordon, Popeye, Superman, and the like] pressed back into service.[24]

This 'great downpour' of sequels and remakes is perhaps more perceived than real. For instance, reviewing a sample of 3,490 films from between

1940 and 1979 Thomas Simonet concludes that far more 'recycled script' films appeared before the conglomerate takeovers of contemporary Hollywood in the 1970s, and perceptions that remaking has increased may be governed by comparisons with the 1960s only.[25] Nevertheless remaking is often taken as a sign of Hollywood film having exhausted its creative potential, leading into 'conservative plot structures'[26] and 'automatic self-cannibalisation'.[27] A recent account of remaking in the popular film monthly *Empire* simply put the motivation for studio remakes down to 'lack of creativity [and] laziness'.[28] Similarly, in previewing the television mini-series remake of *On the Beach* (Russell Mulcahy, 2000), *The Age* newspaper critic Simon Hughes found opportunity not only to express his antipathy toward remake practice in general, but to condemn both the mini-series *and* the earlier, feature film version, *On the Beach* (Stanley Kramer, 1959):

> In the Dearth of Ideas, hard by the dire Lack of Imagination, dwell those alchemists of the entertainment industry who delight in turning gold into base metal. These are the remakers and their awful talent is to be feared. Not only will they not stop at buggering up a classic like *Psycho* . . . they will even transform the second rate – like the original *On the Beach* – into something completely forgettable.[29]

Film remaking is equally seen as a trend that is encouraged by the *commercial* orientation of the conglomerate ownership of Hollywood. In this approach, the Hollywood studios seek to duplicate past successes and minimise risk by emphasising the familiar – 'recreating with slight changes films that have proved successful in the past' – even if this leads to 'aesthetically inferior films'.[30] Mark Kermode similarly reports that remakes, such as *The Texas Chainsaw Massacre* (Marcus Nispel, 2003; Tobe Hopper, 1974), are cynical 'rebranding exercises' and evidence of 'the entertainment industry's artistic laziness and penchant for pre-sold product'.[31] Stern takes this further, pointing to the commercial 'paradox' of remaking:

> Remakes reflect the conservative nature of the industry; they are motivated by an economic imperative to repeat proven successes. But in order to maintain economic viability . . . remakes are also compelled to register variation and difference (from the originals), to incorporate generic developments.[32]

As instantly recognisable properties, remakes (along with sequels and series) work then to satisfy the requirement that Hollywood deliver reliability (repetition) and novelty (innovation) in the same production package.[33] Understood in this way, the remake becomes a particular instance not only of the *repetition effects* which characterise the narrative structure of Hollywood film,[34] but also of a more general repetition – of exclusive stars, proprietary characters, patented processes, narrative patterns and generic elements – through which Hollywood develops its pre-sold audience.[35] In a high-profile example like *Planet of the Apes*, the B-movie aesthetic of the original cult film (and series) becomes an opportunity to revive the franchise as mega-budget ($110 million) blockbuster, complete with stars, special effects and *auteur* themes (see Chapter 3).

In discussions of industry and commerce the surest arbiter of what counts as a film remake is an acknowledgement of copyright, but this limit is complicated by the flexibility of copyright law,[36] and what are commonly referred to as 'unacknowledged remakes' and 'non-remakes'. In *Make It Again, Sam*, Druxman sets out 'to provide a comprehensive dissertation on the remake practice' by 'detailing the film life of [thirty-three] literary properties'.[37] Druxman begins by electing to limit the category of remake 'to those *theatrical* films that were based on a *common literary source* (i.e., story, novel, play, poem, screenplay), but were not a sequel to that material'.[38] This 'seemingly infallible signpost' is, however, complicated by those films that are 'obviously remakes [but] do not credit their origins'.[39] In such cases Druxman adopts a heuristic device – a rule of thumb – which requires that a new film 'borrow more than just an element or two from its predecessor to qualify'.[40] This in turn allows Druxman to distinguish between 'non-fiction films' of a single historical incident or biography of a historical figure (for example, the mutiny on the *Bounty* or the life of outlaw Jesse James) which *differ* because they are based around competing versions of the same incident; and those 'non-fiction films' of a like historical incident which are *similar* even though they are based upon diverse literary sources.[41] As might be expected from an approximate rule which arbitrates according to whether a film's borrowings are 'significant' or only amount to 'an element or two', Druxman ultimately admits that 'there were many marginal situations . . . [in which he] simply used [his] own discretion in deciding whether or not to embrace [a film as a remake]'.[42]

Although Druxman's recognition of 'unacknowledged' remakes introduces a number of methodological difficulties, he further grounds his discussion by viewing (pre-1975) Hollywood remaking practice as a function of industry pragmatism driven by three major factors. First, Druxman argues that the decision to remake an existing film is primarily a 'voluntary one' based on the perceived continuing viability of an original story. However, industry demand for additional material during the studio-dominated era of the 1930s and 1940s, and attempts to rationalise the often high costs of source acquisition prompted studios to consider previously filmed stories as sources for B-pictures, and even for top-of-the-bill productions.[43] As Tino Balio points out, the Hollywood majors 'had story departments with large offices in New York, Hollywood, and Europe that systematically searched the literary marketplace and stage for suitable novels, plays, short stories, and original ideas'.[44] Taking as an example story acquisitions at Warner Brothers between 1930 and 1949, Balio notes that 'the pattern of source acquisition demonstrates two often contradictory goals: [1] the desire to base films on pretested material, that is, low-risk material that was already well known and well received by the public and [2] the desire to acquire properties as inexpensively as possible, especially during declining or uncertain economic circumstances'.[45] In practice this meant that while Warners often invested in expensive pre-sold properties, such as best-selling novels and Broadway hit plays, 'it offset the high costs of pretested properties by using original screenplays written in its screenwriting department and by relying heavily on "the cheapest pretested material of all" – earlier Warner pictures'.[46]

Druxman's second, related point is that the customary studio practice at the time of purchasing the rights to novels, plays and stories *in perpetuity* meant that a company was able to produce multiple versions of a particular property without making additional payments to the copyright holder.[47] Canonised classics of literature, such as *Dr. Jekyll and Mr. Hyde*, *The Count of Monte Cristo* and *The Three Musketeers* not only had pre-sold titles, but because they were in the public domain, had the added advantage of requiring no initial payment for their dramatic rights.[48] While the majority of recycled, previously purchased source material (particularly from those films that had done fair to poorly at the box-office) made its way into B-unit production,[49] high-profile titles were sometimes remade to take advantage of new technologies and practices. Accordingly, Druxman's third and final point relates to the profit potential of redoing established films in order to exploit new stars or screen techniques. For example, following the success of *Captain Blood* and *The Charge of the Light Brigade* (Michael Curtiz, 1935 and 1936) Curtiz's 1938 version of *The Adventures of Robin Hood* is not only a vehicle for co-stars Errol Flynn and Olivia de Havilland, *but also* a sound and Technicolor update of the Douglas Fairbanks silent epic, *Robin Hood* (Allan Dwan, 1922).[50] Expanding screen technologies, including 'the developing technological powers of film to create more convincing representations of reality',[51] and the ongoing appeal of casting star performers in established roles continue to be cited as principal motivations for remaking films.

Druxman's initial definition, and the above factors of industry pragmatism, allow him to posit three general categories of Hollywood remake:

1. the *disguised* remake: a literary property is either updated with minimal change, *or* retitled and then disguised by new settings and original characters, but in either case the new film does not seek to draw attention to its earlier version(s), for example *Colorado Territory* (Raoul Walsh, 1949) is a disguised Western remake of the crime film *High Sierra* (Raoul Walsh, 1941); and *High Society* (Charles Walters, 1956) is a musical retelling of *The Philadelphia Story* (Joseph L. Mankiewicz, 1940);

2. the *direct* remake: a property may undergo some alterations or even adopt a new title, but the new film and its narrative image do not hide the fact that it is based upon an earlier production, for example William Wellman's 1939 remake of *Beau Geste* (Herbert Brenon, 1926), or Charles Vidor's 1957 remake of *A Farewell to Arms* (Frank Borzage, 1932);

3. the *non*-remake: a new film goes under the same title as a familiar property but there is an entirely new plot, for example Michael Curtiz's 1940 version of *The Sea Hawk* (part of the above-mentioned Errol Flynn swashbuckling cycle) is said to bear little relation to First National's 1924 adaptation of the Rafael Sabatini novel, and the 1961 remake of *The Thief of Baghdad* (Arthur Lubin and Bruno Vailati) is little like the 'definitive' 1940 version (directed by Ludwig Berger, Michael Powell and Tim Whelan).[52]

Not surprisingly, Druxman's three categories do not operate without the kind of overlap and exclusion that often attends taxonomism. For instance, an inspection of elements from the second half of James Cameron's *Titanic* (1997) – the band's decision to play on as the ship sinks; Benjamin Guggenheim's preference for his dinner jacket over a life jacket; designer Thomas Andrews's address to a young couple at the fireplace of the first-class lounge – suggest it is a 'direct' remake of the British-made account of the sinking, *A Night to Remember* (Roy Ward Baker, 1958). But the narrative drive of the first half of the film – the establishment of the romance between (fictional) characters Rose DeWitt Bukater (Kate Winslett) and Jack Dawson (Leonardo DiCaprio) – suggests that it is not only a 'non-remake' of *A Night to Remember*, but perhaps a 'disguised' remake of both *It Happened One Night* (Frank Capra, 1934) and *An Affair to Remember* (Leo McCarey, 1957).[53] In addition, any attempt to determine a single precursor text for *Titanic* (even Druxman's method for

distinguishing between types of 'non-fiction' remakes) is further complicated not just by the film's 'inter art intertextuality' (references to paintings, operas and the like),[54] but by various other reworkings of the *Titanic*
disaster: film versions, such as *Saved from the Titanic* (Eclair Film Co.,
1912), *In Nacht und Eis* (Kunstfilm, 1912), *Titanic* (Herbert Selpin, 1943)
and *Titanic* (Jean Negulesco, 1953), and also books (Walter Lord's *A Night
to Remember*), musicals (*The Unsinkable Molly Brown*), TV movies (*S.O.S.
Titanic*) and historical accounts (Steven Biel's *Down with the Old Canoe:
A Cultural History of the Titanic*). In addition to this, the commercial
quality of Cameron's *Titanic* – one of the most expensive and profitable
films ever made – requires that it also take as intertexts broader elements
such as genre (teen romance, action adventure, heritage film), cycle
(millennium disaster movie), stars (Winslett and DiCaprio) and *auteur*
(Cameron).

Although the example of *Titanic* presents difficulties for Druxman's
taxonomy it does, however, support his further claim that, in addition to
industry pragmatism, remaking is located in a film maker's desire to
repeatedly express (and modify) a particular aesthetic sensibility or world
view in light of new developments and interests.[55] In the case of *Titanic*, it
is not only Cameron's 'devotion to and love for the ship at the bottom of
the ocean',[56] but his well-documented 'preoccupation with precision and
historical accuracy'[57] which motivates this particular retelling of the story.
In the anthology *Play It Again, Sam*, Stuart McDougal takes up this type
of approach, describing Alfred Hitchcock as a director who was continuously revising and remaking his own earlier film work.[58] This results not
only in the repetition of specific shots, sequences and themes, but in the
case of Hitchcock's 1955 remake of his own earlier film, *The Man Who
Knew Too Much* (1934), it provides the film maker with an opportunity to
rethink 'the relations between texts, between characters (real and fictional),
and between the work of a younger, more exuberant director and a mature
craftsman'[59] (see Chapter 2). In a similar way, Lloyd Michaels argues that
while it is difficult to conceive of a more ' "faithful" remake' of *Nosferatu,
A Symphony of Horror* (F. W. Murnau, 1922) than Werner Herzog's
Nosferatu, the Vampyre (1979), the latter not only pays homage to
Murnau's silent classic but simultaneously 'resurrects the ghost of
Herzog', remaking in limited ways the director's signature themes and
stylistic traits.[60]

Harvey Roy Greenberg takes this type of authorial approach to remaking a step further, modifying Druxman's commercially grounded remake
categories to locate the motivation for remakes, 'well beyond the profit
principle', in complex, highly personal reasons, based on various 'Oedipal

inflections'.[61] Following Druxman, Greenberg outlines three categories of remaking:

1. *the acknowledged, close remake*: the original film is replicated with little or no change to the narrative, for example *Ben-Hur* (William Wyler, 1959; Fred Niblo, 1925; Sidney Olcott, 1907);
2. *the acknowledged, transformed remake*: there are substantial transformations of character, time and setting, but the original film is variably acknowledged, ranging from a small screen credit to foregrounding in promotion, for example *A Star Is Born* (Frank Pierson, 1976; George Cukor, 1954; William A. Wellman, 1937), *Heaven Can Wait* (Warren Beatty and Buck Henry, 1978; *Here Comes Mr Jordan*, Alexander Hall, 1941) and *Stella* (John Erman, 1990; *Stella Dallas*, King Vidor, 1937; *Stella Dallas*, Henry King, 1925);
3. *the unacknowledged, disguised remake*: minor or major alterations (in character, time and setting) are undertaken but the audience is not informed of the original film version, for example studio-era remakes such as Warner Brothers' *The Wagons Roll at Night* (Ray Enright, 1941) remake of *Kid Galahad* (Michael Curtiz, 1937).[62]

Focusing on the example of Steven Spielberg's *Always* (1990) – an 'acknowledged, transformed' remake of the Second World War fantasy *A Guy Named Joe* (Victor Fleming, 1943) – Greenberg finds in 'the intensely rivalrous spirit inhabiting Spielberg's "homage" . . . an unconscious Oedipally driven competitiveness [which] constitutes the dark side of Spielberg's intense admiration for the original [film] and its director [and father surrogate, Victor Fleming]'.[63] Greenberg's 'symptomatic reading'[64] of film remaking is itself an (acknowledged) elaboration of Harold Bloom's theory of influence (and the Freudian analogies that structure it),[65] and a like attempt to shift the relationship between a text (remake) and its particular precursor (original) to that between an author and his major predecessor(s).[66] In the case of *Always*, Spielberg, at once worshipful and envious of his predecessor (Fleming, and also Spielberg senior, a Second World War veteran), returns to his preferred Second World War locale (the historical setting for *1941* (1979), *Raiders of the Lost Ark* (1981), *Empire of the Sun* (1987), and the later *Schindler's List* (1993) and *Saving Private Ryan* (1998)) and enters into 'an ambiguous, anxiety ridden struggle with a film [*A Guy Named Joe*] he both wishes to honor and eclipse'.[67]

Timothy Corrigan argues that *auteurs* – 'star-directors', such as the above examples of Steven Spielberg and James Cameron – are especially important in contemporary Hollywood because they serve as a '*commercial* strategy for organising [a type of] audience reception . . . [one which is] bound to distribution and marketing aims that identify and address the potential cult status of an *auteur*'.[68] In the case of contemporary remakes, a pre-existing title is relayed and transformed through the 'individual vision' and 'personal perspective' of the film maker.[69] Or, as Catherine Grant puts it, 'contemporary film *auteurs* . . . make aspects of [earlier] texts their own, overwriting them with their own traceable signatures, perhaps reconfiguring them by incorporating references to other (rewritten) inter-texts'.[70] Accordingly, Tim Burton's *Planet of the Apes* is not a remake but a 're-imagining' of Schaffner's film (and Pierre Boulle's novel); George A. Romero's zombie movie *Dawn of the Dead* (1979) is 're-envisioned' by Zack Snyder (2004); and *Solaris*, a 1972 film by Andrei Tarkovsky (from the novel by Stanislaw Lem) is 'revisited' by Steven Soderbergh (2002). In the latter instance, the original material is not only filtered through the per-spective of the film maker, but the contemporary *auteur* remakes *himself* and his earlier remakes:

> [Soderbergh's] *Solaris* is almost if not quite a rerun of *Ocean's Eleven* (out-of-towner invades hi-tech labyrinth in order to win back wife), *The Underneath* (out-of-towner pursues former wife for second chance), *Traffic* (stranger-in-town searches for lost daughter to reunite family), or *The Limey* (trouble-shooter from another continent arrives in town to avenge lost daughter).[71]

Remaking as textual category

While the above factors contribute to an understanding of film remaking, the concept of the remake is never simply reducible to issues of industry and commerce or matters of influence and authorship. A second, general (and related) approach suggests that remakes are located in texts (or struc-tures) that are produced in accordance with the narrative invention of former film models.[72] At its most contracted, a textual approach leads to accounts of remaking which attempt to reduce all narrative structures to a single (Oedipal) logic or variant thereof. Michael Eaton, for instance, notes that 'there are only two possible premises for stories: The Odd Couple and The Fish Out of Water . . . Although Oedipus, if you think about it, is a bit of both'.[73] While Eaton's comment might be tongue-in-cheek, the descrip-tion readily fits any number of recent remakes. For instance, in *Planet of the Apes* astronaut Leo Davidson (Mark Wahlberg) finds himself in a ten-tative ('odd-couple') relationship with chimpanzee Ari (Helena Bonham Carter) on an alien planet dominated by apes. Or in the case of *Insomnia*, Will Dormer (Al Pacino) is the 'fish-out-of-water' city cop who finds himself in the twenty-four hour daylight of an Alaskan summer tracking a murderer (Robin Williams) with whom he becomes complicit. More commonly though (and as for film genre), the desire to confine film remakes to a body of texts or set of textual relationships reveals a tension between 'sharable terms' (shareability) and 'accurate designation' (accuracy).[74] In the case of remaking this is a conflict between a desire to provide exhaustive lists of film remakes, and one (as in Druxman's and other taxonomies) to precisely define the category, or various categories, of the remake.

An example of the former approach – of shareability – is Robert Nowlan and Gwendoline Wright Nowlan's almost one thousand pages long *Cinema Sequels and Remakes, 1903–1987*, a reference work which alphabetically lists 1,025 'primary films' and many more associated remakes and sequels. In a brief (not quite two pages long) introduction, Nowlan and Nowlan make little attempt to define either remake or sequel, but rather take these as received categories. That is, the principal criterion for selection is that a film has been *previously* designated as a remake or sequel in any two or more of a number of unidentified but 'reliable source[s]' which list remakes and sequels of certain genres of films.[75] While this type of loose definition makes for a wide selection of material (shareability), and does not preclude the inferential reconstruction of at least some of the unspecified principles of selection (through an examination of those films that have been included), Nowlan and Nowlan's intuitive approach underscores the extent to which the remake is conceived more through actual usage and common understanding than through rigorous definition. In this respect, Nowlan and Nowlan's account of remaking overlaps with Simonet's survey of recycled scripts (that is, remakes, sequels and series), in which each film is categorised not according to an analysis of its content, but according to its being identified in the text of a film review.[76]

If shareability tends toward exhaustive lists of remakes, then accuracy is inclined toward taxonomism. Robert Eberwein, for instance, provides a recent and elaborate taxonomy of remakes, proposing fifteen categories (many with subdivisions) including sound remakes of silent films, American remakes of foreign films, parodic remakes, pornographic remakes and so on.[77] In the more developed 'Twice-Told Tales', Thomas M. Leitch makes a number of points about the singularity of the remake both among Hollywood films and even among other types of narratives. Leitch argues that:

> The uniqueness of the film remake, a movie based on another movie, or competing with another movie based on the same property, is indicated by the word *property*. Every film adaptation is defined by its legally sanctioned use

of material from an earlier model, whose adaptation rights the producers have customarily purchased.[78]

Putting aside for the moment the fact that this description immediately excludes those 'obvious remakes' (Druxman) which do not acknowledge their previous sources, the point Leitch wants to make is that although adaptation rights (for example, film adaptation rights of a novel) are something producers of the original work have a right to sell, it is only remakes that 'compete directly and without legal or economic compensation with other versions of the same property'[79]:

> Remakes differ from . . . adaptations to a new medium because of the triangular relationship they establish among themselves, the original film they remake, and the property on which both films are based. The nature of this triangle is most clearly indicated by the fact that the producers of a remake typically pay no adaptation fees to the makers of the original film, but rather purchase adaptation rights from the authors of the property on which that film was based, even though the remake is competing much more directly with the original film – especially in these days of video, when the original film and the remake are often found side by side on the shelves of rental outlets – than with the story or play or novel on which it is based.[80]

Taking as an initial proposition the triangular relationship among a remake, its original film and the source for both films, Leitch suggests that any 'given remake can seek to define itself either with primary reference to the film it remakes or to the material on which both films are based'. And then, depending upon 'whether it poses as a new version of an older film or of a story predating either film, it can take as its goal fidelity to the conception of the original story or a revisionary attitude toward that story'.[81] Accordingly, Leitch outlines the following quadripartite taxonomy of the remake:

1. *Readaptation*: the remake ignores or treats as inconsequential earlier cinematic adaptations in order to readapt as faithfully as possible (or at least more faithfully than earlier film versions) an original literary property, for example the film versions of Shakespeare's *Hamlet* (Laurence Olivier, 1948; Tony Richardson, 1969; Franco Zeffirelli, 1990) or *Macbeth* (Orson Welles, 1948; Roman Polanski, 1971).
2. *Update*: unlike the readaptation which seeks to subordinate itself to the 'essence' of a literary classic, the update 'competes directly' with its literary source by adopting an overtly revisionary and transformational attitude toward it, for example *West Side Story* (Robert Wise and

Jerome Robbins, 1961), *China Girl* (Abel Ferrara, 1987) and *William Shakespeare's Romeo + Juliet* (Baz Luhrmann, 1996) as transformed remakes of earlier, 'faithful' filmed versions of *Romeo and Juliet* (George Cukor, 1936; Franco Zeffirelli, 1968).

3. *Homage*: like the readaptation which seeks to direct the audience's attention to its literary source, the homage situates itself as a secondary text in order to pay tribute to a previous film version, for example, Brian De Palma's *Obsession* (1975) and *Body Double* (1986) as homages to Alfred Hitchcock's *Vertigo* (1958), or Rainer Werner Fassbinder's *Fear Eats the Soul* (1974) and Todd Haynes's *Far From Heaven* (2002) as tributes to Douglas Sirk's *All That Heaven Allows* (1956).

4. *True remake*: while the homage renounces any claim to be better than its original, the true remake 'deal[s] with the contradictory claims of all remakes – that they are just like their originals only better – [by combining] a focus on a cinematic original with an accommodating stance which seeks to make the original relevant by updating it', for example Bob Rafelson's 1981 remake of *The Postman Always Rings Twice* (Tay Garnett, 1946) or Lawrence Kasdan's *Body Heat* (1981) as a remake of *Double Indemnity* (Billy Wilder, 1944).[82]

Leitch concludes that, unlike readaptations, updates and homages, which only acknowledge one earlier text (literary in the first two cases and cinematic in the third), 'true remakes [emphasise] a triangular notion of intertextuality, since their rhetorical strategy depends on ascribing their value to a classic earlier text' (that is, an original property such as James M. Cain's novel, *The Postman Always Rings Twice*), 'and protecting that value by invoking a second earlier [film] text as betraying it' (Garnett's version as a watered-down *film noir*, probably due to limitations imposed by the MGM studio and the Production Code of the 1940s).[83]

While Leitch's recognition of the significance of a literary property, and in particular the relationship of a film adaptation and its remake to that property, leads to what at first appears to be a more inflected taxonomy than that developed by Druxman, further consideration reveals a number of difficulties, not only among Leitch's four categories but in relation to his preliminary suppositions. First, while the ubiquity of the Hollywood remake might understandably lead Leitch to conclude that the remake is a particularly cinematic form, one might question to what extent it differs from the remaking of songs in the popular music industry. That is, how does the triadic relationship between (1) the Pet Shop Boys' long remake (of their earlier, shorter remake) of 'Always on My Mind', (2) the 1972 version of the same song by Elvis Presley, and (3) the original property (music and lyrics written by Thompson James Christopher and published by Screen Gems/EMI) differ appreciably from the triangular relationship for the film remake as described by Leitch? Or, to take as another example a case which underscores Leitch's overestimation of the *economic* competition a remake creates for a former adaptation, the Sid Vicious remake of 'My Way' from *The Great Rock'n'Roll Swindle* (Julien Temple, 1980), and even Gary Oldman's remake of that performance for Alex Cox's *Sid and Nancy* (1986), competes *culturally*, but not economically, with Frank Sinatra's earlier adaptation of a property written by Reveaux, Francois and Anka. Director Cameron Crowe draws attention to the affinity between remaking in popular music and film, describing *Vanilla Sky* as a 'cover version' of *Abre Los Ojos*, and Martin Arnold's extraordinary *Alone: Life Wastes Andy Hardy* (1998) remakes the Mickey Rooney–Judy Garland *Andy Hardy* cycle (1937–58) through the methods of music 'sampling'. These examples, and (many) others from the popular music industry, adequately conform to, and so problematise, Leitch's initial claim that *the film remake is unique* because of the fact that its producers 'typically pay no adaptation fees to the makers of the original [version], but rather purchase adaptation rights from the authors [publishers] of the property on which that [version] was based'.[84]

A second limitation is that while Druxman at least acknowledges the difficulty of identifying and categorising those films 'that are obviously remakes [but] do not credit their origins',[85] Leitch remains silent in this respect. For instance, Leitch considers *Body Heat* a 'true remake' of *Double Indemnity*, but he does not comment upon the fact that the film's credits do not acknowledge the James M. Cain novel as a source. Similarly, Leitch takes *Obsession* and *Body Double* to be 'homages' to *Vertigo* but he fails to note that neither of the films credits either the Alec Coppel and Samuel Taylor screenplay, or the Pierre Boileau and Thomas Narceiac novel, *D'entre les morts*, upon which the Hitchcock film is based. Examples such as Sergio Leone's *A Fistful of Dollars* (*Per un pugno di dollari*, 1964) remake of *Yojimbo* (Akira Kurosawa, 1961) – uncredited, but consistently 'acknowledged' in critical commentaries – suggest that taxonomies need attend not only to the nature of textual remakings ('free' or 'faithful'), but to contextual (or extratextual) markers, such as credits and reviews, that enable the identification of the intertext (see Chapters 3 and 5). While the question of categorising unacknowledged remakes is returned to below, Leitch's insistence upon the connection between three elements – a remake, an earlier version and a literary property – presents a further difficulty in that it marginalises those instances in which a *dyadic* relationship exists between a remake and a previous film *that is itself* (at least in the

The Assassin (John Badham, 1994). Courtesy Warner Bros/
The Kobal Collection.

sense conveyed by Leitch) the original property. Although it might be objected that a published original screenplay constitutes a discrete property, the point to be made here is that the remake of an 'original film property', such as John Badham's *The Assassin* [*Point of No Return*] (1994), *does not* 'compete directly and without legal or economic compensation' with its earlier version, but (generally) pays adaptation fees to the copyright holder of the original film upon which it is based (in this example, Luc Besson's *Nikita*, 1990).[86] Indeed, some producers of (foreign) originals, realising the direct financial gains to be made, are actively involved in the production of US remakes.[87] For example, following an unsuccessful attempt to repackage a dubbed version of *Les Visiteurs* (1993) for an English language, multiplex audience, director Jean-Marie Poiré extended the franchise (which included the sequel, *Les Couloirs du temps: Les Visiteurs II*, 1998) through a 2001 French/American remaking, *Just Visiting* (directed under the pseudonym Jean-Marie Gaubert).[88]

The above example of the American remake of *Nikita* (and also *Les Visiteurs*) not only demonstrates that a 'triangular relationship' fails to adequately accommodate remakes of those films based upon original stories and screenplays but highlights the difficulty of Leitch's suggestion that remakes *compete* with earlier versions, and his belief that successful remakes *supersede* and so 'typically threaten the economic viability of their originals'.[89] To stay with the example of the French-Italian production of *Nikita*, it seems doubtful that having successfully played an art-cinema circuit and having been released to home video (variously under the categories of 'cult', 'festival' and 'art-house') the appearance of *The Assassin*, initially as a first-run theatrical release and then as a mainstream video release, would have any appreciable impact (either positive or negative) upon the former's 'economic viability'. Admittedly, *The Assassin* was not *promoted* as a remake of the Besson film, but even a widely publicised remake such as Martin Scorsese's 1991 version of *Cape Fear* did not occasion the burial, or even diminish the cult following, of J. Lee Thompson's earlier (1961) version. On the contrary, the theatrical release of the Scorsese film (accompanied by press releases and reviews foregrounding its status as remake) prompted first a video release and then a prime-time national television screening of the Thompson version. The reciprocity of the two versions is further exemplified by *Sight and Sound* magazine's running together of a lead article by Jim Hoberman on Scorsese and *Cape Fear* and a second briefer article comparing the two versions ('novelist . . . Jenny Diski watches a video of the first *Cape Fear* and the Scorsese remake – and compares them') and giving details of the availability of the (then recently) re-released CIC video of the 1961 version.[90] More recently, the two versions of *Cape Fear* have been released together to DVD in a collector's three-disc boxed set. This does not, however, mean that reciprocity is *always* the case. In the international marketplace a local remake may supplant an earlier foreign language and/or culture version. For instance, the producers of the Brazilian *Costinha e o King Mong* (1977), a parodic

remake of *King Kong* (1933/1976), capitalised on the advertising apparatus and pre-release publicity for Guillermin's 1976 remake to release a
version that ran *simultaneously* with the American remake in Brazilian theatres. [91] While it is likely that both versions benefited from this arrange-
ment, it seems probable too that *King Mong* siphoned off some of its older
sibling's box-office receipts.

The example of *Cape Fear* suggests that contemporary remakes *generally* enjoy a (more) symbiotic relationship with their originals, with publicity and reviews often drawing attention to earlier versions. As Steve
Neale points out, along with the institutionalised public discourses of
press, television and radio, a key role in communicating the narrative image
of a new film is played by the industry itself, 'especially in the earliest
phases of a film's public circulation, and in particular by those sectors of
the industry concerned with publicity and marketing'.[92] In the case of
remakes, official film websites will often draw attention to originals, seeing
this as an opportunity to instantly invest new versions not only with a narrative image, but with aesthetic (and commercial) value. On these sites, film
makers often enthuse about the 'timeless' attributes and 'classic' status of
originals before going on to insist upon their own value-added transformations. For instance, F. Gary Gray, the director of the 2003 version of *The
Italian Job*, says 'I liked a lot of things about the original [*The Italian Job*,
Peter Collinson, 1969]. It had great style and unforgettable performances'.
Gray goes on to add: 'but the film that we've made is for modern audiences,
with updated technology'.[93] Following the 2003 theatrical run of *The
Italian Job*, both versions were simultaneously released to DVD, with
extras on the remake DVD not only drawing attention to the original, but
featuring scenes from it. More than this, the subsequent release of
Paramount Home Video's '*The Italian Job* Gift Set' DVD edition (which
included both 1969 and 2003 versions) suggests that, just as adaptations of
literary properties often lead viewers back to source novels for a first
reading, remakes encourage viewers to seek out original film properties[94]
(see Chapter 5).

While the above examples suggest that Leitch might overestimate the
extent to which some remakes compete with original film versions, his
recognition of the impact that innovations in television technology, particularly home video, have had upon shaping the relationship between a
remake and its earlier versions should not be *under*estimated. Leitch states
that during the studio-dominated era of the 1930s and 1940s it was at least
in part the belief that films had a 'strictly current value' that enabled
studios such as Warners to recycle *The Maltese Falcon* property three times
in ten years (Roy Del Ruth, 1931; *Satan Met a Lady*, William Dieterle,

1936; John Huston, 1941), and release many 'unofficial remakes' of its own films.[95] Although the re-release of successful features, particularly during the late 1940s and early 1950s, gave some films a limited currency outside their initial year of release,[96] the majority of films held in studio libraries were not available for re-viewing until the mid-1950s when the major studios decided to sell or lease their film libraries to television.[97] The release of thousands of pre-1948 features into the television market not only gave the general public the opportunity to see many films that had been held in studio archives since their initial year of release, but provided the possibility of seeing different versions of the same property, produced years or even decades apart, within weeks or even days of each other. Moreover, and in an instance of what has been described as the 'virtual mobility' of contemporary spectatorship,[98] the television broadcasting of films provided the further possibility of viewing remakes outside of the temporal order of their production. That is, the repeated screening of the same features meant that it was inevitable that the broadcast of a remake would *precede* the screening of its original. While Leitch does not address the impact of television, his recognition that a remake and its original circulate in the same video marketplace draws attention to the fact that the introduction of an information storage technology such as videotape (and now DVD) radically extends the kind of film literacy – the ability to recognise and cross-reference multiple versions of the same property – that was inaugurated by the age of television.

The ever-expanding availability of texts and technologies, and the unprecedented awareness of film history among new Hollywood film makers and contemporary audiences, is closely related to the general concept of *intertextuality*, an in principle determination which requires that texts be understood not as self-contained structures but as 'the repetition and transformation of other [absent] textual structures'.[99] In Mikhail Iampolski's discussion of intertextuality and film, the 'semantic fullness' of a text is precisely 'the result of its ability to establish a connection with [these other] texts that came before it, and occasionally with those that came later'.[100] Refusing to reduce this type of semantic productivity to a simple question of influence, Iampolski draws instead upon Ferdinand de Saussure's (and Julia Kristeva's) account of the *anagram* to define the intertextual element – the quotation – as that '*fragment of the text that violates its linear development* [its internal, textual repetitions] *and derives the motivation that integrates it into the text from outside the text itself*'.[101] As this description suggests, the 'semantic anomaly' of the quotation disrupts the linear unfolding of the text impelling the reader toward a non-linear ('tabular') intertextual reading, but one that may ultimately enrich meaning and salvage the very same narrative linearity that was initially compromised.[102] Additionally, Iampolski points out that an 'embedded quotation', one that seems to derive its motivation from the logic of the text and so dissolves into the film's mimetic structure (that is, a quotation known to the author but not the reader) is, paradoxically, *not a quote*, and (conversely) an 'anomalous moment' can *become a quote* through the reader making specific moves of exegesis, regardless of whether this expresses the author's intentions.[103] Adapted to the case of the film remake, this suggests that 'remaking is not necessarily about intended effects, nor necessarily about precise identification of an intertext. It is, or it may be, *a more general intertextual relation*, although this doesn't mean that it is unstructured or imprecise in its operations'.[104]

Robert Stam takes up the concept of intertextuality in film drawing upon Gérard Genette's description of *transtextuality* as 'all that which puts one text into a relation, manifest or secret, with other texts' to describe several types of textual transcendence.[105] Among these categories, the term 'intertextuality' specifically describes the 'literal presence of one text within another', principally as 'quotation' (or 'the explicit summoning up of a text that is both presented and distanced by quotation marks'), but also through 'plagiarism and allusion of various kinds'.[106] In its most literal and contracted form, *remaking as quotation* would describe the (acknowledged) insertion of segments from one film into another. There are countless instances of direct quotation in feature films. Examples include: Nana (Anna Karina) watching images of Maria Falconetti from *La Passion de Jeanne d'Arc* (Carl Theodor Dreyer, 1928) in *Vivre sa vie* (Jean-Luc Godard, 1962); Allan (Woody Allen) transfixed upon the ending from *Casablanca* (Michael Curtiz, 1942) in *Play it Again, Sam* (Herbert Ross, 1972); Donnie (Jake Gyllenhaal) and Gretchen (Jena Malone) 'sleeping' through *The Evil Dead* (Sam Raimi, 1981) in *Donnie Darko* (Richard Kelly, 2001); and, in one of the most expansive of recent examples, scenes from *Shock Corridor* (Sam Fuller, 1963), *À bout de souffle* (Jean-Luc Godard, 1959), *Queen Christina* (Rouben Mamoulian, 1933), *Bande à part* (Jean-Luc Godard, 1964), *Blonde Venus* (Josef von Sternberg, 1932) and others interspersed throughout *The Dreamers* (Bernardo Bertolucci, 2003). The *unauthorised* but direct use of material in experimental films – for example, clips from *East of Borneo* (George Melford, 1931) in *Rose Hobart* (Joseph Cornell, 1936); fragments from *The Wild One* (László Benedek, 1951) in *Scorpio Rising* (Kenneth Anger, 1964); and soundbites from *Ali Baba and the Forty Thieves* (Arthur Lubin, 1944) in *Flaming Creatures* (Jack Smith, 1963) – would constitute a kind of quotation as *appropriation*.[107] By contrast, *plagiarism* – the direct *but unacknowledged* use of segments from another film – is (by definition) a less obvious but no less prevalent strategy. Plagiarism might include the use of stock footage (establishing shots, action sequences and the like) in genre films and B-movies. For instance, *Flying Leathernecks* (Nicholas Ray, 1951) makes extensive use of US Navy newsreel footage for its battle sequences, and stock footage recurs in the various versions of the *Titanic* story.[108] Finally, while Genette seeks to restrict intertextuality to *direct and localised* instances of citation, *allusion* suggests a wide range of practices, and a potential overlap with the forms of imitation, pastiche and parody reserved by Genette for the category of 'hypertextuality' where a hypertext 'transforms, modifies, elaborates, or extends' an anterior hypotext[109] (see Chapter 3). Employed here in a restricted sense, allusion describes 'a verbal or visual evocation of another film',[110] and includes such strategies as the mention of films and film makers in dialogue, the display of film titles on marquees and posters, and the recreation of classic scenes, shots and lines of dialogue from earlier movies. For instance, Omar Calabrese claims that Spielberg's *Raiders of the Lost Ark* includes 350 allusions to old Hollywood films.[111] Or, to give a more recent and specific example, in the 2030 sequence in *The Time Machine* (Simon Wells, 2002) Alexander Hartdegen (Guy Pearce) asks Vox, a holographic guide at the New York public library, about time travel and is referred not only to *The Time Machine* by H. G. Wells but also to the original 1960 film directed by George Pal.

Genette's 'highly suggestive' category of intertextuality leads Stam to speculate upon sub-categories within the same paradigm.[112] Some of these terms can be productively adapted for a discussion of remaking. The first sub-category, *celebrity intertextuality*, defines those situations in which the presence of a film or television star or celebrity evokes an earlier version of a film property. This is evident in many contemporary remakes where actors from original films lend themselves to cameo appearances. For instance, Robert Mitchum and Gregory Peck – stars of J. Lee Thompson's version of *Cape Fear* (1961) – take minor roles in Martin Scorsese's 1991 remake. In another example, two of the four actors who played the 'survivors' in George A. Romero's *Dawn of the Dead* (1978) appear in different roles in the 2004 remake, and a third actor from the original (Gaylen Ross) has a clothing store in the mall named after her. A second, similar sub-category of intertextuality is referred to as *genetic intertextuality*. In this case, the appearance of a well-known actor's child (or other relative) evokes the memory of an earlier film version. For example, in *Swept Away* (Guy Ritchie, 2002) Adriano Giannini takes on the role played by his father, Giancarlo, in Lina Wertmüller's original *Swept Away . . . by an Unusual Destiny in the Blue Sea of August* (1974).

In a related example, Simon Wells, director of the 2002 remake of *The Time Machine*, is great-grandson to H. G. Wells, author of the book from which the film versions are derived. Stam's next category, *intratextuality*, might be employed to describe the way in which a remake refers to the *process* of remaking – in particular, the status of originals and copies – through strategies of mirroring or *mise-en-abyme* structures. For example, Laura Grindstaff says that Luc Besson's *Nikita* (1990) is an 'adaptation of the Pygmalion myth in which a woman is subjected to a dramatic make-over', and as such 'the Nikita narrative stands as a synecdoche for the relation between original film and its copies [*The Assassin* and *Black Cat*]'.[113] Similar arguments have been made about the way in which science fiction remakes like *The Fly* (Kurt Neumann, 1958; David Cronenberg, 1986) and *Invasion of the Body Snatchers* (Don Siegel, 1956; Philip Kaufman, 1978) act out the logic of the original and the copy.[114] Finally, the category of *autocitation* would refer to a film maker's self-quotation through the remaking of his/her own earlier film. Examples include Alfred Hitchcock's *The Man Who Knew Too Much* (1955, 1934), George Sluizer's *The Vanishing* (1993, 1971) and Takashi Shimizu's *The Grudge* (2004, *Ju-On: The Grudge*, 2003).

Film remaking can be regarded as a specific (institutionalised) aspect of the broader and more open-ended intertextuality described above. It can range from the limited repetition of a classic shot or scene, for example the many reprises of the Odessa Steps sequence of *The Battleship Potemkin* (Sergei Eisenstein, 1925) – *Bananas* (Woody Allen, 1971), *Brazil* (Terry Gilliam, 1985), *The Untouchables* (Brian De Palma, 1987), *Steps* (Zbigniew Rybczynski, 1987) and *Naked Gun 33⅓: The Final Insult* (Peter Segal, 1994) – to the 'quasi-independent' repetitions of a single story or popular myth,[115] for example the successive versions of Dracula or Robin Hood or the *Titanic* story. More often, though, film remakes are understood as (more particular) intertextual structures which are stabilised, or *limited*, through the naming and (usually) legally sanctioned (or copyrighted) use of a particular literary and/or cinematic source which serves as a retrospectively designated point of origin and semantic fixity. In addition, these intertextual structures (unlike those of genre) are highly particular in their repetition of *narrative units*, and these repetitions most often (though certainly not always) relate to the content ('the order of the message') rather than to the form (or 'the code') of the film.[116] Brian De Palma's *Obsession* (1976) provides an example of both, repeating not only the narrative invention of Alfred Hitchcock's *Vertigo* (1958), but 'resurrecting' some of Hitchcock's most visible stylistic characteristics, such as doubling effects and the voyeuristic use of point-of-view shots.[117]

While these factors yield some degree of consensus, any easy categorisation of the remake is frustrated (as seen above) by a number of factors. First, there is the problem of those films which do not credit an 'original' text, but which do repeat both general and particular elements of another film's narrative unfolding, for example *Body Heat* as an uncredited remake of *Double Indemnity*; *The Big Chill* (Lawrence Kasdan, 1983) as an unacknowledged remake of *The Return of the Secaucus Seven* (John Sayles, 1980); and *Flying Tigers* (David Miller, 1942) and *all major combat films* of the early 1940s as unacknowledged remakes of *Only Angels Have Wings* (Howard Hawks, 1939).[118] Second, there is the difficulty of those films based on a like source – a literary (or other) work or historical incident – but which differ significantly in their treatment of narrative units, for example *The Bounty* (Roger Donaldson, 1984) as a non-remake of *Mutiny on the Bounty* (Frank Lloyd, 1935 and Lewis Milestone, 1962); Tony Richardson's *The Charge of the Light Brigade* (1968) as a non-remake of Michael Curtiz's 1936 version; and *The King and I* (Richard Rich, 1999) as a remake of the Rogers and Hammerstein musical, *but not* of the film versions based on Margaret Landon's book or Anna Leonowens's diaries. Moreover, in a contemporary context, remakes increasingly take *only* the pre-sold title of an original property as a point of departure to create a non-remake, with all new characters, settings and situations. A third complication (discussed further below) arises from the fact that originals are never pure or singular. For instance, Michaels notes that Herzog's remaking of *Nosferatu* is complicated by the fact that the negative of the Murnau 'original' was destroyed, and that all existing prints are copies (*remakes*) reproduced from Murnau's shooting script.[119] Furthermore, the intertextual referentiality between either 'non-remakes' or 'unacknowledged remakes' and their 'originals' is to a large extent *extratextual*,[120] being conveyed through institutions such as film reviewing, marketing, distribution and exhibition. For example, the BFI/National Film Theatre's programme describes four films from Paul Schrader scripts – *Taxi Driver* (Martin Scorsese, 1976), *Rolling Thunder* (John Flynn, 1977), *Hardcore* (Schrader, 1979) and *Patty Hearst* (Schrader, 1988) – as 'updates', or remakes, of *The Searchers* (John Ford, 1956).[121] And Schrader has since added that his later *Mishima: A Life in Four Chapters* (1985) is in turn a 'remake' of *Taxi Driver*.[122] In a more complicated example, reviewers consistently refer to *The Big Chill* as a remake of *The Return of the Secaucus Seven*,[123] even though director John Sayles does not admit to the description: 'I never felt like it [*The Big Chill*] was a rip-off. It goes in such a different direction. It's like saying if my movie had an Indian and a horse in it: "Oh, it's a rip-off of *Shane*" '.[124]

Remaking as critical category

The above comments suggest that remakes do not consist simply of bodies of films but, like genres, are located too in 'expectations and audience knowledge'[125] and in 'the institutions that govern and support specific reading strategies'.[126] The concept of intertextuality needs, for instance, to be related to the ever-expanding availability of texts and technologies, the tendency of contemporary Hollywood film makers to combine the commercial necessity of generic patterns of repetition with more direct patterns of borrowing (allusion and quotation), and the unprecedented awareness of film history both among film makers and contemporary audiences.[127] As seen in Leitch's taxonomy, a remake can be categorised according to whether its intertextual referent is *literary* (the 'readaptation', the 'update') or *cinematic* (the 'homage', the 'true remake'). In the latter case, Leitch states that while homages, such as *The Thing* (John Carpenter, 1982) and *Invaders from Mars* (Tobe Hooper, 1986), establish direct intertextual relations to their original films (*The Thing from Another World*, Christian Nyby, 1951; *Invaders from Mars*, William Cameron Menzies, 1953), these quotations or 'rewards . . . take the form of throwaway jokes whose point is not necessary to the [film's] continuity, and which therefore provide an optional bonus of pleasure to those in the know'.[128] This seems consistent with what Umberto Eco describes as the 'intertextual dialogue', that is the instance where a quotation is explicit and recognisable to an increasingly sophisticated, ciné-literate audience.[129] But what Leitch does not sufficiently stress here is that his examples of the homage (and of the true remake) – all drawn from the new Hollywood cinema – suggest a historically specific response to a postmodern circulation and recirculation of images and texts. This does not mean that the classical Hollywood remake never takes an earlier film as its intertextual referent, but rather that, as the continuity system develops through the pre-classical period (1908–17), direct intertextual referentiality is mostly displaced by an industrial imperative for standardisation which prioritises the intertextual relation of genres, cycles and stars. Accordingly, as the classical narrative strives to create a coherent, self-contained fictional world according to specific mechanisms of internal (or *intra*textual) repetition, direct *inter*textual referentiality to earlier film versions (and other textualised sources) becomes an *extra*textual referentiality, carried by such apparatuses as advertising and promotional materials (posters, lobby cards, commercial tie-ins, etc.), film magazines, review articles and academic film criticism (see Chapter 5).

What seems to happen with contemporary Hollywood cinema, particularly in the case of remakes, is that while the intratextual mechanisms of

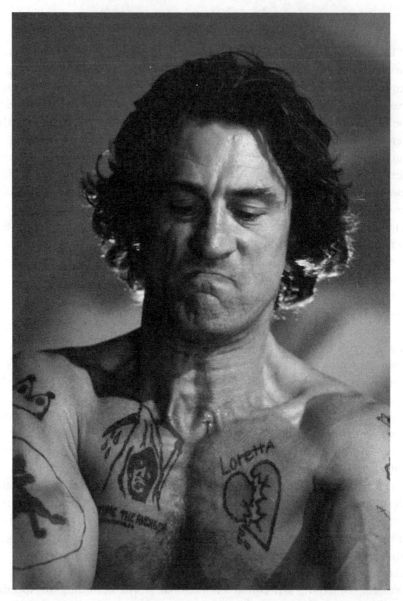

Cape Fear (Martin Scorsese, 1991). Courtesy Universal/The Kobal Collection.

classical continuity are mostly respected, intertextual referentiality
(to genres, cycles and stars) is sometimes complemented by what is
perceived – *within specific interpretive communities*[130] – as the explicit and
recognisable intertextual quotation of plot motifs and stylistic features
peculiar to earlier film versions. To take a general example, and one that

underscores the assertion that 'allusion constitute[s] . . . the very briefest form of "remaking"',[131] the narrative of *Unforgiven* (Clint Eastwood, 1992) assumes as its primary intertexts the revisionist Westerns of the 1960s and 1970s and the Eastwood star persona, but (re)viewers additionally see the film as a kind of sequel (the Will Munny character as the now aged 'Man-with-no-name' from Eastwood's spaghetti Westerns), and as a homage to the films of both Sam Peckinpah and John Ford. For instance, Pat Dowell states that *Unforgiven* is 'inescapably Fordian' in its mood, lifting a 'signature scene' – the man silhouetted against the sunset, looking over the grave of his beloved wife – from *She Wore a Yellow Ribbon* (1949) and *Young Mr Lincoln* (1939).[132] More specifically, Martin Scorsese's remake of *Cape Fear* may be said to work perfectly well as a conventional thriller (a psychopath attacks a 'normal' – in this case, dysfunctional – American family), but the new *Cape Fear* also 'assumes [in its reworking of the original Bernard Herrmann score, and the casting of original lead players in cameo roles] that the viewer has seen the earlier one, perhaps even as recently as Scorsese himself'.[133] Another example, Jim McBride's *Breathless* (1983), displays a 'neo-*noir*' predilection for *l'amour fou*, but also quotes its Godard original (*A bout de souffle*, 1959) in its smallest detail (a character's name, a player's gesture), and more generally embraces Godard's enthusiasm for American pop-cultural iconography: the title song, 'Breathless', by the 'Killer', Jerry Lee Lewis; the direct quotation from Joseph H. Lewis's *Gun Crazy* (1950); the Roy Lichtenstein-type lifts from Marvel Comics' *The Silver Surfer*; the collectable American automobile – the 1957 Ford Thunderbird, the 1959 Cadillac Eldorado (see Chapter 6). While it is possible to find instances of 'direct' quotation in the classical cinema, the above examples demonstrate that 'at whatever level of generality the intertext exists (or rather can be posited), every remake simultaneously refers to and remakes the genre to which that intertext belongs, and this genre may itself be the only intertext'.[134]

The type of intertextual referentiality that characterises contemporary American film circulates in a historically specific context. Accordingly, the identification of (and indeed the commercial decision to remake) an earlier film is located in particular extratextual, institutional or discursive practices. As in Noël Carroll's discussion of new Hollywood 'allusionism', the question of intertextual referentiality needs to be related to the radical extension of film literacy and the enthusiasm for (American) film history that took hold in the United States during the 1960s and early 1970s.[135] Partly made possible by the release of Hollywood features to television and the wider accessibility of new technologies (for example, 16 mm film projection), this re-evaluation, or legitimisation, of Hollywood cultural product was underwritten by such additional factors as the importation of the French *politique des auteurs*, the upsurge of repertory theatre short seasons, the expansion of film courses in American universities and the emergence of professional associations such as the American Film Institute. Accordingly, and this is evident from the above examples – *Unforgiven, Cape Fear, Breathless* – the selection and recognition of films, and bodies of films, for quotation and reworking (for example, the work of *auteurs*, Ford and Peckinpah; the cult movie, *Cape Fear*; the *nouvelle vague* landmark, *A bout de souffle*) can be located in the institutionally determined practice of film canon formation and its contributing projects – the determination to comment upon and conserve a film heritage, the discussion and citation of particular films in popular and academic film criticism, the selective release and re-release of films to theatrical and video distribution windows, the proliferation of talk and websites on the Internet and (in circular fashion) the decision of other film makers to evoke earlier films and recreate cinema history.[136]

An understanding of the formation and maintenance of the film canon in turn goes some way toward explaining why remakes of highly institutionalised *film noirs* – for example, *D.O.A.* (Rocky Morton and Annabel Jankel, 1988), *No Way Out* (Roger Donaldson, 1987) and *Against All Odds* (Taylor Hackford, 1984) – are discussed with reference to their originals (*D.O.A.* (Rudolph Maté, 1949), *The Big Clock* (John Farrow, 1948) and *Out of the Past* (Jacques Tourneur, 1947), respectively), while films such as Martin Scorsese's version of *The Age of Innocence* (1993) and James Dearden's remake of *A Kiss Before Dying* (1991) defer, not to their little known or (now) rarely seen earlier film versions – *The Age of Innocence* (Wesley Ruggles, 1924; Philip Moeller, 1934) and *A Kiss Before Dying* (Gerd Oswald, 1961) – but to the authority of an established literary canon: *The Age of Innocence* is based on Edith Wharton's 1920 Pulitzer Prize winning novel and *A Kiss Before Dying* is adapted from a best-selling novel by Ira Levin. Indeed, and in accordance with the canonisation of the work of Alfred Hitchcock, the more direct intertextual referent for the remake of *A Kiss Before Dying* is Hitchcock's *Vertigo* – a clip from the film appears diegetically on a character's television screen, and in addition to the 'figure' of the *doppelganger* there is allusion to Hitchcockian plot structure and motif: 'liberally alluding to Hitchcock by killing off his leading actress in the first reel, Dearden includes subtler references like the washing out of hair-dye and the cop who just won't leave'.[137] Steven Soderbergh's remake of *Solaris* is similarly likened not only to its direct precursor (the Tarkovsky version), but is 'reminiscent of Hitchcock's *Vertigo*',[138] and has 'more than a touch of *Vertigo*'s *l'amour fou* as *déjà vu*'.[139] In another example, Kolker suggests that Scorsese's *Cape Fear* is not simply a 'direct remake' of the 1961 version, but a 'secret remake' of three 'minor' Hitchcock films: *Stage Fright* (1950), *Strangers on a Train* (1951) and *I Confess* (1953): '[*Cape Fear*] adopts the plot of its predecessor while gaining a deeper structure through an allusive tag game with [these] three Hitchcock films'.[140]

The endless chain of connections – both voluntary and involuntary – which characterises film remaking is further sketched in Lesley Stern's *The Scorsese Connection*. Stern argues, for instance, that Scorsese's version of *Cape Fear*, in its reworking of elements of horror and *film noir*, is as much a remake of *The Night of the Hunter* (Charles Laughton, 1955) as it is of Thompson's earlier film version.[141] Additionally, Stern sees Max Cady (Robert DeNiro) from *Cape Fear* as a 'reincarnation' of *Taxi Driver*'s Travis Bickle (also played by DeNiro) who, in turn, is a kind of 'resurrected' Ethan Edwards, the John Wayne character from *The Searchers*.[142] Moreover, Stern states that 'it is not just characters who are reincarnated: ideas persist, questions that are not answered, anomalies that drive by night through a variety of cinematic landscapes [return].'[143] In the case of *The Searchers*, Stern traces an elaborate exchange, 'a network of similarities, a kind of cinematic scar tissue [it is the Indian Chief 'Scar' whom Ethan pursues] that stretches, extends over the continuity of the celluloid surface'.[144] In *The Searchers* and *Taxi Driver*, this exchange is not just (to give two examples) an oscillation between the terms of 'home' and 'away', or the reproduction of a prohibition against contamination and miscegenation, but more broadly the ghostly return of 'a troubling scenario of irresolution . . . The repetition . . . (aimless yet compulsive) . . . of the obsessive structure of the films [of all films] themselves'.[145]

The above examples of *A Kiss Before Dying*, *Cape Fear* and *The Searchers/Taxi Driver* demonstrate that 'the intertext, the precursor text, is never singular and never a moment of pure origin'.[146] This is nowhere more evident than in *Breathless*, the American remake of *A bout de souffle*. At one level, *Breathless* is a genre movie, an outlaw romance which draws heavily on the romantic star persona developed by Richard Gere in films like *American Gigolo* (Paul Schrader, 1980) and *An Officer and a Gentleman* (Taylor Hackford, 1982). For a contemporary audience, the *Breathless* update is a 'suitably jazzy, sexy entertainment',[147] but its identification as remake may be the occasion for an *interpretive shift*, restricting attention to particular scenes and to a comparative analysis of the remake to its original. For instance, Gilbert Adair says that 'whatever its precise status – homage, pastiche, paraphrase, vulgarisation' – the McBride film is in 'no significant sense' a remake of *A bout de souffle*, but rather 'a wet, pulpy, squelching kiss lovingly applied to Hollywood's backside'.[148] Reviewers thus appeal to originals not only in order to establish the (greater or lesser) worth of the remake, but also to secure the value of the film medium by relating it to deeply established precursors (the canon).[149] The identification of a source can *secure* the former version as a kind of fixity (against which the remake is evaluated), but 'there can never be a simple original uncomplicated by the structure of the remake'.[150] Just as *Breathless* admits to other intertexts – its makers screened *Gun Crazy*, *High Sierra* (1941), and *Killer's Kiss* (1955) during pre-production[151] – *A bout de souffle* draws upon classic *film noirs* – *Whirlpool* (1949), *The Enforcer* (1951), *The Harder They Fall* (1956), *Ten Seconds to Hell* (1959) – and a host of inter-art intertexts, among them: Paul Klee's *The Timid Brute* (1938), Picasso's *The Lovers* (1923), Faulkner's *The Wild Palms* (1939) and Maurice Sachs's *Abracadabra* (1952).[152] Understood in relation to a vast body of critical writing on Godard, *Breathless* is but one moment in an elaborate chain of reworkings: Godard as critic rewrites Hollywood cinema; Andrew Sarris rewrites Godard as critic; Godard remakes Hollywood cinema in *A bout de souffle*; Godard remakes *A bout de souffle* in *Pierrot le fou* (1965); McBride remakes Godard in *David Holzman's Diary* (1967); McBride remakes *A bout de souffle* in *Breathless*; Quentin Tarantino remakes everyone in *Pulp Fiction* (1994) (see Chapter 6).

Like all critical constructs (genre included), remaking – quotation, allusion, adaptation – is created and sustained through the repeated use of terminology.[153] The suggestion that the very limited direct intertextual referentiality between the remake and its original is organised according to an extratextual referentiality, located in historically specific discursive formations – especially film criticism and reviewing, but also copyright law and authorship, canon formation and film literacy – has consequences for purely textual descriptions of the remake, particularly those which seek to ground the category in a rigid distinction between an original story and its new discursive incarnation.[154] Aside from the questionable move of assuming that the unchanging essence of a film's story can somehow be abstracted from the mutable disposition of its expression,[155] demarcation along the lines of story and discourse is evidently frustrated by those remakes which repeat not only the narrative invention of an original property but seek, for instance, to recreate the expressive design of an earlier film (for example, *Far From Heaven* as a recreation of Sirkian *mise-en-scène*) or to rework the style of an entire *oeuvre* or genre (for example, *Miller's Crossing* (Joel Coen, 1990) as the 'essential' Hammett, or *Body Heat* as the archetypal recreation of the *film noir*). More importantly, while it might appear 'an elementary and intuitively given fact that a story can be told in different ways and remain, in an important sense, the same story',[156] the identification of exactly which elements shall count as the fundamental units of narrative in the determination of the similar and the same – that is, in the identification of the remake and its original – becomes (especially in the absence of a screen credit acknowledging an original property) a theoretical construct, or a function of the discursive context of the film's production and reception. These 'contextual forms of intertextuality',[157] which include film industry and other public discourses, shift attention from purely textual markers to the identification of an interpretive frame. That is, while a general narrative and cinematic competence enables the construction of an intratextually determined hierarchy of story descriptions, which range from the most succinct to the most detailed, the construction of a particular intertextual relation between a remake and its presumed original is *an act of interpretation*, one which is 'limited and relative – not to a [viewing] subject but to the interpretive grid (the regime of reading) through which both the subject position and the textual relations are constituted'.[158] Finally, and as Frow argues generally in relation to the concept of intertextuality,[159] what is important to an account of the remake is not the detailed 'identification of particular . . . intertextual source[s]', which function as retrospectively designated points of origin, but the determination of 'a more general discursive structure' – *the genre of re-viewing labelled 'remake'*.

To sum up, it seems necessary to stress the need for detailed (historical) investigation and research into the concept of film remaking, in both its legal-industrial and critical-interpretive definitions. As Stern points out, there may be no simple answer to what it is about the term 'remaking' that makes it 'peculiarly cinematic', but the pursuit of just what defines film remaking and characterises its intersection with other practices of repetition would need to include '[an engagement] with the industrial nature of the cinema (questions of what constitutes a "property" and questions of copyright, for instance), [an engagement with] the peculiarity of cinematic genre, with the nature of cinematic quotation, and with how to conceive of cinematic intertextuality as a question of cultural history'.[160] Beyond textual approaches to film remaking, beyond the identification of endlessly proliferating patterns of repetition and difference, inquiries into the nature of remaking would locate it (as has been argued above) not only in industrial fields and textual strategies, but in cinematic (and general) discursive fields, in such historically specific technologies as copyright law and authorship, canon formation and media literacy, film criticism and film reviewing.

Reflecting the organisation of this introduction, this book draws out and develops various approaches to film remaking across its three broad sections. Part I develops the idea of *remaking as an industrial category*. Chapter 1 (Commerce) takes up the case of the remaking of television series as feature films in order to investigate the commercial strategies behind the rebranding of previously market-tested properties such as *The Addams Family* and *Charlie's Angels* as new cross-media franchises. Chapter 2 (Authors) takes this production-oriented approach further to look at the way in which the film remake can be understood as a category of authorship by investigating the case of *Psycho* and the general remaking of the films of Alfred Hitchcock. Part II investigates *remaking as a textual category*. Chapter 3 (Texts) attends to the question of the transformation of earlier textualised sources by investigating issues of adaptation and drawing these out through extended case studies of the remaking of *Yojimbo* and *Planet of the Apes*. Chapter 4 (Genres) continues this approach but attends to the remaking of broader generic structures by investigating the case of the remaking of classic *film noirs* such as *The Postman Always Rings Twice* and *Double Indemnity*. Part III casts an even wider net to look at *remaking as a critical category*. Chapter 5 (Audiences) looks at a wide range of contemporary remakes to consider the contribution that audience knowledge and industry discourses (publicity, exhibition, reviewing) make to an understanding of remakes. Chapter 6 (Discourse) further develops this contextual approach to investigate the role of the film canon in a chain of remakings extending from *Gun Crazy* and *A bout de souffle* to *Bonnie and Clyde* and *Breathless*. The book's conclusion (Remaking Everything) at once extends and revisits some of these issues by attending to the persona and films of arch-remaker Quentin Tarantino.

Notes

1. Mazdon, *Encore Hollywood*, p. 2.
2. Grindstaff, 'A Pygmalion Tale Retold', p. 134.
3. Horton and McDougal, *Play It Again, Sam*, p. 3.
4. Stam, *Film Theory*, p. 202.
5. Wills, 'The French Remark', p. 148.
6. Altman, *Film/Genre*, p. 84.
7. Whelehan, 'Adaptations', p. 3.
8. Neale, 'Questions of Genre', p. 51.
9. Altman, *Film/Genre*, pp. 83–4.
10. Ibid., p. 85.
11. Ibid., p. 120.

12. Frow, *Marxism and Literary History*, and 'Intertextuality and Ontology'.
13. Stern, *The Scorsese Connection*, and '*Emma* in Los Angeles'.
14. See online reviews of *Play It Again, Sam* by Frow and Stern in *Screening the Past* and *Modernism/Modernity*, respectively.
15. Altman, *Film/Genre*, p. 86.
16. Ibid., p. 84.
17. Ellis, *Visible Fictions*, p. 30.
18. Altman, *Film/Genre*, p. 112.
19. Bahrenburg, *The Creation of Dino De Laurentiis' King Kong*, pp. 13 and 112–13.
20. Patterson, 'Second Time Lucky', p. 6.
21. Vincendeau, 'Hijacked', p. 24.
22. See Balio, 'Introduction to Part II'; Hoberman, 'Ten Years That Shook the World', pp. 34–59; and Silverman, 'Hollywood Cloning', pp. 24–30.
23. Schatz, 'The New Hollywood', pp. 17–25.
24. Hoberman, 'Facing the Nineties', pp. 1–2.
25. Simonet, 'Conglomerates and Content', p. 161.
26. Harvey, 'Can't Stop the Remakes', pp. 50–3.
27. Miller, 'Hollywood: The Ad', pp. 59–62.
28. Murray, 'Let's Do It Again', p. 64.
29. Hughes, 'Apocalypse now. Please!', p. 1.
30. Simonet, 'Conglomerates and Content', p. 154.
31. *Cinefantastique*, quoted in Kermode, 'What a Carve Up!', p. 14.
32. Stern, '*Emma* in Los Angeles', p. 226.
33. Simonet, 'Conglomerates and Content', p. 155.
34. See Bellour, *The Analysis of Film*.
35. See Kolker, 'Algebraic Figures', p. 36; Neale, 'Questions of Genre', p. 56; and Altman, *Film/Genre*, p. 115.
36. See Friend, 'Copy Cats', pp. 51–7.
37. Druxman, *Make It Again, Sam*, p. 9.
38. Ibid.
39. Ibid.
40. Ibid.
41. Ibid.
42. Ibid.
43. Ibid., p. 13.
44. Balio, *Grand Design*, p. 99.
45. Robert Gustafson, quoted in ibid.
46. Ibid. See also Schatz, *Boom and Bust*, pp. 40–1 and 64–5.
47. Druxman, *Make It Again, Sam*, p. 15.
48. Ibid., pp. 18–20.
49. Balio, *Grand Design*, p. 100.
50. Druxman, *Make It Again, Sam*, p. 15.
51. Corrigan, 'Which Shakespeare to Love?', p. 163.

52. Druxman, *Make It Again, Sam*, pp. 13–15.
53. Lubin, *Titanic*, pp. 36 and 72.
54. Ibid., p. 120.
55. Druxman, *Make It Again, Sam*, p. 20.
56. Keller, ' "Size Does Matter" ', p. 133.
57. Wyatt and Vlesmas, 'The Drama of Recoupment', p. 35.
58. McDougal, 'The Director Who Knew Too Much', p. 52.
59. Ibid., pp. 53 and 67.
60. Michaels, '*Nosferatu*', p. 245.
61. Greenberg, 'Raiders of the Lost Text', p. 165.
62. Ibid., p. 170.
63. Ibid., pp. 166–7.
64. Bordwell, *Making Meaning*, p. 9.
65. Bloom, *The Anxiety of Influence*.
66. See Culler, *The Pursuit of Signs*, pp. 107–10; and Worton and Still, 'Introduction', pp. 27–9.
67. Greenberg, 'Raiders of the Lost Text', p. 170.
68. Corrigan, *A Cinema Without Walls*, p. 103. See also Corrigan, 'Auteurs and the New Hollywood'.
69. Corrigan, 'Which Shakespeare to Love?', p. 168.
70. Grant, 'Recognising *Billy Budd* in *Beau Travail*', p. 58.
71. Strick, 'Rev. of *Solaris*', pp. 54–5.
72. Altman, *Film/Genre*, p. 84.
73. Eaton, 'Condemned to Repeats', p. 4.
74. Altman, *Film/Genre*, p. 87.
75. Nowlan and Nowlan, *Cinema Sequels and Remakes*, pp. xi–xii.
76. Simonet, 'Conglomerates and Content', p. 156.
77. Eberwein, 'Remakes and Cultural Studies', pp. 28–31.
78. Leitch, 'Twice-Told Tales', p. 138.
79. Ibid.
80. Ibid., p. 139.
81. Ibid., p. 142.
82. Ibid., pp. 142–5.
83. Ibid., p. 147.
84. Ibid., p. 139.
85. Druxman, *Make It Again, Sam*, p. 9.
86. The titles to *The Assassin* state that it is 'based on Luc Besson's "Nikita" ' (the latter was both written and directed by Besson). While the payment of copyright fees is *generally* the case, there are exceptions. For instance, *Black Cat* (Stephen Shin, 1991), a Hong Kong film that closely follows the narrative unfolding of *Nikita*, does not acknowledge Besson's film.
87. Vincendeau, 'Hijacked', p. 24.
88. Newman, 'Rev. of *Just Visiting*', p. 47.
89. Leitch, 'Twice-Told Tales', p. 139.

90. Hoberman, 'Sacred and Profane'; and Diski, 'The Shadow Within'.
91. Vieira and Stam, 'Parody and Marginality', p. 94.
92. Neale, *Genre and Hollywood*, p. 39.
93. http://www.italianjobmovie.com/flash/index.html.
94. Corrigan, 'Which Shakespeare to Love?', p. 164.
95. Leitch, 'Twice-Told Tales', p. 139.
96. See McElwee, 'Theatrical Re-issues'.
97. Lafferty, 'Feature Films on Prime-Time Television', pp. 235–56.
98. Friedberg, *Window Shopping*.
99. Frow, 'Intertextuality and Ontology', p. 45.
100. Iampolski, *The Memory of Tiresias*, p. 8.
101. Ibid., p. 31, emphasis in original.
102. Ibid.
103. Ibid., pp. 32–5.
104. Frow, 'Rev. of *Play It Again, Sam*', emphasis added.
105. Stam, *Film Theory*, p. 207.
106. Macksey, 'Foreword', p. xviii.
107. Wees, *Recycled Images*, pp. 32–48.
108. Thompson, 'Songe de Titanic', p. 66.
109. Stam, *Film Theory*, p. 209.
110. Ibid., p. 208.
111. Calabrese, *Neo-Baroque*, pp. 173–9.
112. Stam, *Film Theory*, p. 337, n. 2.
113. Grindstaff, 'A Pygmalion Tale Retold', p. 161.
114. Roth, 'Twice Two'.
115. Georgakas, 'Robin Hood', p. 70.
116. Frow, 'Intertextuality and Ontology', p. 45.
117. Rosenbaum, 'Rev. of *Obsession*', p. 217.
118. Ray, *A Certain Tendency of the Hollywood Cinema*, pp. 119–20.
119. Michaels, '*Nosferatu*', p. 241.
120. Friedberg, *Window Shopping*, pp. 175–6.
121. '*The Searchers*: A Family Tree', pp. 2–6.
122. Schrader commentary on *Mishima*, Warner Home Video, Region 1 DVD, 2001.
123. For example, Newman, 'Rev. of *The Big Chill*', p. 41.
124. Sayles and Smith, *Sayles on Sayles*, p. 57.
125. Neale, 'Questions of Genre', p. 51; and *Genre and Hollywood*, p. 31.
126. Altman, *Film/Genre*, p. 91.
127. Kolker, 'Algebraic Figures', p. 36.
128. Leitch, 'Twice-Told Tales', p. 141.
129. Eco, 'Innovation and Repetition', pp. 161–84.
130. See Fish, *Is There a Text in This Class?*
131. Biguenet, 'Double Takes', p. 131.
132. Dowell, 'Rev. of *Unforgiven*', p. 72.

133. Hoberman, 'Sacred and Profane', p. 11.
134. Frow, 'Rev. of *Play It Again, Sam*'.
135. Carroll, 'The Future of Allusion', pp. 51–81.
136. Staiger, 'The Politics of Film Canons', p. 4.
137. Strick, 'Rev. of *A Kiss Before Dying*', p. 50.
138. Martin, 'Soderbergh's Planet Casts Psychic Spell', p. 5.
139. Taubin, 'Steven Soderbergh Follows Andrei Tarkovsky into Space for a Walk with Love and Death', p. 22.
140. Kolker, 'Algebraic Figures', p. 40.
141. Stern, *The Scorsese Connection*, p. 198.
142. Ibid., pp. 49 and 170.
143. Ibid., p. 49.
144. Ibid., p. 58.
145. Ibid., pp. 33–4.
146. Frow, 'Rev. of *Play It Again, Sam*'.
147. *Variety Movie Guide*, p. 121.
148. Adair, 'Rev. of *Breathless*', pp. 241–2.
149. Altman, *Film/Genre*, p. 127.
150. Wills, 'The French Remark', p. 157.
151. Carson, '*Breathless* Diary', pp. 33–8.
152. Andrew, '*Breathless*: Old as New', pp. 3–20; and Kline, *Screening the Text*, pp. 184–221.
153. Altman, *Film/Genre*, p. 84.
154. Leitch, 'Twice-Told Tales', p. 143.
155. See Brunette and Wills, *Screen/Play*, p. 53; and Gabbard, 'The Ethnic Oedipus', p. 96.
156. Culler, 'Defining Narrative Units', p. 123. See also Andrew, 'Adaptation', p. 34; and Ray, 'Film and Literature', pp. 121–2.
157. Klinger, 'Digressions at the Cinema', p. 7.
158. Frow, *Marxism and Literary History*, p. 155.
159. Frow, 'Intertextuality and Ontology', p. 46.
160. Stern, 'Rev. of *Play It Again, Sam*'.

Part I Remaking as Industrial Category

CHAPTER 1

Commerce

A number of essays in the recent Thomas Elsaesser and Kay Hoffmann anthology, *Cinema Futures*, consider the *mutual dependence* – both cultural and economic – of the institutions of cinema and television.[1] In particular, Elsaesser describes two related strategies of *media repetition*. The first, *serialisation*, is a *textual* strategy employed by both television (serials, series, sagas) and cinema (series, sequels, remakes) to deliver and bind a global audience to its product and its own institution. The second, *multi-plication*, is a *marketing* strategy that connects these institutions, and their audiences, beyond textual and national boundaries via adjacent discursive fields.[2] In other words, Elsaesser describes a globalised entertainment industry (dominated by Sony, News Corp, Time-Warner and the like) in which film and television franchises exceed boundaries (textual, national, institutional) to be *reiterated* – expanded and exploited – across an array of media platforms: from music and print media to theme parks and electronic games.[3] This is, for instance, the strategy of the *Batman* remaking (Tim Burton, 1989) of the television property and feature film of the 1960s (*Batman*, ABC, 1966–68; and *Batman*, Leslie Martinson, 1966, respectively). Both versions (1960s and 1980s) have their foundation in Bob Kane's comic books for Detective Comics in the late 1930s, and the Burton remake (earning $250 million domestically and $160 million overseas) revived the franchise, spinning it out through sequels (*Batman Returns*, 1992; *Batman Forever*, 1995; *Batman and Robin*, 1997; *Batman Begins*, 2005) and a host of media texts (including a new *Batman* tele-series, 1992–95) and merchandising items.[4]

As described in the introductory chapter, remakes are often thought of as commercial products that repeat successful formulas in order to minimise risk and secure profits in the marketplace. Some properties, such as *King Kong* (Peter Jackson, 2005), are selected for (commercial) remaking because they are inherently spectacular and so suited to the developing technological powers of (digital) film. Other properties are reworked to offer up vehicles for top-line stars, or to open up and exploit new markets, or (as in the example of *Batman*) to revive and create cross-media franchises. This chapter takes particular interest in the remaking of classic television series – such as *The Addams Family*, *The Fugitive*, *The Flintstones*, *Mission: Impossible*, *Charlie's Angels* and *Scooby Doo* – as new theatrical features and potential cross-media platforms. On one hand, this cycle of television remakes relates to cultural memory and to the archival function of television, but on the other it seems a function of the conservative production and marketing strategies of a globally dominant (and, what critics see as, artistically challenged) contemporary Hollywood. That is, since the mid-1970s, the North American film industry invests – whether because of 'creative atrophy, conglomerate domination, commercial timidity, or all three at once'[5] – in various strategies of recycling. In the case of television remakes, critics despair at 'the pillaging of television vaults for movie ideas', a tendency they characterise as 'a kind of latter-day tomb raiding'.[6] In the context of defensive production practices, old television series (along with comic books and computer games[7]) provide recognisable, and relatively inexpensive, self-promotional devices with which to market and *brand* new 'high-concept' feature films and media franchises. For instance, producer-star Tom Cruise's second instalment in the *Mission: Impossible* film series is described as 'a franchise in the making, taking over, perhaps, where James Bond Inc. left off'.[8] *Mission: Impossible* and other successful properties generate then not only sequels – *Addams Family Values*, *A Very Brady Sequel*, *U.S. Marshals*, *The Flintstones in Viva Rock Vegas*, *Mission: Impossible 2*, *Charlie's Angels: Full Throttle*, *Scooby Doo 2: Monsters Unleashed* – but revived television series, music videos, film soundtracks, video games, comic books and other brand-name products.

The term 'television features' is used in this chapter to refer to an industrial cycle of feature films, mostly from the 1990s (and beyond), derived from television series of the late 1950s, 1960s and early 1970s. Variously described as adaptations, updates, homages, remakes, recyclings, recreations, resurrections, sequels and spin-offs, these television features are heavily imbricated – like the tele-series that inspire them – with patterns of repetition. In the 1950s, the major Hollywood studios – restructuring in their shift to independent production and in response to the emergence of commercial television – gradually realised the potential for transferring some of their mass production techniques to television, and began to supply standardised episodic series to the major television networks.[9] These *tele-series* constituted a form of television characterised by the recurrence of a narrative scheme, a fixed situation with a restricted set of regular pivotal characters – the Clampett family in *The Beverly Hillbillies* (CBS, 1962–71), the castaways on *Gilligan's Island* (CBS, 1964–67), the three female detectives in *Charlie's Angels* (ABC, 1976–81) – around which a secondary set of characters revolved.[10] In the example of *The Beverly Hillbillies* the tele-series is a *sitcom*, a domestic comedy which unfolds in the specific physical world of the Clampett's mansion, and the 'situation' itself is built into this (principally) domestic space and develops there through confusion and complication, eventually toward its resolution.[11] More specifically, it has been noted that *The Beverly Hillbillies*, the most popular television comedy of the 1960s, and a series which generated 216 half-hour episodes (or approximately ninety hours of television), can be reduced to just five (repeated) narrative lines. These are:

1. shrewd city folks try to swindle Jed Clampett and family out of their fortune;
2. variously inappropriate – corrupt and/or mercenary – suitors come courting for the hand of Jed's daughter, Elly May;
3. Jed's moronic nephew, Jethro, tries his hand at various careers, including international spy and brain surgeon;
4. Jed, a widower, meets a potential bride; and
5. Granny, the family matriarch, battles to protect her backwoods traditions against the forces of post-industrial culture.[12]

While the above description already suggests strong patterns of textual repetition in the US tele-series, it is necessary to make a distinction between, on the one hand, thirty-minute sitcoms like *The Beverly Hillbillies* and *Gilligan's Island*, and on the other hand, sixty-minute action-adventure series like *Maverick* (ABC, 1957–62), *The Fugitive* (ABC, 1963–67) and *Mission: Impossible* (CBS, 1966–73). This is because, while in the latter instance there is still a restricted set of characters – brothers Bart and Bret Maverick (and sometimes their English cousin, Beau), Dr Richard Kimble and his nemesis Lt Philip Gerard, or the members of the IMF (Impossible Mission Force) team – other elements, such as situations, settings and adversaries ('special guest stars'), can vary considerably. The more important point, though, is that in the case of the tele-series (especially the variety found in the 1960s), the structure of each episode is always basically the same, and 'each episode contains a complete story, [while] the series as a whole possesses no story' (that is, there is no antici-pated series conclusion).[13] The episodes in the series can thus be produced and 'programmed infinitely' (and to some extent broadcast in any order) because 'the [narrated] time of each episode' (which can vary from the space of a few hours to that of several weeks) 'exists outside of history [or historical time] and is identical to itself, and each episode has no recollection of the others'.[14]

While the above comments provide something of a model, it is immediately evident that some television series (especially more recent ones) set up a more complex relationship between episode time, series time, and narrated time. In order to accommodate this variation it is necessary to turn to a second category of television, that of the *saga*. The saga differs from the series (as described above) mostly in so far as it concerns 'the "historical" lapse of time', or (in other words) the saga becomes a document of the history of its characters.[15] In this case, the structure of individual episodes is substantially the same as before, but 'the general time of the series changes': that is, 'the entire series is constructed according to a single narrative program that foresees a final solution, [but] each episode is [still] produced according to [its own] working narrative program'.[16] Unlike the *serial* (most commonly associated with television soap opera), where the overall narrative programme translates into *plot*, in the case of the saga, the overall timescale is transformed into 'a mechanism of mutation that modifies *the status of characters* from one episode to the next', so encouraging viewers to keep up with the changing knowledge of the characters.[17] It is, therefore, difficult to miss an individual episode without missing something of importance, but each episode still has meaning for the more casual viewer. Examples of the saga would be, then, programmes like *The Life and Legend of Wyatt Earp* (ABC, 1955–61) which developed its characters over a period of several years in an ongoing story of politics and family relations, alongside of its standard, episodic Western action; or (more recently) *Star Trek: The Next Generation* (syndicated, 1987–94), where each episode deals with a particular mission of the starship *Enterprise*, but equally each episode is organised around a number of sub-plots dealing with principally familial relationships that develop across the entire series (Worf's connection to his son; Deanna Troy's relationship with her mother; the episode dealing with Data's 'daughter', and so on). In these cases, the character of the US television series is such that it is able to produce an *episodic* narrative while at the same time working toward a satisfying (if endlessly deferred) *finalised* narrative.[18] Moreover, from the late 1970s onwards, and influenced by the 'legitimisation' of the *serial* form in the guise of prime-time soap operas such as *Dallas* (CBS, 1978–91), *Dynasty* (ABC, 1981–89) and (differently) *Twin Peaks* (ABC, 1990–91), the tele-series more often than not admits to a historical dimension.

The above comments begin to indicate how some aspects of repetition can be understood as structural mechanisms for generating television texts, but there is also the issue of how repetition translates into questions of programming and reception. That is, the seriality of the tele-series (or saga) is not just textual, but can be further understood by way of the reception category of the *rerun*. Defined as the 'repetition of a recorded performance',[19] the television rerun dates from 1953 when CBS first began putting repeats of *The Lone Ranger* (ABC, 1949–57) on its Saturday afternoon schedule, and the phenomenon gained intensity when, in 1957, CBS scheduled reruns of *I Love Lucy* (CBS, 1951–57) five days a week during the afternoon.[20] Within the context of US television, this type of repetition can mean either: (1) the syndicated rerun of a current network tele-series (or sometimes a tele-series that has recently gone out of production) which is sold on a station-by-station basis and aired at whatever time of the day chosen by that station; or (2) reruns may be taken up by networks themselves, both as summer repeats and/or as fillers for the peripheral slots of daytime or late night television (in other words, before or after prime time).[21] In the latter instance, series that formerly aired on a weekly basis (and to fill thirty-nine weeks of programming) are often shown on a daily basis, and sometimes on a continuous loop. Cheap and convenient time fillers, these reruns can remain in circulation well beyond a series' first-run, and come to account for much of television's programming time. Additionally, some tele-series become 'perennial rerun success stories' and others – like *Leave It to Beaver* in the 1980s and *The Brady Bunch* in the early 1990s – enjoy 'renaissances of sorts'.[22]

This relocation (or *dis*location) of tele-series as reruns – the free mixing of episodes outside of the chronology of their production – both underscores and complicates the (at least) minimal amount of temporal continuity that does seem to exist in tele-series and/or sagas. That is, removed from a context of linear, weekly and/or seasonal progression, what are perhaps intended as subtle series developments can become quite substantial intrusions.[23] Furthermore, encountering a programme as rerun rather than as *first-run* (even when the rerun is encountered *as* first-run) underscores the fact that the programme refers principally to televisual conventions and to a personal and/or cultural history.[24] This may in turn encourage specific *protocols of viewing*. That is, if the repetitive nature of the television text already encourages viewers to take pleasure not so much in the programme's limited narrative invention, but rather in its repetition of character and motif, gesture and signature line, then the repetition of the series as rerun has a further impact, encouraging an intensification of what might be called a *telephilic* protocol of viewing, one which celebrates or fetishises particular televisual moments.[25] Additionally, and in what has been described as 'an intense comedy of obsolescence',[26] the tele-series as rerun, framed by contemporary televisual codes and practices, can be encountered as anachronism and as cliché. This in turn may encourage – in specific viewing communities – a kind of ironic sensibility or historically contingent category of cultural taste commonly associated with the reading protocols of neo-camp, or 'bad taste'.[27] Such technologies of viewing are extended – especially from the mid-1980s onward – by the expansion of cable television (which repackages tele-series as nostalgia and/as high camp), and also by the entrenchment of home video (and now DVD), which contributes significantly to the archiving of tele-series. For instance, in 1985 the Nickelodeon channel successfully introduced its *Nick at Nite* programming as a 'friendly habitat' for the showcasing of reruns (a move that coincided with the appearance of 'evergreen' divisions in other syndication companies).[28] These types of developments are in turn attended to by such ephemera as cult television magazines (*Cult TV*), music compilations (*Television's Greatest Hits*) and web pages (both official and fan-based).

These endless repetitions – both textual and contextual – of tele-series and/or sagas not only provide specific occasions for criticism, but generate (and are generated by) other kinds of textual materials. These are not only the paratexts or epiphenomena of the television guide and TV magazine, but also texts produced through opportunities for merchandising. Initially, in the 1950s and 1960s, this included products like novelisations, comic books, trading cards and board games, but *Batman* (ABC, 1966–68) extended this to include over five hundred different 'Bat-products' (produced by more than sixty manufacturers) that earned in excess of $60 million.[29] More importantly (but linked to this), the ongoing circulation of television programmes and other textual materials has generated what mostly get referred to as *extension* or *reunion* episodes. These are typically two hours of television (shown either as a single instalment or in two parts) which bring the original cast (or most of the original cast) of a tele-series together – usually several years after the show's cancellation – for a special extended episode. This extension (or reunion) episode can be characterised in the following ways:

1. The extension episode often operates as a kind of sequel to the tele-series, that is because actors – especially child-actors – age, the extension episode addresses the historical lapse of time.
2. Commonly, the extension episode will deal with some special event over and above the narrative invention that characterised the textual repetitions of the tele-series.

3. Sometimes the extension episode will function as a *pilot* episode to generate the revival of the tele-series, or perhaps something like an animated version of that series.
4. Although initially shown in prime-time network slots, these extension
episodes (like some tele-series pilots) are, in foreign markets, often promoted and broadcast as televised movies.

Examples of extension episodes include programmes like: *The Return of
the Beverly Hillbillies* (CBS, 1981, broadcast ten years after the end of the
series' first-run); *Halloween with The Addams Family* (NBC, 1977, broadcast eleven years after the end of that series); and *The Wild, Wild West
Revisited* and *More Wild, Wild West* (CBS, 1979 and 1980, broadcast ten
and eleven years after the end of the series' first run).

A more elaborate example of the extension episode is the case of
Gilligan's Island. The first-run of *Gilligan's Island* was on the CBS network
from 1964 to 1967 and it generated 98 episodes in total. Ten years after
Gilligan's Island first came to air, the ABC network launched *The New
Adventures of Gilligan* (1974–77), the first of two animated series. The following year (1978) the NBC network began a cycle of three extension
episodes. The first of these was *Rescue From Gilligan's Island*, a two-hour
reunion episode screened as a two-part Saturday evening special (14 and
21 October 1978) in which the castaways of *Gilligan's Island* (all original
cast members, except in the role of Ginger) are finally rescued from the
tropical desert island upon which they have been captive for ten years. Back
in civilisation, the castaways make the mistake of going on a reunion cruise
(on the *SS Minnow II*) and get shipwrecked again on the same island, thus
paving the way for a sequel. The second of the extension episodes – *The
Castaways on Gilligan's Island* (NBC, 1979, 90 min.) – thus picks up from
the above, and rescued a second time the castaways (on this occasion) vol-
untarily return to the island in order to convert it (with the help of
Thurston Howell III's millions) into a tourist resort. The third extension
episode – *The Harlem Globetrotters on Gilligan's Island* (NBC, 1981,
120 min.) – has the famous basketball team drop in on the resort where they
join forces with the castaways to battle an evil billionaire who plans to use
'Superium', a rare energy source found on the island, to control the
world.[30] These three extension episodes were immediately followed up by
Gilligan's Planet (CBS, 1982–83), a second animated series (and kind of
extension of the earlier animated series) in which, in a desperate attempt
to get off the island, the Professor builds a rocket ship for the castaways but
a defect in its solar panels leads to them becoming marooned on an
unknown planet.[31] Scheduled alongside reruns, these extension episodes

and animated series have contributed to the programme's ongoing cultural currency, not only occasioning 'appearances' by Gilligan on *The Simpsons* and *South Park*, but contributing to various intertextual dialogues. Examples of the latter include conjecture in *Dazed and Confused* (Richard Linklater, 1993) as to how the castaways might by now have partnered off and spawned a whole mess of kids; a reference in *The Brady Bunch Movie* (Betty Thomas, 1995) to Peter being a babe in 'a Gilligan sort of way', and ongoing speculation as to whether *Gilligan's Island* might not inspire a new theatrically released, feature film with someone like Jim Carrey in the Gilligan role. Most recently, *Gilligan's Island* has been remade as a reality TV programme – *The Real Gilligan's Island* (TBS, 2004) – which assembles two complete sets of castaways (contestants) to work through elimination challenges (modelled on some of the situations that occurred in the original series) and attempt to find a way off the island.[32]

A variation on the idea of the extension episode is the tele-series that is transformed into a full-blown theatrically released feature film, complete with big (or bigger) budget production values and promotional strategies. Examples of the theatrically released extension episode include features such as *McHale's Navy* (Edward J. Montagne, 1964), *McHale's Navy Joins the Air Force* (Edward J. Montagne, 1965) and the *Get Smart* movie, *The Nude Bomb* (Clive Donner, 1980). The latter, which was televised as *The Return of Maxwell Smart* (NBC, 1982), is an unusual example of the extension episode in so far as it brings together only Don Adams (Maxwell Smart) and George Karvelas (Larraby) of the principal original cast. It is, however, in its own way a clever extension of the TV series (and its spoof of Cold War espionage). *The Nude Bomb* includes a title sequence in imitation of James Bond (complete with Bond-type title song, 'You're Always There' by Lalo Schifrin), Sylvia Kristel (between performances in the *Emmanuelle* movies) as Smart's partner Agent 34 and, as a set piece, a chase through its production company's (Universal's) popular studio tour. A second, more conventional reunion episode – *Get Smart, Again* (ABC, 1989) – brought together not only Adams and Karvelas, but Barbara Feldon (as Agent 99) and Dick Gautier (as Hymie, the robot). And in 1995, Fox briefly revived the tele-series *Get Smart*, with Maxwell Smart (Adams) now chief of CONTROL, Agent 99 (Feldon) as a congresswoman, and their son, Zach (Andy Dick), as a newly recruited CONTROL agent. [33]

The best known and most successful of the theatrically released extension episodes is *Star Trek: The Motion Picture* (Robert Wise, 1979), and the five *Star Trek* features that followed (from 1982 to 1991). As in the case of broadcast extension episodes, *Star Trek: The Motion Picture* is the occasion for a reunion: in this case, when news reaches Starfleet headquarters that a malignant force within a cloud-like formation is headed for Earth, James T. Kirk (now an Admiral) takes charge of his old starship *Enterprise*, is reunited with his former crew and together they confront the alien menace. The long-awaited, big-budget feature of the discontinued *Star Trek* tele-series (NBC, 1966–69) generated not only the aforementioned features but also four further tele-series (*Star Trek: The Next Generation*, *Deep Space Nine*, *Voyager*, *Enterprise*) and the first of these led to a further series of feature films, most recently *Star Trek Nemesis* (Stuart Baird, 2002). A more recent attempt to translate a tele-series into a fan-based *Star Trek*-like franchise is *The X-Files Movie* (Rob Bowman, 1998), but in this case the tele-series was still in production and the interrelatedness of Fox's media interests had merged to the point that the tele-series occasioned the feature, but the feature directly generated the next season's series. Other attempts to transpose a still current tele-series into a feature film (with the 'same' cast and without a substantial gap between the broadcast time of the first-run series and the release of the feature) include films such as *Teenage Mutant Ninja Turtles* (Steve Barron, 1990) and its two sequels (1991 and 1993), and *Mighty Morphin Power Rangers: The Movie* (Bryan Spicer, 1995) and its sequel (1997). More recent examples include (but are not limited to) *The Rugrats Movie* (Norton Virgien and Igor Kovalyov, 1999) and sequels (2000 and 2003), *South Park: Bigger, Longer & Uncut* (Trey Parker, 1999) and *Jackass The Movie* (Jeff Tremaine, 2002).

As described above, the extension episode creates a circuit with its tele-series reruns, sometimes providing the opportunity for a revived series. For example, *Still the Beaver*, the 1983 CBS extension episode of *Leave It to Beaver* (CBS 1957–58; ABC 1958–63), led to a new cable tele-series (again with most members of the original cast) titled *Still the Beaver* (aka *The New Leave It to Beaver*, Disney, 1985–86 and WTBS, 1986). But equally – and in particular over the past decade or more – the rerun and the extension episode, and especially the ways these continue to circulate as 'snippets' from the televisual past,[34] have provided the occasion for an entire new cycle of feature film versions of original tele-series (and other television properties). As Ina Rae Hark points out, whereas the aforementioned theatrically released, extension episodes involved a *transfer* from one medium to another, these new adaptations 'involved *remaking* the television series as films'.[35] This cycle of remakings had precursors throughout the 1980s in features such as *The Legend of the Lone Ranger* (William A. Fraker, 1981) and *Twilight Zone: The Movie* (Joe Dante, John Landis, George Miller and Steven Spielberg, 1983), *Dragnet* (Tom Mankiewicz, 1987) and *The Untouchables* (Brian De Palma, 1987). But the cycle picked up momentum with the successful release of *The Addams Family* (Barry Sonnenfeld, 1991), which took $113 million at the US box-office.[36] This cycle of features continued throughout the 1990s with films like: *Addams Family Values, Dennis the Menace, The Fugitive, The Beverly Hillbillies, Car 54, Where Are You?* (all 1993); *The Flintstones, Maverick, The Cisco Kid, Lassie, The Little Rascals, Richie Rich* (all 1994); *The Brady Bunch Movie, Casper* (both 1995); *A Very Brady Sequel, Sgt. Bilko, Mission: Impossible, Flipper* (all 1996); *The Saint, Mr. Magoo, McHale's Navy, George of the Jungle, Leave It to Beaver* (all 1997); *Lost in Space, The Avengers, The Mask of Zorro* (all 1998); and *My Favorite Martian, The Mod Squad, Inspector Gadget, The Wild, Wild West* (all 1999). These remakings continue into the present decade with features such as: *The Adventures of Rocky & Bullwinkle, Charlie's Angels, Mission: Impossible 2* (all 2000); *I Spy, Scooby-Doo* (both 2002); *Charlie's Angels: Full Throttle, S.W.A.T.* (both 2003), and *Scooby-Doo 2: Monsters Unleashed, Starsky & Hutch, Thunderbirds* (all 2004).

At one level, this cycle of feature films – derived from tele-series (and animated cartoon anthologies) that have 'moulded the childhood aesthetics of baby-boomers and Gen-Xers alike'[37] – relates to the archival function of television. But at another, it can be seen to respond (as previously noted) to the conservative production and marketing strategies of contemporary Hollywood, whereby tele-series of the 1960s and early 1970s provide recognisable, 'bankably inexpensive, high-concept, self-promotional devices with which to market feature films'.[38] Old television programmes have ready-made audiences on cable and DVD as well as fan support on the Internet, and often boast 'a strong set-up for a film and lend themselves to clever updating'.[39] David Marc adds that such properties provide investors with the reassurance of a *quantifiable* track record, including figures on 'the profitability of the series in the syndicated rerun market; the demographic character of its viewership; product licensing reports; [and] public perception of the property's position on the family viewing/adult entertainment grid'.[40] This seems generally true of the features grouped above, which provide titles, character names (and sometimes situations) for 're-casting'. Moreover, an understanding of the phenomenon of tele-series remakes, or television features, can be taken further by broadly identifying two commercial strategies for the remaking of these old television properties.

The first strategy of remaking would seem to be an attempt to create a circuit between, on the one hand, a generation (or two) of viewers who encountered these tele-series as first-runs and/or reruns through the 1960s and beyond (that is, an audience largely made up of parents and grandparents), and on the other hand a younger generation of filmgoers – children and/or grandchildren of the first group – who may have little or no knowledge of the original tele-series but whose narrative image of that property is developed through the feature film's promotion and cross-promotion. This 'family viewing' category of television features can be further divided into two sub-sets: (1) a group of features derived from television sitcoms: *The Addams Family*, *The Beverly Hillbillies* (Penelope Spheeris, 1993), *Dennis the Menace* (Nick Castle, 1993), *The Flintstones* (Brian Levant, 1994), *The Brady Bunch Movie*, *Leave It to Beaver* (Andy Cadiff, 1997), and *My Favorite Martian* (Donald Petrie, 1999); and (2) a group of features based on characters that (mostly) originate in media *other than television* (for example, comics and theatrical shorts), but which nonetheless have a strong television identity as children's adventure series or animated cartoon series: *The Little Rascals* (Penelope Spheeris, 1994), *Richie Rich* (Donald Petrie, 1994), *Lassie* (Daniel Petrie, 1994), *Casper* (Brad Silberling, 1995), *Flipper* (Alan Shapiro, 1996), *Mr. Magoo* (Stanley Tong, 1997), *George of the Jungle* (Sam Weisman, 1997) and *Inspector Gadget* (David Kellogg, 1999).

These features can be further categorised according to whether they are remakes of live action tele-series or remakes of animated cartoon series, although this is complicated by the fact that some – *The Addams Family*, *Dennis the Menace*, *The Brady Bunch*, *My Favorite Martian* – are both. That is, *The Addams Family* (ABC, 1964–66) was followed by an animated series (*The Addams Family*, NBC, 1973–75), and a second animated series, also titled *The Addams Family* (ABC, 1992–95), followed the release of the first television feature. *Dennis the Menace* (CBS, 1959–63) was briefly revived as an animated cartoon (CBS, 1987–88), and a second animated series, *The New Dennis the Menace* (CBS, 1993–94), followed the release of the feature film version. *The Brady Bunch* (ABC, 1969–74) ran in tandem with *The Brady Kids* (ABC, 1972–74), a Saturday morning animated series featuring the voices of the six Brady children. *My Favorite Martian* (CBS, 1963–66) inspired an animated series, *My Favorite Martians* (CBS, 1973–75), which featured three Martians: uncle Martin, his nephew Andy and their dog, Oakie Doakie.[41] This initial grouping does, however, seem consistent in so far as: (1) all the features are remakes of what were thirty-minute tele-series or collections of animated cartoon series; (2) even though several of these tele-series had a prime-time first-run, all of these have also circulated as reruns in weekday afternoon and/or Saturday morning viewing slots that identify them as 'children's television'; and (3) these tele-series (and this is why remakes of *Car 54, Where Are You?*, *Sgt. Bilko* and *McHale's Navy* are excluded from this grouping) feature children and animals, ghouls and aliens, which contribute to the remake's appeal, marketability and merchandising opportunities among its target audience. Not surprisingly, these features are consistent, too, in their release pattern, with both theatrical and home video releases coinciding with school vacations and holiday seasons.

If this first production strategy is to take what were principally thirty-minute sitcoms and animated cartoons, and remake them for a family audience, then the second category is derived from mostly sixty-minute prime-time television dramas, and the remake is pitched at cinema's largest target audience, the eighteen to twenty-four year old group. In this instance, the tele-series as pre-sold property becomes the occasion for a big budget, high-concept remake, complete with an emphasis on established genres, production design, star image, special effects and attendant advertising and merchandising campaigns. In this case (even more than the first), the formulaic combinations of television (*serialisation*) are extended not just linearly, but multi-dimensionally as the blockbuster becomes a point of dispersal (*multiplication*) for cross-platform production: print materials, recorded music, toy manufacture, fashion design, theme parks and (revived) television series.[42] This second 'adult viewing' category includes top-line features such as: *The Fugitive* (Andrew Davis, 1993), *Maverick* (Richard Donner, 1994), *Mission: Impossible* (Brian De Palma, 1996), *The Saint* (Phillip Noyce, 1997), *Lost in Space* (Stephen Hopkins, 1998), *The Avengers* (Jeremiah Chechik, 1998), *The Mod Squad* (Scott Silver, 1999), *The Wild, Wild West* (Barry Sonnenfeld, 1999), *Charlie's Angels* (McG [Joseph McGinty Nichol], 2000) and *Starsky & Hutch* (Todd Phillips, 2004).

The dramatic tele-series upon which this second group draws have probably circulated less widely (on broadcast television) than the first, and are characterised (as noted above) by their greater attention to the narrative plotting of individual series episodes. Accordingly, there is often less attention in these remakes to the kind of sedimented detail that recurs in the thirty-minute sitcom, and which gets expressed in a variety of ways in the remakings. In the case of *The Beverly Hillbillies* feature this is the incorporation of four of the five aforementioned narrative lines, or in the examples of *Sgt. Bilko* and *The Addams Family* it is the repetition of a character's gesture (Ernie Bilko's wave of the hands) or signature line (Gomez Addams's 'Tish, that's French'). Rather than drawing out the detail and/or ambience of the tele-series, this second group of 'high concept' remakes (as the label suggests) takes up the pre-sold title and basic premise – a man wrongly accused of killing his wife becomes a *fugitive* from the law; a family of inter-galactic travellers becomes *lost in space*, a group of delinquent teenagers is recruited as a police *mod-squad* – and remakes it within the parameters of a like contemporary genre: an action-pursuit adventure, a science-fiction spectacular and an urban police drama, respectively. This provides, too, the opportunity to extend the more humble means of the tele-series into, say, a star vehicle (Mel Gibson in *Maverick*, Tom Cruise in *Mission: Impossible*, Owen Wilson and Ben Stiller in *Starsky & Hutch*) or into a big special effects picture (the train derailment in *The Fugitive*, the opening battle in *Lost in Space*, the martial arts sequences in *Charlie's Angels*). There may in these films still be the opportunity (as in the first cat-egory) for an intertextual joke, for instance television's Bret Maverick (James Garner) shows up as feature film Maverick's (Mel Gibson's) father; several of the original cast members of *Lost in Space* appear in cameo roles in the film's opening sequences (June Lockhart as a school official, Mark Goddard as a General, Marta Kristen and Angela Cartwright as reporters); and Starsky and Hutch are given a new Ford Gran Torino by the original Starsky and Hutch (Paul Michael Glaser and David Soul). But these are (in the main) remakes less interested in recreating the detail of their origi-nals than in adapting the (previously market tested) source material to the conventions and expectations of the contemporary genre movie and/or blockbuster.

As in the case of taxonomies generally, these two production tenden-cies – the family entertainment movie and the high-concept blockbuster – for the remaking of tele-series admit to overlap and exclusion. For instance (as noted above), the first grouping does not readily accommodate the mid-1990s remaking of the thirty-minute police and military service sitcoms, *Car 54, Where Are You?* (Bill Fishman, 1993), *Sgt. Bilko* (Jonathan Lynn, 1996) and *McHale's Navy* (Bryan Spicer, 1997). In these examples, the original tele-series do not have substantial pre-existing fan bases, nor the appeal for young viewers of revived domestic (and/or fantasy) sitcoms and adventure series. In the opposite direction, thirty-minute animated series such as *The Bullwinkle Show* (1961–73) and *Scooby Doo, Where Are You!* (1969–72) have had their title characters digitally recreated in the (other-wise) live action remakes *The Adventures of Rocky and Bullwinkle* (Des McAnuff, 2000) and *Scooby-Doo* (Raja Gosnell, 2002). These films cer-tainly hold appeal for child–parent units but are also pitched – in the example of *Scooby-Doo* through the (re)casting of the teen-movie personas of Freddy Prinze Jr, Sarah Michelle Gellar and Matthew Lillard in the roles of Fred, Daphne and Norville – to a teenage and young adult audience.

No other series remaking focuses the tactics of the high-concept ten-dency of the television feature better than the recent *Charlie's Angels* (2000) and its sequel *Charlie's Angels: Full Throttle* (McG, 2003). The 2000 feature film was developed from the five-season Aaron Spelling series (*Charlie's Angels*, ABC, 1976–81) about a trio of female crime-fighters who work for the mysterious Charlie. Spelling had tried to revive the series as

Charlie's Angels (McG, 2000). Courtesy Columbia/The Kobal
Collection/Darren Michaels.

Angels '88 (a concept that got as far as casting and a rumoured, but never
seen, pilot), and in 1999 a thirteen-episode Spanish-language remake titled
Àngeles aired on Telemundo. Following these ventures, Sony had the
feature film in development for several years, testing the market with the
re-release of the original shows on video and a range of *Charlie's Angels* gift
ideas (for Christmas 1997).[43] When it finally did reach the big screen, the
feature's impressive $40 million opening weekend box-office (in November
2000) was the biggest non-summer debut in movie history.[44] A preview of
the *Charlie's Angels*' marketing machine that contributed to this result was
seen some nine months earlier when the (new) Angels – Dylan (Drew
Barrymore), Alex (Lucy Liu) and Natalie (Cameron Diaz) – appeared at
the Academy Awards, 'all frocked-up and sexy', to present an Oscar.[45]
Momentum built in the lead up to the US opening with such events as the
world premiere of the theatrical trailer on *Entertainment Tonight*, the
release of the song (and music video) 'Independent Woman, Pt 1' by
Destiny's Child, and the attendant publicity from such ephemera as
spreads in *Elle*, *Mademoiselle* and *Jane* magazines, featuring fashions
inspired by the TV series.[46] As Mariana Mogilevich points out, the high-
concept premise – 'three beautiful crime-fighting babes fight crime and
look hot' – anchored in, and multiplied through, tie-ins and media hype
makes the film text the lubricant that oils the machine: 'there are so many

threads anchoring [*Charlie's Angels*] in our collective unconscious . . . that one hardly needs to see the film to, in a way, have already seen it'.[47]

Aside from its basic premise, and the original's strategy of putting the Angels into a host of sexually suggestive undercover poses – prison gang inmates, showgirls, prostitutes – the remake is less concerned with transforming this material into a new *textual unit* than with engaging in a constellation of televisual images and an expanding array of multimedia texts. As Mogilevich describes it, *Charlie's Angels* 'is not a closed, finite work, but rather a footnote, a set of citations'.[48] Accordingly the film lifts sounds and images not only from the *Charlie's Angels* tele-series (notably a chain-gang routine from the 'Angels in Chains' episode), but also snippets from movies and grabs of popular music. For instance, Bosley's (Bill Murray's) imprisonment in the tower references – in the space of seconds – *The Birdman of Alcatraz* (John Frankenheimer, 1962), *The Great Escape* (John Sturges, 1963) and *Take the Money and Run* (Woody Allen, 1969), and the soundtrack includes not only a host of 'angel' songs – 'Angel of the Morning', 'Heaven Must be Missing an Angel', 'Undercover Angel' – but features such episodes as Drew Barrymore's 'Billie Jean' moonwalk rip. In addition to this, *Charlie's Angels* makes reference to the very practice of remaking tele-series. In the opening airplane sequence, the character played by LL Cool J, having discovered that the in-flight entertainment is *T. J. Hooker: The Movie*, complains: '[not] another movie from an old TV show'. His reaction – he is in fact Angel Dylan (Barrymore) in *Mission: Impossible*-type disguise – is to 'walk out', dropping himself (and the audience) into a gob-smacking parachuting and water rescue action sequence. The net effect is to announce itself to a knowing (and perhaps cynical) youth-audience as an exuberant high-concept remaking: a repetition informed as much by (television) serialisation as it is by (cross-media) amplification and multiplication.

While the example of *Charlie's Angels* (and the above account of two broad production strategies) say something about commercial approaches to remaking tele-series as feature films and adapting them to a theatrical film market, each of the groupings nonetheless reveals various (and different) approaches for transforming the narrative invention of the source materials. As Marc points out, the nature of long-running tele-series was such that the major investment for viewers was not the narrative, the basic set-up of which was left untouched from one week to another, but rather the milieu and characters (and the way television personalities came to inhabit these).[49] This provides a unique problem for remakers, and narrative strategies range from the adaptation of particular series episodes (or parts thereof) to the invention of entirely new narrative situations for recycled characters and milieus. In the first instance, the strategy for adaptation includes the replaying of the narrative invention of: (1) a tele-series pilot, for example *Lost in Space* remakes its first episode, 'The Reluctant Stowaway'; (2) a specific series episode, for example *Leave It to Beaver* remakes the episode titled 'Beaver's Bike'; or (3) several series episodes, for example *The Brady Bunch Movie* remakes, among others, episodes titled, 'The Tattletale', 'Her Sister's Shadow', 'The Not So Rose Coloured Glasses', 'Getting Davy Jones', 'Dough-Re-Mi', 'The Subject was Noses', 'Amateur Night', 'Alias Johnny Bravo' and 'Try, Try Again'.[50] In some cases, the feature's borrowings of narrative elements may be even more particular; for example, Kim Newman notes that *The Avengers* takes, from the 'A Surfeit of H_2O' episode, its narrative kernel concerning the weather, but also lifts such things as the disorienting labyrinth from 'The House that Jack Built', the tropical enclave from 'Small Game for Big Hunters', an invisible spy from 'The See Through Man', and so on.[51] In other cases, the feature eschews the narrative invention of its tele-series altogether, creating new situations for familiar characters. For example, *Mission: Impossible* deals with a new assignment for Jim Phelps's IMF team; *The Saint* takes up the latest challenge for gentlemanly thief, Simon Templar; the Angels' new assignment reveals a plot to kill Charlie. In some instances (and viewed more cynically), the recycling of the narrative might be of no consequence, but (in the case of *Charlie's Angels*) 'a mere peg on which to hang a series of showy action sequences and [remembering that star Drew Barrymore was also co-producer] a succession of stardom-enhancement moments for the leads'.[52] Additionally, in some cases the feature-as-remake may adopt narrative strategies more typical of the 'retake' or sequel. For instance, the Angels play the *next* generation in the same all-female detective agency. And in *Maverick* and *McHale's Navy*, the entire narrative is retrospectively coded as a family saga, that is the closing segments of these two films explain that James Garner and Ernest Borgnine (television's Maverick and McHale, respectively) are in fact fathers to Mel Gibson (Bret Maverick) and Tom Arnold (Quint McHale).

In addition to these various textual strategies, it is necessary to realise that while some of these feature films remake properties that formerly have a (principally) television identity, others draw upon multiple sources and in some ways resist being categorised as remakes of television properties. It would seem (as is the case with film remakes generally) that a textual marker – acknowledgement in the form of a credit – would be the surest arbiter of what would (or would not) count as a remake of a tele-series. In many instances this is the case: the credits of *McHale's Navy* state that it is 'based on the television series'; the credits of *Leave It to Beaver* read: 'based on the TV series created by Bob Mosher and Joe Connelly'; the credits for *Sgt. Bilko* read: 'based on the television series created by Nat Hiken'; and so on. In other instances, it is the character(s) rather than the programme which get the acknowledgement: *The Brady Bunch Movie* is based on characters created by Sherwood Schwartz; *The Fugitive* is based on characters created by Roy Huggins; *The Addams Family* on characters created by Charles Addams; *Dennis the Menace* on characters created by Hank Ketcham; *Dick Tracy* on characters created by Chester Gould. The difficulty here is that while in the first two instances – *The Brady Bunch* and *The Fugitive* – these characters are created *for* television, in the latter instances the characters originate in other media: the Addams Family in a cartoon; Dennis the Menace in a comic strip; and Dick Tracy originates as a character in a newspaper comic strip but is featured in a radio series (1935–48), a fifteen-chapter movie serial (1937), several feature films (late 1930s and 1940s), a live action tele-series (early 1950s) and animated cartoons for television (1960s), before eventually making it (back) into feature films as *Dick Tracy* (Warren Beatty, 1990). This final example – the case of Dick Tracy – holds for several other features – *The Legend of the Lone Ranger*, *Mr Magoo*, *The Saint* and even *The Mask of Zorro* (Martin Campbell, 1998) – all of which might be considered remakes of tele-series but which originate in media other than, and have strong identities outside of, television.

The question of identifying remakes of tele-series becomes, then, not simply one of textual evidence, or even of legally sanctioned use (in the form of a copyright credit), but rather a question of how these properties continue to circulate – as texts and as memories – and how they are identified in film industry and other public discourses, such as film reviewing and media coverage. Accordingly, there would be a strong argument for including *The Addams Family* as part of a 1990s cycle of remakes of television series, even though it acknowledges (in its credits) *only* the Charles Addams characters from which the tele-series is derived. As reviewers of the feature have pointed out, the film's director, Barry Sonnenfeld, claims he 'never cared much' for the TV programme and that he placed more emphasis on evoking the style of the old cartoons.[53] Sonnenfeld's feature in fact begins – in imitation of one of Charles Addams's most famous New Yorker cartoons – with the 'eponymous ghouls preparing to pour boiling oil over an unbearably merry group of carol singers'.[54] But the employment of features like Vic Mizzy's original TV theme and performances by lead players Anjelica Huston and Raul Julia (as Morticia and Gomez Addams), which develop the former performances of Caroline Jones and John Astin, coupled with things like advertising copy and film reviews that refer back to the tele-series, ensure that the film has a strong television identity. *The Addams Family* feature, in fact, becomes pivotal in an ongoing dialogue between television and feature film. Against the backdrop of continuing reruns of the original ABC tele-series, the success of the first feature prompted the release of a (second) animated cartoon series, also titled *The Addams Family* (ABC, 1992–95). This was accompanied by a second, theatrically released feature film, *Addams Family Values* (Barry Sonnenfeld, 1993), and the two features were, in turn, followed up with a direct-to-video feature (with different lead actors) titled *Addams Family Reunion* (1998) and then *The New Addams Family* (Fox, 1998–99), an updated 1990s version of the original *The Addams Family* tele-series.

These arguments would seem true of television features derived from characters that have an even stronger presence in other media, say the Lone Ranger, The Saint or even Batman, but they can be equally persuasive in the opposite direction. For instance, the release of the 1990 version of *Dick Tracy* was accompanied by a well-publicised record of Warren Beatty's effort to capture the detail of a fictional world created in comic strips by Chester Gould: 'to spare no expense to reproduce the primary colour scheme, the two-dimensional characters, the abstract décor of that world'.[55] This translates, in the context of high concept, into an emphasis on production design, but also an endeavour in Beatty's version to surpass all earlier adaptations – including the 1950–51 tele-series with Ralph Byrd (who had already played Tracy in serials and feature films) – by returning to the 'authority' of the original comic strips for its characters and most of its visual style. By contrast, and for different viewerships, the principal identity of a feature like *Flipper* (Alan Shapiro, 1996) might (variously) reside in the 1964–67 tele-series, or the updated 1995 tele-series, or even in the 1963 feature film that preceded both. But other viewers might see it (generically) alongside a cycle of 1990s films featuring semi-domesticated aquatic animals, such as *Andre* (George Miller, 1993) and especially *Free Willy* (Simon Wincer, 1993), its sequels (*Free Willy 2: The Adventure Home*, 1995 and *Free Willy 3: The Rescue*, 1997) and animated tele-series (*Free Willy*, ABC, 1994).[56] The difficulty encountered here applies equally to the likes of *The Mask of Zorro*, not only because of the character's many incarnations – different audiences would remember Zorro as played by Douglas Fairbanks Sr (1920), Tyrone Power (1940), Guy Williams (1957–59), Frank Langella (1974), even George Hamilton (in *Zorro, the Gay Blade*, 1981) – but also because this most recent feature (like the Hamilton version) operates as much as a sequel as a remake. The murkiness of origins becomes even more pointed when arguing for the inclusion of features such as *Wyatt Earp* (Lawrence Kasdan, 1994) or the 1994 *Lassie* movie, films that deal with 'characters' who circulate in the public domain over and above their particular realisations in historic and/or fictional documents. And yet even in these cases textual and contextual factors work to encourage some identifications over and above others. At the beginning of *Lassie*, a clip from the CBS television series (1954–74) is seen playing in the Turner home, prior to the family adopting a stray Collie they name Lassie. And the 1994 version of *Wyatt Earp* coincided with *Wyatt Earp: Return to Tombsto*ne (1994, CBS), a two-hour extension episode of the tele-series *The Life and Legend of Wyatt Earp*, that brings back Hugh O'Brien as Earp – *forty years later* – by digitally combining new footage with colourised segments from the original series.

To conclude, the industrial imperative behind the remaking of television properties is perhaps nowhere more evident that in those (commercially) successful features which realise the potential for transferring the serial methods of television into the feature film sequel and franchise. The 2003 *Charlie's Angels* sequel – *Charlie's Angels: Full Throttle* – provides one of the most recent and profitable examples, taking over $100 million at the US box-office and spinning further profits in overseas markets and through DVD sales and rentals. Textually speaking, the sequel provided opportunities for the 'three crazy beautiful girls' (to quote a Mongol from the film's *Indiana Jones*-type overture) to put *on display* all that had pleased audiences of the first instalment. For many reviewers this resulted in a film even more incoherent than the first, but one that furthered its strategy, not so much of recycling the television series, but of recycling *everything* to provide 'a garish compost heap of pop-culture references'.[57] More pointedly, the sequel enabled Sony to extend the franchise through the *Charlie's Angels: Full Throttle* Play Station 2 game, the *Angel X* online game and a prequel to *Charlie's Angels: Full Throttle* in the form of *Charlie's Angels Animated Adventures*. The latter – delivered online[58] – was a series of six, two-minute animated cliffhangers written by *Full Throttle* associate producer Stephanie Savage and designed to 'capture the essence of the film [by] incorporating visual references from the movie into its story-line'.[59] Further profits were generated by a wide range of official (licensed) products, including bobble-head figurines, lunch boxes, shot glasses, women's T-shirts, mini-purses, back packs and a *Full Throttle* book for pre-teen readers. The example of the *Charlie's Angels* franchise underlines the (earlier) point that the linearity of serial-time (of *serialisation*), and the relationship between TV series and TV features, is complicated by a multi-dimensional strategy of media repetition (of *multiplication*). Finally, *Charlie's Angels*, and the example of the television feature generally, suggests some of the ways in which industrial and commercial approaches can contribute to – but do not exhaust – an understanding of cinematic remaking.

Notes

1. See Elsaesser, 'Fantasy Island'; Eaton, 'Cinema and Television'; Ellis, 'Cinema and Television'.
2. Elsaesser, 'Fantasy Island', pp. 143–58.
3. Schatz, 'The Return of the Hollywood Studio System', pp. 73–5.
4. Ibid., pp. 93–4; and Meehan, ' "Holy Commodity Fetish, Batman!" ', p. 49.
5. Neale, *Genre and Hollywood*, p. 247.
6. Maddox, 'Television a Tomb with a View'.
7. See Atkinson, 'Delirious Inventions', pp. 12–16.
8. Hawker, 'Rev. of *Mission: Impossible 2*', p. 5.
9. See Anderson, *Hollywood TV*.
10. Eco, *The Limits of Interpretation*, p. 85.
11. See Marc, *Comic Visions*, pp. 84–154.
12. Marc, 'Sibling Rivalry', p. 8.
13. Calabrese, *Neo-Baroque*, p. 35.
14. Ibid.
15. Eco, *The Limits of Interpretation*, p. 87.
16. Calabrese, *Neo-Baroque*, p. 37.
17. Ibid., p. 38, emphasis added.
18. Ibid., p. 38.
19. Nelson, 'The Dislocation of Time', p. 81.
20. Simon, 'The Eternal Rerun', p. 51.
21. Nelson, 'The Dislocation of Time', p. 81.
22. Williams, 'The Evolution of the Television Rerun', p. 173.
23. Nelson, 'The Dislocation of Time', p. 85.
24. Ibid., p. 84.
25. See Willemen, 'Through the Glass Darkly', pp. 229–30.
26. Marc, *Demographic Vistas*, p. 8.
27. See Sconce, ' "Trashing" the Academy', pp. 371–80.
28. Williams, 'The Evolution of the Television Rerun', p. 173.
29. Javna and Javna, *60s!*, p. 216.
30. Marc and Thompson, *Prime Time, Prime Movers*, pp. 38–48.
31. McNeil, *Total Television*, p. 327.
32. Carter, 'Marooned Again with Gilligan', p. 19.
33. McNeil, *Total Television*, p. 324.
34. Marc, 'Sibling Rivalry', p. 6.
35. Hark, 'The Wrath of the Original Cast', p. 173.
36. O'Hehir, 'Gleaning the Tube', p. 18.

37. Ibid., p. 16.
38. Marc, 'Sibling Rivalry', p. 6.
39. Maddox, 'Television a Tomb with a View'.
40. Marc, 'Sibling Rivalry', p. 8.
41. See McNeil, *Total Television*; and Brooks and Marsh, *The Complete Dictionary to Prime Time Network and Cable TV Shows*.
42. Elsaesser, 'Fantasy Island', pp. 146–8 and 157.
43. 'Puppet Love', p. 32.
44. McCarthy, 'Where Angels Don't Fear to Tread', p. 7.
45. Perkin, 'Charlie Who?', p. 18.
46. Tulloch, 'Flipping Out Over Angels Remake', p. 1.
47. Mogilevich, 'Charlie's Pussycats', p. 38.
48. Ibid., p. 39.
49. Marc, 'Sibling Rivalry', p. 8. See also Hark, 'The Wrath of the Original Cast', p. 176.
50. Eisner and Krinsky, *Television Comedy Series*, pp. 146–52.
51. Newman, 'Rev. of *The Avengers*', p. 39.
52. Medhurst, 'Rev. of *Charlie's Angels*', p. 44.
53. Newman, 'Rev. of *The Addams Family*', p. 37.
54. Ibid.
55. Combs, 'Rev. of *Dick Tracy*', p. 216.
56. Newman, 'Rev. of *Flipper*', p. 44.
57. Hoberman, 'They're Back'.
58. http://www.animatedangels.com.
59. Sony press release quoted at http://www.charliesangels.com.

CHAPTER 2

Authors

Much of the talk leading up to, and following, the release of Gus Van Sant's 1998 remake – or 'replica' – of the Alfred Hitchcock film *Psycho* (1960) was an expression of outrage and confusion at the defilement of a beloved classic. For instance, and most prominently, the '*Psycho*: Saving a Classic' website described the remake as a 'disgrace' and urged audiences to express their dissatisfaction by boycotting the opening weekend.[1] Reviewers and 'Hitchcockians' alike agreed that Van Sant had made two fundamental mistakes: the first was to have undertaken to remake a treasured landmark of cinematic history; and the second to have followed the Hitchcock original (almost) shot by shot, line by line. As a reviewer for the *New York Post* remarked: 'if you're going to be hubristic enough to remake *Psycho*, you should at least have the courage to put your own spin on it'.[2] But even for those who noted that the shooting script for the remake was only about ninety per cent the same as Hitchcock's,[3] Van Sant's revisions were thought to have added nothing to what remained (for them) an *intact* and undeniable classic, a semantic fixity against which the new version was evaluated and dismissed as a degraded copy. For these fans and critics – for these *re*-viewers – the *Psycho* remake was ultimately nothing more than a blatant rip-off: not only an attempt to exploit the original film's legendary status, but (worse) a cheap imitation of 'one of the best and best known of American films'.[4]

This reaction to Van Sant's *Psycho* remake is consistent with the vast majority of critical accounts of film remakes which understand remaking as a one-way process: a movement from authenticity to imitation, from the superior self-identity of the original to the debased resemblance of the copy. Critics and viewers privileged the 'original' *Psycho* over its remake, measuring the success of the Van Sant remake according to its ability to realise what were taken to be the *essential* elements of the Hitchcock text. Rather than follow these reductive trajectories, this chapter adopts a broader approach to the concept of remaking, which – in its more general application – might be regarded as a specific aspect of a wider and more open-ended intertextuality. As Lucy Mazdon inquires: 'how can it be possible to criticise the remake as non-original, as a [degraded] copy, when all films [once inserted in an ongoing dialogical process] can in some way be seen as copies?'[5] Approached in this way, remaking might refer to any number of cultural and industrial activities, ranging from practices of allusion and quotation, to the patterns of repetition (and variation) that attend the process-like nature of genre and serial filmmaking. As a particular instance of this logic of cinematic repetition, the *Psycho* remake is a text initiated, negotiated and stabilised – but never *totally* limited – by a series of technologies, such as copyright law and authorship, that are essential to the existence and identification of film remakes.

In recognition of these arguments around the nature of cinematic remaking, this chapter seeks to sketch a *broad circuit* between *Psycho 60* and *Psycho 98*, focusing in particular on remaking as a category of *authorship*, and on Hitchcock's status as one of cinema's most celebrated and influential practitioners. Rather than accept the negative view of the majority of descriptions of the *Psycho* remake, this chapter seeks to understand *both* versions of *Psycho* as 'aspect[s] of a much wider process of cinematic reproduction'.[6] The chapter falls into four parts. The first looks at Alfred Hitchcock's artistic and authorial persona, and the way in which the author remakes himself (and *Psycho*) across a vast body of film and television work. The second part attends to Hitchcock's legacy to the horror genre (especially the contemporary slasher film), and to how the *Psycho* sequels of the 1980s – *Psycho II, III* and *IV* – revisit (and *remake*) not only their precursor but the conventions of the slasher movie genre. The third section looks at the canonised figure of Alfred Hitchcock and the nature of cinematic homage, specifically as it plays out across three films by Brian De Palma – *Dressed to Kill* (1980), *Blow Out* (1981) and *Body Double* (1984) – that remake aspects of *Psycho*. The fourth and final part considers the ongoing influence that Alfred Hitchcock, and his masterpiece *Psycho*, have had on contemporary art and popular film, in particular Pierre Huyghe's *Remake* (1995), Douglas Gordon's *24 Hour Psycho* (1993) and Gus Vant's *Psycho 98* replica.

Psycho is by no means the first or the only film of Alfred Hitchcock's to be remade.[7] For instance, *direct, acknowledged remakes* of films from Hitchcock's early 'British period' include such titles as: *The Thirty-Nine Steps* (Hitchcock, 1935; Ralph Thomas, 1956; Don Sharp, 1978); *The Lady Vanishes* (Hitchcock, 1938; Anthony Page, 1979); and Hitchcock's own

1956 American remake of his earlier, *The Man Who Knew Too Much* (1934). Many other Hitchcock films – including *Notorious* (1946), *Strangers on a Train* (1951) and *Rear Window* (1954) – have been remade for television, and recent theatrically released films include the *A Perfect Murder* (Andrew Davis, 1998) remake of *Dial M for Murder* (1954), and a new version of *Sabotage* (1936) filmed under the title of its source material, *The Secret Agent* (Christopher Hampton, 1996). This type of remaking can be understood as a function of industry and commerce, a type of economic pragmatism whereby existing films are thought to minimise risk by providing successful formulas for the development of new studio (or television) based projects. In a commercial context, Van Sant's *Psycho* remake is pre-sold to its audience, with viewers not only expected to recognise the title but assumed to have some prior experience of the original *Psycho*, one of the most widely known and profitable films of all time. Even viewers with no direct experience of *Psycho* are likely to possess a 'narrative image' of the film,[8] or have some familiarity with the famous shower sequence and/or Bernard Herrmann's musical accompaniment of shrieking violins. This commercial orientation, whereby a new film seeks to duplicate past success and reduce risk by emphasising the familiar, might account for the ubiquity of (Hollywood) remakes. But Hitchcock's revision of *The Man Who Knew Too Much* suggests, too, that remaking might be located in a film maker's desire to repeatedly express and modify a particular aesthetic sensibility and world view in light of new developments and interests.[9] This view is supported by Michael Tarantino who notes that during the early 1940s (the period in which Hitchcock was under contract to producer David Selznick) there was talk of remaking not only *The Man Who Knew Too Much* but also *The Lodger* (1926), *The Thirty-Nine Steps* and *The Lady Vanishes*.[10]

Stuart McDougal takes up this type of authorial approach to remaking, describing Hitchcock as a director 'who was continuously and obsessively remaking his own work'.[11] This results not only in the ongoing repetition of cinematic techniques (shots, transitions and sequences) and underlying themes (pursuit and rescue, guilt and punishment), but also in 'loose' remakings, for example the revision of *The Thirty-Nine Steps*, first as *Saboteur* (1942) and again as *North by Northwest* (1959).[12] In the more direct remaking of *The Man Who Knew Too Much*, Hitchcock *transforms* his earlier version not only in recognition of prevailing 'social, political and geographical dynamics', but through the *personal* (authorial) filter of a more mature film maker, to create a work structurally similar to, but thematically more consistent, than the original.[13] The sense of cohesion across Hitchcock's body of work is not only evident at the level of a particular shot or individual film, but also at a broader, generic level. For instance, Robert Kapsis notes that while Hitchcock's reputation as a director of thrillers can be traced back to *The Lodger* and *Blackmail* (1929), the 1934 version of *The Man Who Knew Too Much* inaugurated a cycle of six British thrillers now known as the 'classic thriller sextet'.[14] The high degree of continuity and consistency across these six films – *The Man Who Knew Too Much*, *The Thirty-Nine Steps*, *The Secret Agent* (1936), *Sabotage* (1936), *Young and Innocent* (1937) and *The Lady Vanishes* – can be attributed to the house style of British Gaumont, but it also supports McDougal's claim that 'Hitchcock remade his early work in a variety of ways, combining . . . the expressive potential of film with a desire for technical perfection'.[15] Indeed, McDougal argues that it was Hitchcock's dissatisfaction with the climax of the earlier version of *The Man Who Knew Too Much* that led, first, to its *disguised and limited* remaking in the ending of *The Thirty-Nine Steps* and later to its *official and direct* remaking in *The Man Who Knew Too Much*.[16] And, more recently, Laura Mulvey has suggested that '*Psycho* takes the plots that characterised Hitchcock's English thriller series, which he continued to recycle in Hollywood, and uses them in a way that is shocking both in its novelty and in its strange familiarity'.[17] These comments, and the example of the classic thriller sextet, would appear to suggest that Hitchcock's authorship 'lies in his ability to continually *remake* or recombine a basic repertory of narrative situations and cinematic techniques, thus creating a *characteristic "world"*'.[18]

Although *Psycho* might be seen as an amalgamation – a revision – of the bleaker tone of (the slightly earlier) *The Wrong Man* (1957) and the ironic, anti-romance of *Vertigo* (1958), several critics claimed that it 'marked a darkening in the world view of the director [Hitchcock]'.[19] *Psycho* certainly appears to be a departure from the interests and conventions of the 'standard' Hitchcock thriller, especially the lavish, Hollywood productions of the 1950s – *The Man Who Knew Too Much*, *To Catch a Thief* (1955) and *North by Northwest* – that immediately preceded it. Hitchcock purchased the film rights to Robert Bloch's (then recently published) novel *Psycho* in 1959, but unable to secure an agreement under his existing contract with Paramount, he turned to Universal Studios, where his television series, *Alfred Hitchcock Presents* (CBS, 1955–65), was being filmed. Working within the constraints of a low budget, Hitchcock approached *Psycho* as an experiment in the making of a feature film along the lines of an expanded television episode, employing some of his regular television crew and working with multiple camera set-ups.[20] Both Kapsis and James Naremore point to a number of continuities between Hitchcock's television work and *Psycho*, including such features as the film's 'black-and-white photography, the moments of suspense, the sardonic wit and macabre humour, the ordinariness of its characters and the drabness of its setting'.[21] Naremore argues that *Psycho* was 'clearly influenced' by the format of *Alfred Hitchcock Presents*, and even finds in the film's first minutes 'some echoes' of 'Banquo's Chair', a 1959 episode of the television series 'which opens [like *Psycho*] with the camera travelling across a row of buildings and moving in toward a doorway while words announce an exact place, date, and time'.[22] In addition to this, Hitchcock's introduction and epilogue for each of the episodes for *Alfred Hitchcock Presents* had made him something of a household name. As Kapsis points out, the publicity campaign for *Psycho* – which included a six-minute trailer featuring Hitchcock leading a 'tour' through the Bates house and motel[23] – would have given audiences familiar with the television series every reason to believe 'that *Psycho* would be in the tradition of Hitchcock's macabre little teleplays'.[24]

Psycho opened in the summer of 1960 to mixed critical reactions but immediately began to break box-office records, rapidly developing into a national phenomenon. Stephen Rebello states that '*Psycho* tapped into the American subconscious' provoking: 'Faintings. Walk-outs. Repeat visits. Boycotts. Angry phone calls and letters'.[25] *Psycho*'s massive domestic and international success ensured that it was one of the most talked about films of 1960, cited in discussions on a range of topics, including 'the rise in crime; the decline in sales of opaque shower curtains; the alarming upswing in violence, particularly toward women; [and] the downturn in motel stays'.[26] *Psycho* immediately spawned a number of imitations: Rebello makes note of William Castle's *Homicidal* (1961), and Kolker describes J. Lee Thompson's *Cape Fear* (1962) as 'a film that plays upon . . . the atmosphere of *Psycho* and its reception'.[27] In the wake of *Psycho*'s success Hitchcock was interviewed and profiled as never before, but as Rebello notes 'critical enshrinement for the movie and its director still lay several years ahead'.[28] This is to say that it was not until *after* the re-evaluation of Hitchcock's work by the *Cahiers du cinéma* critics, and Andrew Sarris's popularisation of the *politique des auteurs* (or theory of authorship) that Hitchcock would become one of Hollywood's most influential and imitated directors.[29] As Noël Carroll points out, the forging of a canon of films and film makers by *auteur* critics enabled allusion to film history, 'especially as that history was crystallised and codified in the sixties and seventies', to become a major expressive device.[30] The recognition of Hitchcockian themes and motifs enabled a film maker like Martin Scorsese to 'recalculate' the Hitchcock formula (at least) twice: '*Taxi Driver* (1976) reformulates *Psycho* (while it simultaneously situates its narrative pattern in *The Searchers* [John Ford, 1956])', and *Cape Fear* (1992) directly remakes the aforementioned 1962 Universal picture of the same name, but within this is 'embedded a kind of remake of three minor Hitchcock films from the early fifties: *Stage Fright* (1950), *I Confess* (1953), and *Strangers on a Train* (1951)'.[31]

While the canonisation of *Psycho* might account for the way in which the former version of a film property can come to function as a kind of fixity (a point of origin) against which its remake is evaluated, the suggestion that Hitchcock continually remakes or recombines a limited number of personal themes and cinematic techniques equally suggests that 'there can never be a simple original uncomplicated by the structure of the remake'.[32] More than this, John Frow argues that, at whatever level the intertext can be posited (shot, sequence, entire film), every remake is simultaneously a remaking of the conventions of the genre to which it belongs, and (for those viewers unfamiliar with the presumed original) the genre may be the only point of reference.[33] Taking this approach, Carol Clover situates *Psycho* within the broader context of film genre, describing it as the 'immediate ancestor' to the cycle of slasher movies initiated by *The Texas Chainsaw Massacre* (Tobe Hooper, 1974) and *Halloween* (John Carpenter, 1978), and celebrated in the sequels and series that followed: notably, *Halloween* II–VI (plus *H20* and *Halloween: Resurrection*), *A Nightmare on Elm Street* I–V (plus *Freddy's Dead: The Final Nightmare*) and *Friday the 13th*, Parts I–VIII (plus *Jason Goes to Hell: The Final Friday*). *Psycho* is taken as the benchmark for surveying each of the component categories of the slasher film genre: Norman Bates (Anthony Perkins) is the original *killer*, 'the psychotic product of a sick family, but still recognisably human'; the Bates mansion is the *locale*, 'the terrible place [that] enfolds the history of a mother and son locked in a sick attachment'; the carving knife is the killer's preferred *weapon*; Marion Crane (Janet Leigh) is the first *victim*, 'the beautiful, sexually active woman'; and her sister, Lila (Vera Miles), is the *survivor*, 'the final girl' or 'the one who looks death in the face [but] survives the murderer's last stab'.[34] As Clover points out, none of these generic particulars is exclusive to *Psycho*, 'but the unprecedented success [*notoriety and canonisation*] of Hitchcock's particular formulation, above all the sexualisation of both motive and action, prompted a flood of imitations and variations'[35]:

> The spiritual debt of all the post-1974 slasher films to *Psycho* is clear, and it is a rare example that does not pay a visual tribute, however brief, to the ancestor – if not in a shower stabbing, then in a purling drain or the shadow of a knife-wielding hand.[36]

Psycho's influence is nowhere clearer than in John Carpenter's low-budget stalker film, *Halloween*, which 'returns to the visual dynamic of the famous shower scene and extends it throughout the entirety of the new film'.[37] Steve Neale sees *Halloween* as an exemplary instance of the process-like nature of genre, arguing that the character of Michael brings together what were formerly two mutually exclusive elements of horror: the supernaturally defined monster of (for instance) *Dracula* (Todd Browning, 1930) and the psychologically defined evil of *Psycho*.[38] More than this, Adam Lowenstein suggests that the shift from the (more respectable) psychological suspense of *Psycho* to the tasteless graphic horror of *Halloween* (and beyond) is anticipated by Hitchcock himself is his own *Psycho* revision, *Frenzy* (1972). Lowenstein says 'if *Psycho* represents a watershed in Hitchcock's project of manipulating the sensory responses of his audience, then *Frenzy* represents a stunning revaluation [*remaking*] of that watershed'.[39] But it was *Halloween*'s enormous commercial success – $47 million on an estimated budget of $325,000 – that made it the (more) immediate prototype for the slasher movies of the late 1970s and early 1980s. For instance, *Friday the 13th* (Sean S. Cunningham, 1980) was described as a 'bare-faced duplication of *Halloween*',[40] and the sequel *Friday the 13th, part II* (Steve Miner, 1981) was seen as 'a virtual remake of the earlier movie'.[41] The legacy of *Halloween* and its cycle in turn continued into the self-referential series of neo-slasher films of the 1990s, inaugurated by *Scream* (Wes Craven, 1996) and culminating in the gross-out humour of *Scary Movie* and *Scary Movie 2* (Keenen Ivory Wayans, 2000 and 2001).

Halloween begins in a small Illinois town in 1963 where Judith Myers is brutally murdered by her six-year-old brother, Michael. Fifteen years later Michael escapes from the asylum in which he has been held since the killing, and makes his way back to his hometown where, on All Hallow E'en, he stalks a babysitter, Laurie Strode (Jamie Lee Curtis), and her teenage friends, Annie and Lynda. Laurie is the only one to escape Michael's murderous knife attacks, and with the help of Dr Sam Loomis (Donald Pleasence), the psychotic killer is stopped, at least for the moment. *Halloween* repeats a number of the conventions or 'rules' of the slasher genre pioneered by *Psycho* (and enumerated and parodied in *Scream*), but at the same time Carpenter's film transforms and expands the formula, enlarging (in the character of Laurie) the role of the 'final girl'.[42] Although *Halloween* escaped what some critics saw as the 'excesses' of Brian De Palma's early homages to Hitchcock (discussed below), it nonetheless acknowledged its debt to *Psycho*. It did this not only by way of theme and technique, but (more directly) through the naming of the character of Dr Sam Loomis after Marion Crane's lover, and by engaging in a kind of 'genetic intertextuality'[43] through the casting of Jamie Lee Curtis, daughter of *Psycho* star Janet Leigh, in the role of final girl, Laurie Strode.

The late 1970s interest in the slasher movie sub-genre, coupled with the burgeoning home-video and cable TV markets of the early 1980s, saw the character of Norman Bates revived for a number of *Psycho* sequels. The first of these, *Psycho II* (Richard Franklin, 1983), was a low-budget, joint venture between Universal Studios and a US cable television company.[44] *Psycho II* takes up the story of Norman Bates (played again by Anthony Perkins) and tells of his return to the Bates Motel after spending twenty-two years in a mental institution for the murder of Marion Crane (and others). Norman secures a job at a local diner, but his attempt to begin a new life is gradually undermined by Marion Crane's sister, Lila Loomis (Vera Miles), and her daughter, Mary Samuels (Meg Tilly), who together conspire to drive Norman back to the institution by masquerading as the deceased Mrs Bates. Back in the Bates mansion, Norman's behaviour becomes increasingly erratic and following several grisly knife murders (subsequently blamed by police on Lila and Mary), Norman is visited by the kindly Mrs Spool, who explains that she is his real mother and the one actually responsible for the recent murders. Norman kills her with a shovel and carries the body up to Mrs Bates's room while the 'voice' of mother gives Norman instructions on reopening the motel (thus anticipating a further sequel). The film ends with a brooding (replicated) shot of the *Psycho* house and a scarecrow-like Norman silhouetted against the night sky.

Psycho II elects to provide part of its back story by opening with a black and white shot of the Bates Motel neon sign (showing a vacancy) followed by a replaying of the *Psycho* shower sequence, almost in its entirety. The prologue begins with Marion Crane entering the bathroom and moving toward the shower, and details her violent murder, omitting just two shots – the water running past her legs to the bath drain and the famous dissolve to a close-up shot of her eye – cutting instead directly to a shot of Marion's dead face pressed against the tile floor. The first of the sequel's titles appears at the end of the shower sequence as Hitchcock's camera begins its slow movement from Marion's body in the bathroom to the folded newspaper with the stolen money on the night table and then out an open window to a silhouetted view of the *Psycho* house and Norman's distant shouts of 'Mother! Oh God, Mother! Blood!' There follows a cut to the main title – *Psycho II*, in the same bold, shattered letters of the original – and then the remainder of the credits are played out against a dark silhouette of the house (the first of the recreated shots), the night sky gradually turning through several colours to reveal a daylight view of the threatening mansion.

The sequel's post-credit sequence takes up and develops the story of Norman's rehabilitation and release, but *Psycho II* also goes on to carefully remake further aspects of Hitchcock's *Psycho* through imitation and exact pastiche. Not only is there a replaying of elements of the shower sequence and its lead up – Mary is treated by Norman to a supper of sandwiches and milk; Mary disrobes and showers as an eye watches through a hole drilled in the wall – but there is also the repetition of such details and shots as the silhouetted *Psycho* house, the overhead view of Norman carrying his invalid mother to the cellar, even a suitcase tumbling backwards down the stairs in imitation of Arbogast's body.[45]

While the publicity campaign for *Psycho II* attempted to identify the sequel as a 'quality film' (in the tradition of the Hitchcock thriller), upon its release it was dismissed by critics for its escalating violence, for instance Mrs Bates stabs Lila Loomis through the mouth and Norman draws his own hand across the blade of a large knife.[46] These aspects were seen to link the film to the (then) recent excesses of the slasher cycle, which included the heightening violence and multiple murders of such films as *Prom Night* (Paul Lynch, 1980) and *Motel Hell* (Kevin Connor, 1980). More than this, and despite its ending with a 'paratextual' dedication – 'The producers wish to acknowledge their debt to Sir Alfred Hitchcock' – the sequel (like *Psycho 98* fifteen years later) was condemned for its exploitative imitation of the master: 'You don't have to be a Hitchcock idolater to see [that] this dumb, plodding pseudo-camp bore is a callous, commercial parasite'.[47] *Psycho II* (and the Norman Bates 'franchise') nonetheless found enough of an audience to justify further sequels, both featuring Perkins. *Psycho III* (Anthony Perkins, 1986) picked up from the narrative twist that Mrs Bates was Norman's adoptive mother, and *Psycho IV: The Beginning* (Mick Garris, 1990) functioned (through the use of numerous flashbacks) as a kind of 'prequel' to the 1960 film. In addition to this, there was *Bates Motel* (Richard Rothstein, 1987), an unsuccessful television feature and pilot for a proposed tele-series, in which Norman hands over management of the motel to a fellow mental hospital inmate (played by the wide-eyed Bud Cort).

Like the *Psycho* sequels of the 1980s (each of which can be seen as a colour update of *Psycho 60*) Van Sant's 1990s replica remakes Hitchcock's *Psycho*. But at the same time, at a higher level of generality, each one of these films repeats – *replays and expands* – the generic corpus of the slasher film.[48] Released alongside such films as *Scream 2* (Wes Craven, 1997) and *Halloween H20* (Steve Miner, 1998), *Psycho 98* might (as noted above) take the genre as its *only* intertext. Indeed, some of the transformations that *Psycho 98* effects upon its precursor are best understood in relation to the conventions of the contemporary slasher movie and its reformulation of the Hitchcock thriller. Although Hitchcock's forthright treatment of Marion and Sam's sexual encounter and the shocking violence of the shower scene may have challenged (and contributed to the breakdown of) Hollywood's self-regulatory code of ethics, Hitchcock nonetheless had to work within the guidelines of the Production Code administered by the Motion Picture Association of America. For instance, Hitchcock had to remove, from Joseph Stefano's screenplay, a line of dialogue to be spoken to Marion by Cassidy, the Texas oilman: 'Bed? Only playground that beats Las Vegas'.[49] This was restored to Van Sant's version, and a number of other *Psycho 98* modifications – nudity in the opening motel and central showers scenes, Norman masturbating as he watches Marion undress – would not have surprised a contemporary audience familiar with the amount of nudity and number of sexual themes that attend the slasher film. In a similar way, the role of the 'final girl', prefigured only rudimentarily in *Psycho*'s Lila Crane, is reinterpreted in Julianne Moore's performance of Lila as the 'spunky inquirer',[50] familiar to viewers of the genre from *Halloween*'s Laurie Strode to *Scream*'s Sidney Prescott (Neve Campbell).

In the early 1970s (and into the following decade) Brian De Palma earned himself a reputation as a film stylist in the tradition of Hitchcock by embarking upon a cycle of films seen to be heavily indebted to the Hitchcock thriller. *Sisters* (1972) was a 'very Hitchcock thriller' inspired by both *Rear Window* and *Psycho*, and *Obsession* (1975) was described by De Palma and co-writer Paul Schrader as 'an homage to *Vertigo*'.[51] The latter film – *Obsession* – can be seen as a kind of *generic* Hitchcock, reconstructing not only the 'mood and manner' of *Vertigo*, but recreating, too, some of Hitchcock's most visible stylistic characteristics: 'tight plot construction, extended *doppelgänger* effects, precise control of point-of-view'.[52] Moreover, Hitchcock's reputation by this time was such that De Palma's allusions were consistently commented upon in critical and promotional materials attending the films. For instance, following the first reviews for *Obsession*, advertisements included an endorsement from the *New York Daily News*: 'Like Hitchcock at the top of his form'.[53] De Palma's next film, *Carrie* (1976), took this further, its distributors developing 'a promotional campaign for the film which presented [De Palma] as a "new master of suspense" – rivalling . . . Hitchcock'.[54] Like *Sisters* and *Obsession*, *Carrie* liberally borrowed from 'the old master'. In particular, the film's opening was a variation on *Psycho*'s shower sequence, with Carrie White (Sissy Spacek) becoming hysterical when she discovers (in the high-school showers) that she has bleeding from her menstrual cycle. Across three subsequent

films – *Dressed to Kill* (1980), *Blow Out* (1981) and *Body Double* (1984) –
De Palma would go on to elaborately rework Hitchcock's famous shower
sequence.

Released just a few months after Hitchcock's death in 1980, *Dressed to
Kill* polarised viewers and critics alike, and demonstrated the extreme critical reaction to De Palma's ongoing revision of Hitchcock's *oeuvre*.[55]
Dressed to Kill was De Palma's most detailed invocation – a 'virtual
remake'[56] – of *Psycho*. Andrew Sarris described *Dressed to Kill* as 'a shamefully straight steal from *Psycho*' and noted several 'Hitchcockian parallels
in the plot', most notably the bloody slashing of the principal character,
Kate Miller (Angie Dickinson), just a third of the way into the film, but
also the nervously played meeting between Kate and Dr Robert Elliott
(Michael Caine) that has its equivalent in *Psycho*'s parlour room scene and
the psychiatrist's final revelation that Elliott is a transsexual driven to
homicidal fury by any woman who arouses his masculine side.[57] It is around
these borrowings that the battle lines over *Dressed to Kill* – whether De
Palma was 'a consummate film maker or a rip-off artist' – were drawn.[58] On
one side, and in near identical terms to the kind of criticism levelled against
Psycho 98, Sarris (and others) condemned 'De Palma's shot-by-shot rep-
licas for the cheap, skimpy imitations they [were]'.[59] On the other side, rival
New York-based critics such as Jim Hoberman and Pauline Kael celebrated De Palma's ability to 'recalculate'[60] the grammar of Hitchcock's
work. Quoting the film maker, Hoberman noted: 'De Palma reasonably
asserts that his work is "not a slavish imitation . . . [Hitchcock] pioneered
correct grammar. I use it because it's the best there is"'.[61]

The beginning of *Dressed to Kill* – Kate Miller in a languorous shower
masturbation fantasy that ends in a violent awakening – is not just an out-
rageous reworking of *Psycho*'s famous murder sequence, but also a reprise
of De Palma's own earlier tribute to Hitchcock: *Dressed to Kill*'s 'showerbath sequence, with its swooning soft-porn atmosphere and adolescently
over-active camera, actually starts out as a *hommage* to *Carrie* before it
becomes a cod [or empty] *hommage* to *Psycho* (with an attack that isn't)'.[62]
De Palma reprises the shower sequence at the end of *Dressed to Kill* in the
nightmare Liz Blake (Nancy Allen) has of Elliott escaping from the mental
institution and slitting her throat in the shower. It can be argued that,
rather than slavishly imitating *Psycho*'s originary scene, this final sequence
(like the larger gesture of *Psycho 98*) contributes to an elaborate circuit of
cinematic repetitions in which 'De Palma will become Hitchcock will
become De Palma, *ad infinitum*'.[63] More than this, De Palma cannily
engages here not only with a sequence – the showerbath murder – that is
part of a collective tradition but with its pro-filmic event. That is, a 'body

double' was used for Angie Dickinson in some of the shower shots just as Hitchcock had hired, for the nude filming of *Psycho*'s shower scene, Marli Renfro, a professional dancer-model, to double for Janet Leigh.[64]

De Palma's next film, *Blow Out* (1981), is widely recognised as a variation on (an *unacknowledged remake* of) both *Blow Up* (Michelangelo Antonioni, 1966) and *The Conversation* (Francis Ford Coppola, 1974), but in addition to this it replays – again – the *Psycho* shower sequence *and* its pro-filmic event. *Blow Out* begins – *Halloween*-style – with a knife-wielding murderer stalking young women through a dormitory to its steamy shower room. As the stalker draws back the shower curtain and raises his knife to strike, his victim lets out a pathetic scream. At this point, the scene cuts to a shot of Jack Terry (John Travolta), a sound recordist, watching a work-print of what is in fact a low-budget slasher movie titled (in a further reference to Hitchcock) *Co-Ed Frenzy*. Jack's endeavour to replace some of the film's sound effects – the scream, but also eerie, ambient night sounds – leads him to a secluded spot where he witnesses an 'accident' in which a presidential candidate is drowned when his car plunges from a bridge. (The plotting of this sequence remakes, too, the Chappaquiddick incident of 1969 that effectively ended the presidential prospects of Senator Edward Kennedy.) Jack rescues a female passenger, Sally Badina (Nancy Allen), from the water but (at the very end of the film) she is murdered while helping Jack attempt to unravel the conspiracy surrounding the candidate's death. In the film's final sequence – and in an ironic reprise of the beginning – Jack finds his 'voice-double' through the dubbing of Sally's dying screams onto the soundtrack of his tawdry slasher movie.

De Palma's 1984 film, *Body Double*, is not only an extended reworking of the voice and body doubles of *Blow Out* and *Dressed to Kill* but arguably De Palma's 'densest appropriation of Hitchcock's cinematic vocabulary and themes: voyeurism, pursuit, rescue, guilt, punishment, and the use of multiple identities or disguises'.[65] More particularly, De Palma repeats in *Body Double* elements of the narrative invention of both *Rear Window* and *Vertigo*. In the latter film – *Vertigo* – a wealthy industrialist, Gavin Elster (Tom Helmore), hires a former police detective, John 'Scottie' Ferguson (James Stewart), to watch his beautiful wife, Madeleine (Kim Novak), because he believes she is suicidal. This triangular relationship of two men focused on a single woman is replayed in *Body Double*, where Sam Bouchard (Gregg Henry) points out to fellow actor, Jake Scully (Craig Wasson), that a woman in a distant house does a nightly dance and masturbatory routine that insists on being watched. As Carol Squiers points out, in both films the 'watching' is a deliberate set-up by the first man to

Body Double (Brian De Palma, 1984). Courtesy Columbia/The Kobal
Collection.

make the second a witness to murder in order to cover up his role as the
murderer. In both cases, the second man is stricken with a phobia that
limits his actions at crucial moments. In both cases, the second man discovers that the woman he watched (in the lead up to the murder) was a
stand in – *a body double* – for the murdered wife.[66] More than this, in both
cases, the first man is a 'body double' for Hitchcock (and De Palma), the

man who directs the audience – for which the second man is the body double – to watch the violence that the first has orchestrated and inflicted upon the woman.

Commenting on Hitchcock's films of the 1950s, Dave Kehr explains that if cinema itself is the central metaphor that informs *Vertigo*, then 'the dream of *Vertigo* – the dream of . . . a beautiful illusion that gives way to nothingness – is also the dream of the movies'.[67] De Palma begins and ends *Body Double*, but also *Dressed to Kill* and *Blow Out*, with just such an illusion: a dream, a film-within-a-film. At the end of *Body Double*, De Palma returns to the horror movie set of the film's opening: a bat descends upon a bathroom where a young woman is showering and transforms itself into a vampire played by the actor Jake Scully. Just as the vampire is about to strike, the film's director (Dennis Franz, a De Palma regular) appears in the bathroom window, shouting for Jake to freeze. Jake holds a rigid pose as the actress in his clutches is replaced with a body double. The filming resumes and we see a montage: shots of Jake and the actress intercut with body shots of Jake and the Body Double, Jake sinking his fangs into the slender neck of the actress, blood streaming down the perfect breasts of the Body Double. At this point, *Body Double* does not lead in any direct way back to *Psycho*, but establishes instead the larger circuit of what Gilles Deleuze describes as a 'dream-image',[68] a *transtextual* relay in which each image becomes legible only in relation to the seriality of cinematic representation.

Gus Van Sant's version of *Psycho* was released in December 1998 following an intense promotional campaign and reports that Van Sant had not only followed the original film shot-for-shot, but adhered to Hitchcock's six-week shooting schedule and insistence that there be no advance press screenings. The official website for the film announced that Van Sant's daring remake of 'an intact [and] undeniable classic' would be 'part tribute to Hitchcock, part new introduction for younger audiences, part bold experiment'.[69] Questioned as to why he had undertaken such a project, Van Sant answered:

> I felt that, sure, there were film students, cinephiles and people in the business who were familiar with *Psycho* but that there was also a whole generation of movie-goers who probably hadn't seen it. I thought this was a way of popularising a classic . . . It was like staging a contemporary production of a classic play while remaining true to the original . . . There is an attitude that cinema is a relatively new art and therefore there's no reason to 'restage' a film. But as cinema gets older there is also an audience that is increasingly unpractised at watching old films, silent films, black and white films.

> *Psycho* is perfect to refashion as a modern piece. Reflections are a major theme in the original, with mirrors everywhere, characters who reflect each other. This version holds up a mirror to the original film: it's sort of its schizophrenic twin.[70]

Critics were prompt to point out that Van Sant's statements were disingenuous. Naremore objected, stating that 'movies have as much in common with novels as with theatre', and added that Van Sant's *Psycho* was not simply a refilming of the original Joseph Stefano script, but 'an elaborate quotation of things that were literally printed on another film'.[71] And Steven Schneider noted that the phrase 'popularising a classic' was inappropriate not only because *Psycho* was already 'one of the most profitable films of all time, and one that [had] haunted American culture's collective consciousness ever since its release', but also because Universal had actively worked against this, withdrawing the original from circulation in the lead up to the release of the remake.[72]

As noted at the outset, the critical reception of Van Sant's *Psycho* was uniformly one of bemusement or hostility. Adrian Martin announced that no matter what 'clever justifications' might be advanced for the remaking, the 'experiment' was noteworthy only in so far as it proved 'that you can mechanically copy all the surface moves of a screen "classic" and yet drain it of any meaning, tension, artistry and fun'.[73] Jonathan Rosenbaum (similarly) stated that *in theory* 'a nearly shot-by-shot, line-by-line remake of any movie could produce something marvellous, fresh, and revelatory, at least if an artist had a viable artistic program to go with it', but that *in practice* Van Sant's *Psycho* was 'a piece of dead meat'.[74] Perhaps the most withering comments came from William Rothman, who had devoted some one-hundred pages of his *auteurist* study, *Hitchcock – The Murderous Gaze*, to a close analysis of *Psycho*[75]:

> Van Sant . . . deserves all the blame anyone might heap on him for making his dreadful version of *Psycho* . . . In Hitchcock's films the figure of the author is an important – perhaps the most important – character . . . What is missing . . . from every moment of Van Sant's film . . . are those motifs or signs or symbols . . . whose presence participates crucially in the films' philosophical meditations [and which] taken together, simply signify that these are Hitchcock films. They function as Hitchcock's signatures, like his name in the credits or his cameo walk-ons.[76]

Each of these critical reactions echoes the call for 'lovers of film . . . lovers of Hitchcock . . . lovers of the original *Psycho*' to boycott what was seen to amount to 'the worst, most offensive idea in the history of film'.[77] It seems curious, though, that few of the commentaries at the time of the release of *Psycho 98* (Rosenbaum's excepted) drew attention to the ways in which *Psycho 60* had *already* been variously 'remade'. As outlined above, these broader, intertextual relations range from the generic repetitions of *Halloween*, *Scream* and (countless) other slasher movies to the careful acts of homage evident in De Palma's work of the 1980s – *Body Double*, *Dressed to Kill* and *Blow Out*. More recently De Palma has returned to the style and themes of these earlier films with another labyrinth thriller – at once a tribute to *film noir* and to cinema but also another Hitchcock remaking – in *Femme Fatale* (2002). The film begins with an elaborate, fifteen-minute heist sequence (incorporating a homage to the *Psycho* shower sequence) in which an icy blonde (Hitchcockian) heroine, Laure Ash (Rebecca Romijn-Stamos), is enlisted in the robbery of a $10 million piece of jewellery during a premiere screening at the Cannes Film Festival Palais. Double-crossing her accomplices, Laure absconds to Paris where she becomes a brunette, assumes the identity of a woman (Lily) she closely resembles, and escapes to a new life in America. It is not until ten minutes before the end of *Femme Fatale* that one (fully) realises that all of what has gone before (that is, all that comes after her assuming Lily's identity) is Laure's dream. Upon waking, Laure elects for a 'second chance', steering events away from the premonition of her (nightmarish) future toward a (*Vertigo*-like) ending that reworks and reprises the dream vision. As Gavin Smith points out, if there are two things one can be sure of in a De Palma film, these are that 'nothing is ever as it seems and someone is *always* watching'.[78] With *Femme Fatale*, De Palma devises another seductive deception, reworking Hitchcock (and others), but also revisiting his own signature style (split screen, gliding steadicam) and themes: pursuit and surveillance, mistaken identities and doublings, and (like Hitchcock) an obsession of *seeing* all that is forbidden.

In addition to these personal (signature) De Palma movies, other 'limited' remakings of *Psycho* can be found in such varied examples as: the shower scene spoof in *High Anxiety* (Mel Brooks, 1977), the 'murder' of the heroine in Sally Potter's experimental film *Thriller* (1979), Maggie's *Psycho*-like mallet attack on Homer in the 'Itchy & Scratchy & Marge' episode of *The Simpsons* (season 2, 1990), Martin Arnold's short *Psycho* trailer for Viennale film festival (1997), and the masochistic parody of the shower murder in the short film *Psycho Too* (Andrew Gluck Levy, 1999). In addition to these, *Psycho* has been revisited in *Hitchcock: The Final Cut* (2002), a video game featuring extracts from six Hitchcock films (*Psycho*, *Frenzy*, *Torn Curtain*, *Rope*, *Saboteur* and *Shadow of a Doubt*), and – in the most meticulous remaking prior to *Psycho 98* – Richard Anobile's

Femme Fatale (Brian De Palma, 2002). Courtesy Quinta Comm./
The Kobal Collection/Etienne George.

(pre-video age) reconstruction of *Psycho*: 1,300-plus frame enlargements
and every word of dialogue in book form.[79] Van Sant's version of *Psycho*
might well closely follow the form and narrative of Hitchcock's film and
also (as mentioned above) repeat a number of its contexts: same sound-
stage, similar order of shooting, no advance screenings and so on. But each
of the aforementioned *other* revisions of *Psycho* suggests that the 'original'
text is never fixed or singular and that Van Sant's *Psycho* remake differs textually (from this larger circuit of remakings) not *in kind* but only *in degree*.
As stated in the introductory chapter, remaking might refer to *any number*
of industrial and cultural practices, and the remake can be seen as but a particular institutional form of the logic of repetition that is possible *for all
films*. Understood in this way, a broad conception of the remaking of *Psycho*
would acknowledge, too, any of the several re-releases of *Psycho* (from
1965 onward) and its subsequent licensing by MCA for network and syndicated television screenings, and (later) sale to video tape and disc, as
further revisions – or remakings – of the film.

While all of the above establishes a much broader set of relations
between *Psycho 60* and *Psycho 98* (than that accorded it by most of its
reviewers), there is another, perhaps more interesting, way to approach
the Van Sant version. Rather than suggest, as many of its detractors have,
that *Psycho 98* follows Hitchcock's film too closely – that it steers near to

plagiarism, adding nothing to the 'original' – it can be argued that Van Sant's *Psycho* is *not close enough* to the Hitchcock version. Such an evaluation is implicit in the Martin and Rosenbaum reviews cited above, and is even more clearly expressed by *Chicago Sun Times* critic, Roger Ebert, who states:

> Curious, how similar the new version [of *Psycho*] is, and how different . . .
> The movie is an invaluable experiment in the theory of cinema, because it demonstrates that a shot-by-shot remake is pointless; *genius apparently resides between or beneath the shots*.[80]

This suggestion – that an irreducible difference plays simultaneously between the most mechanical of repetitions – is best demonstrated by two earlier (and lesser known) remakes of Hitchcock's work: *Remake* (Pierre Huyghe, 1995) and *24 Hour Psycho* (Douglas Gordon, 1993). The first of these, *Remake*, is a shot-by-shot remake, a 'home-made' video reproduction – 'complete and literal but nonchalant, with a few jumps and discrepancies owing to its [deliberate] amateurism'[81] – of Hitchcock's *Rear Window*. As in the case of Van Sant's *Psycho*, where the duration of the actors' performances were timed against those of a video monitor replay of their predecessors' movements, Huyghe instructed his non-professional actors 'to repeat, to be doubles, to *reproduce* [to create anew]'.[82]

The second work, *24 Hour Psycho*, is a new version – an 'exact' remake – of *Psycho 60*, but one that (as its title suggests) takes a full day to run its course. More specifically, Gordon's version is a video installation piece that re-runs *Psycho 60* at approximately two frames per second, just fast enough for each image to be pulled forward into the next,[83] placing it 'somewhere between the stillness of the photograph and the movement of the cinema'.[84] As Stéphane Aquin points out, 'stripped of its soundtrack, slowed down to the limit of tolerability, the film plays like a regression through the history of cinema, back to that threshold where black and white photography haltingly becomes a moving image'.[85] Drawing upon the formal precedents of the North American 'structural' film (notably George Landow's *Film in which there appear sprocket holes, edge lettering, dirt particles, etc.*, 1966; and Ken Jacobs' *Tom, Tom, the Piper's Son*, 1969), but also the new technologies of viewing introduced by home video, Gordon's strategy is to demonstrate that each and every film is remade – that is, *dispersed and transformed* – in its every new context or configuration. Accordingly, Gordon does not set out to imitate *Psycho* but to *repeat* it – that is, to change nothing, but at the same time allow an absolute difference to emerge. Understood in this way, *Psycho 98* might be thought of not as a *perversion* of an original identity, but as the production of a new event, one that adds to (rather than corrupts) the seriality of the former version. If Hitchcock's work holds for its viewers some ongoing fascination then it is perhaps because these viewers remake the work in its every reviewing, and this re-viewing may be no more or less than the genre labelled 'remake'.

Each of the above mentioned works – *Remake*, *24 Hour Psycho* and *Psycho 98* – is a kind of homage to Hitchcock, 'a recognition of the deep structure of his accumulated works, which speaks across generations and across artistic media'.[86] As Paula Cohen notes, when critics (like Naremore[87]) declare that a better solution to Van Sant's remaking of *Psycho* would have been to re-release a 35 mm print of that film, they fail to realise that a *re*-viewing of *Psycho 60* is itself 'a form of homage rather than a recreation of the original experience': 'Van Sant's film [is] a mechanism for catalysing homage, as ingeniously designed to draw admiring attention to the original as anything Hitchcock might have come up with himself'.[88] More than this, *Psycho 98* – indeed, *all* of the *Psycho* remakes – are a reminder both of Hitchcock's place as a major figure in theories of film authorship and of his ongoing influence in and through (popular) film and (high) art, and the exchange between the two. Finally, Hitchcock's example underscores the importance of an understanding of the author-producer in accounts of remaking, drawing attention to the very nature of cinema, to the nature of cinematic quotation and artistic production, and to the fact that every film – every film viewing – can be understood as a type of remaking.

Notes

1. 'Psycho: Saving a Classic', accessed 12 February 1999.
2. Ibid.
3. See, for example, Harkness, 'Psycho Path'.
4. '*Psycho*: Saving a Classic', accessed 12 February 1999.
5. Mazdon, *Encore Hollywood*, p. 151. See also Sutton, 'Remaking the Remake', pp. 69–70.
6. Ibid.
7. See Condon and Sangster, *The Complete Hitchcock*.
8. Neale, 'Questions of Genre', p. 48.
9. Druxman, *Make it Again, Sam*, p. 20.
10. Tarantino, ' "How He Does It" ', p. 25.
11. McDougal, 'The Director Who Knew Too Much', p. 52.
12. Ibid., p. 53.
13. Ibid., pp. 58–61.
14. Kapsis, *Hitchcock*, p. 22.

15. McDougal, 'The Director Who Knew Too Much', p. 52.
16. Ibid., pp. 57–8.
17. Mulvey, 'Death Drives', p. 233.
18. Naremore, 'Remaking *Psycho*', p. 5, emphasis added.
19. Rebello, *Alfred Hitchcock and the Making of* Psycho, p. 47.
20. Krohn, *Hitchcock at Work*, p. 224; and Rebello, *Alfred Hitchcock and the Making of* Psycho, pp. 25–30.
21. Kapsis, *Hitchcock*, p. 60.
22. Naremore, *Filmguide to* Psycho, p. 26.
23. See Rebello, *Alfred Hitchcock and the Making of* Psycho, pp. 152–6.
24. Kapsis, *Hitchcock*, p. 60.
25. Rebello, *Alfred Hitchcock and the Making of* Psycho, p. 162.
26. Ibid., p. 172.
27. Kolker, 'Algebraic Figures', p. 40.
28. Rebello, *Alfred Hitchcock and the Making of* Psycho, p. 169.
29. Ibid., pp. 168–74.
30. Carroll, 'The Future of Allusion', p. 52.
31. Kolker, 'Algebraic Figures', p. 40.
32. Wills, 'The French Remark', p. 157.
33. Frow, 'Rev. of *Play It Again, Sam*'.
34. Clover, 'Her Body, Himself', pp. 192–205.
35. Ibid., p. 192.
36. Ibid., p. 194.
37. Dika, *Recycled Culture*, p. 208.
38. Neale, 'Questions of Genre', p. 56.
39. Lowenstein, 'The Master, The Maniac, and *Frenzy*', p. 185.
40. Pulleine, 'Rev. of *Friday the 13th*', p. 132.
41. Pulleine, 'Rev. of *Friday the 13th, part 2*', p. 138.
42. Clover, 'Her Body, Himself', p. 204.
43. Stam, *Film Theory*, p. 337, n. 2.
44. Kapsis, *Hitchcock*, p. 172.
45. Milne, 'Rev. of *Psycho II*', pp. 245–6.
46. Kapsis, *Hitchcock*, pp. 174–5.
47. Jack Kroll (*Newsweek*), quoted in ibid., p. 175.
48. Neale, 'Questions of Genre', p. 56.
49. Rebello, *Alfred Hitchcock and the Making of* Psycho, p. 77.
50. Clover, 'Her Body, Himself', p. 203.
51. Kapsis, *Hitchcock*, pp. 193–6.
52. Rosenbaum, 'Rev. of *Obsession*', p. 217.
53. Quoted in Kapsis, *Hitchcock*, p. 196.
54. Ibid., p. 197.
55. Ibid., p. 201.
56. Combs, 'Rev. of *Dressed to Kill*', p. 213.
57. Sarris, 'Rev. of *Dressed to Kill*', pp. 42 and 44.

58. Kapsis, *Hitchcock*, p. 201.
59. Sarris, quoted in ibid., p. 207.
60. Kolker, 'Algebraic Figures', pp. 34–51.
61. Hoberman, 'Rev. of *Dressed to Kill*', p. 44. See also Kael, 'Master Spy, Master Seducer', pp. 68–71.
62. Combs, 'Rev. of *Dressed to Kill*', p. 213.
63. Ibid.
64. Rebello, *Alfred Hitchcock and the Making of* Psycho, p. 104.
65. Squiers, 'Over Brian De Palma's Dead *Body Double*', p. 97.
66. Ibid.
67. Kehr, 'Hitch's Riddle', p. 16.
68. Deleuze, *Cinema 2*, pp. 44–67.
69. '*Psycho*, Official Universal Pictures website'.
70. Ibid.
71. Naremore, 'Remaking *Psycho*', p. 6.
72. Schneider, 'A Tale of Two *Psycho*s'.
73. Martin, 'Norman's not Stormin'', p. 20.
74. Rosenbaum, 'Hack Job'.
75. Rothman, *Hitchcock*, pp. 245–341.
76. Rothman, 'Some Thoughts on Hitchcock's Authorship', pp. 29–33.
77. '*Psycho* Boycott, The'.
78. Smith, 'Dream Project', p. 28.
79. Anobile, *Alfred Hitchcock's* Psycho.
80. Ebert, 'Rev. of *Psycho*', emphasis added.
81. Royoux, 'Remaking Cinema', p. 22.
82. Ibid.
83. See Taubin, 'Douglas Gordon', p. 69.
84. Mulvey, 'Death Drives', p. 231.
85. Aquin, 'Hitchcock and Contemporary Art', p. 174.
86. Tarantino, ' "How He Does It" ', p. 25.
87. Naremore, 'Remaking *Psycho*', p. 12.
88. Cohen, 'The Artist Pays Homage', p. 131.

Part II Remaking as Textual Category

CHAPTER 3

Texts

In a seminal essay on adaptation, Dudley Andrew argues that the defining feature of film adaptation – 'the matching of the cinematic sign system to prior achievements in some other system' – can be shown to be typical of all representational film.[1] This is to say that every film – indeed, *every representation* – can be regarded as an adaptation because no film 'responds immediately to reality itself' but rather adapts, or *re-presents*, some pre-existing model.[2] As Andrew points out, adaptation theory typically *limits* representation, first by focusing on the transference of novels into film, and then by targeting those cases in which the prior model is a highly regarded literary classic or a widely read popular novel.[3] More recently, some critics have suggested that writing about adaptation should provide a more 'flexible [and] animating discourse in film studies'.[4] James Naremore notes that while adaptation is mostly thought about in relation to canonical literature, it might also accommodate adaptations of other textualised materials.[5] A broader approach to adaptation could include, for example, films derived from songs (*The Indian Runner*, Sean Penn, 1991), letters (*The Last Time I Committed Suicide*, Stephen Kay, 1996), newspaper articles (*Biker Boyz*, Reggie Rock Bythewood, 2003), comic books (*Spiderman*, Sam Raimi, 2002), computer games (*Laura Croft: Tomb Raider*, Simon West, 2001), adventure rides (*Pirates of the Caribbean: The Curse of the Black Pearl*, Gore Verbinski, 2003), television series (*Charlie's Angels*, McG, 2000) and films derived from other films – *remakes*. This chapter sketches a broad approach to adaptation and/as remaking before attending to two extended case studies – the remaking of *Yojimbo* and *Planet of the Apes* – and concluding with some historical notes around the concept of remaking.

Robert Eberwein points to the affinity between the terms 'adaptation' and 'remaking' when he defines the latter as 'a kind of reading or rereading of the original [text]'.[6] This definition seems equally applicable to both, but what typically distinguishes the two concepts is the relation between the new version (adaptation or remake) and the medium of the original arte-fact. A remake is generally considered *a remake of another film*, whereas one of the principal arguments of adaptation theory is concerned with the movement between *different semiotic registers*, most often between literature and film.[7] That is, adaptation does not simply involve a retelling (*reread-ing*) of a story but 'entails a move from one [expressive] medium to another and therefore the "adjustment" of the narrative to the [new] expressive language'.[8] This seems straightforward enough when dealing with the matching of written and cinematic signs, but any easy demarcation (between adaptation and remake) is complicated when sources derive from other (visual) media, such as graphic novels, computer games, television programmes and even serial, experimental and animated films (for example, the *Twelve Monkeys* (Terry Gilliam, 1995) remake of *La Jetée* (Chris Marker, 1962)). Even more problematic is the fact that many liter-ary adaptations have themselves been previously adapted to film, as in the case of the multiple versions of *Little Women* (1933, 1949, 1994) or *The Man in the Iron Mask* (1929, 1939, 1998). As Lesley Stern points out, a chain of remakings often makes the more recent film version 'by default a remake, and particularly in a case in which the source is not a classic [lit-erary] text, the reference point will be the earlier film'.[9]

Stern's comment indicates that a crucial issue when dealing with adap-tations and remakes is the identification and status of the original text. A second animating discourse of adaptation theory is typically concerned with the degree to which the adaptation relates to the (literary or other) original. Recently, critics have taken up a metaphor of translation to describe the way in which accounts of adaptation (remaking) usually centre on issues of fidelity and freedom. The former designates a strategy that seeks to stay as close as possible to the text being translated in order to facilitate a *faithful* adaptation. The latter departs from the original text, investing in its fertility to inspire or stimulate a *free* adaptation.[10] In either case, the similarity to, or difference from, the text being translated ulti-mately serves to affirm the identity and integrity of the (presumed) origi-nal. More than this, a highly canonised text (film *or* novel) is not only considered more worthy of translation, but generates more concern over the accuracy of the translation.[11] In an endeavour to shift the debate, Eric Cazdyn follows Walter Benjamin to assert that the task of the translator is *not to transmit meaning*, but rather to *liberate* a 'pure language', one 'that is imprisoned in the original *as well as* . . . in the language of the transla-tion'.[12] Cazdyn says that 'this pure language is not the original in its pris-tine state that is then defiled by the translation', but something larger that can only be hinted at by the *supplementary* relationship of the original and the translation.[13] He thus proposes a third strategy of translation, one of *transformative* adaptation, in which every film 'as it adapts an original text, inevitably transforms the original text itself'.[14]

Robert Stam similarly takes up the concepts of translation and transformation to describe adaptation as 'a principled effort of inter-semiotic [*or inter-textual*] transposition, with the inevitable losses and gains typical of any translation'.[15] Adaptations need not be concerned with the faithful rendering of some original text, but can now take 'an activist stance toward their source[s] . . . inserting them into a much broader intertextual dialogism'.[16] More particularly, Stam draws upon Gérard Genette's category of *hypertextuality* to describe adaptation as a relationship between a given text (a 'hypertext') and an anterior text (a 'hypotext') that the former transforms, inviting a double reading.[17] Film adaptations – we could include remakes – are understood as hypertexts (new films) derived from pre-existing hypotexts (literary or other textualised sources) that have been transformed through a particular series of operations, including 'selection, amplification, concretisation, actualisation, critique, extrapolation, analogisation, popularisation, and reculturalisation'.[18] Furthermore, in the case of subsequent adaptations of properties – re-adaptations and/or remakes – new hypertexts do not necessarily refer back to original hypotexts, but rather encompass the entire chain of remakings that form a 'larger, cumulative hypotext'.[19] As in Cazdyn's account of transformative adaptation, every reorganisation – every remaking – not only transforms the original but also its anterior adaptations: 'each adaptation organises the elements of the original literary text in a certain way in order to wrap it up with meaning' yet the transformative adaptation 'implies that the original is not only what it is, but also that it exceeds itself'.[20] Like adaptations, then, film remakes 'are caught up in the ongoing whirl of intertextual reference and transformation, of texts generating other texts in an endless process of recycling, transformation, and transmutation, with no clear point of origin'.[21]

The language of translation suggests that the film adaptation (film remake) is not 'a faded imitation of a superior, authentic original . . . [but] a '"citation" grafted into a new context and thereby inevitably refunctioned' or 'disseminated'.[22] While it might often be the case that 'the critic treats the original and its meaning . . . as a fixity, against which the remake is measured and evaluated',[23] more interesting questions pertain to the factors that enable the identification of the intertext and to the nature of the transformations that are worked upon it. As Stam describes it, the intertext or 'source text forms a dense informational network . . . that the adapting text [the remake] can then take up, amplify, ignore, subvert, or transform'.[24] These transformations are conducted within the limitations of a specific historical situation, and the remake performs these transformations along multiple axes, 'absorbing and altering the genres and inter-texts available through the grids of ambient discourses and ideologies, and as mediated by a series of filters: studio style, ideological fashion, political constraints, auteurist predilections, charismatic stars, economic advantage or disadvantage, and evolving technology'.[25] In this way the translation – adaptation or remake – is less interested in its fidelity to the original than in the potential of the original to generate further, and sometimes un-predictable, cultural production. Moreover, in addition to tracking the changes to particular films, a transformative approach to remaking would take an interest in how the very concept of remaking has been transformed over time.[26]

Textual descriptions of remaking, in particular taxonomies, seek to locate remakes in the structural repetition of specific narrative features, drawing an (implicit) distinction between what genre analysis describes as the film's semantic and syntactic elements.[27] A semantic approach defines a film or genre according to a list of common traits, character types, objects, loca-tions and the like, that comprise the film's iconography. A syntactic approach takes an interest in the various relationships that are established between these semantic elements, the way these are organised in a similar manner to create a narrative structure. In taxonomies of remaking, *close* or *direct* remakes ('faithful adaptations') are those that seek to reduce difference between themselves and their originals by sharing both syntac-tic elements (plot structure, narrative units, character relationships, etc.) *and* semantic elements (specific names, settings, time frames, etc.). For example, Lloyd Michaels describes *Nosferatu, the Vampyre* (Werner Herzog, 1979) as a 'faithful' remake of *Nosferatu: A Symphony of Horror* (F. W. Murnau, 1922), claiming that it not only repeats the narrative syntax of the original, but 'closely' follows the semantics of its 'visual design', copying its costuming, make-up, performance style and locations.[28] By contrast, *transformed* or *disguised* remakes ('free adaptations') are those that might only make minor alterations to key syntactic elements, but more substantially transfigure the semantic elements, altering character names, gender and/or race, cultural setting, temporal setting and even the genre of the original. For instance, Stern says *Clueless* is 'remarkably faithful' in its structural repetition of the syntactic elements of *Emma*, that is 'plot and the way it is articulated through the figuring of characters and the combin-ations they enter into'. But the remake is 'inventively divergent in terms of incidentals' or the semantic aspects of title, character name, location, time-frame and genre.[29] A third category, *non-remakes*, describes those films that open up so substantial a difference – semantic *and* syntactic – between themselves and their designated originals that they may have more in common with the narrative attributes of a genre or production cycle than with a particular precursor text, *even though* the remake may have a like title and credit a common source. Recent examples might include films such as *Ocean's Eleven* (Steven Soderbergh, 2001) and *The Italian Job* (F. Gary Gray, 2003) which function independently of their originals as generic heist movies. Finally, one needs to acknowledge that the difference between these categories is only ever one of *degree* (not kind) and that the three positions are best understood as points along a *continuum* with the close remake (at one end) seeking to keep the semantic and syntactic plurality of an original in place through a process of 'repetitional transferral' and the non-remake (at the other end) adopting a tactic of 'differential dispersal'.[30]

As in the case of genre, the most productive textual accounts of remaking locate the remake not simply in a similar (and/or divergent) semantics or syntax, but in the 'intersection of a common semantics and a common syntax'.[31] Additionally, some textual accounts of remaking attend to a commonality (or otherwise) of stylistic elements or the way a film's use of cinematic devices can indicate a hypertextual relationship. In these cases, a likeness at the level of the composition of the shot and editing relations can communicate something of the tone, values and rhythm of a precursor text. For instance, Brian De Palma's interest in Hitchockian themes, in particular voyeurism, is inscribed in his reworkings of *Psycho* and *Vertigo* not only at a semantic-syntactic level but in the 'manner' of point-of-view structures. In another example, Shawn Levy says that Steven Soderbergh's 2001 *Ocean's Eleven* remake adopts little more than its title and (similarly) high wattage talent – George Clooney, Julia Roberts, Brad Pitt, Matt Damon, Andy Garcia – from the original (Lewis Milestone, 1960), which starred Hollywood Rat-Pack members Frank Sinatra, Dean Martin, Peter Lawford and Sammy Davis, Jr. But, he adds, 'in being so true to the frivolous impetus of the first [film] the new *Ocean's Eleven* is a faithful remake'.[32] In a different example, Jonathan Demme's *The Truth About Charlie* (2002) closely follows the structure of *Charade* (Stanley Donen, 1963), retaining all of its key narrative units – characters, events, motivations – but is consistently likened in terms of 'style' and 'spirit' to the films of the French New Wave, especially those of François Truffaut.[33]

The central elements for a narrative analysis of genre – lexicon, syntax and style – provide a key to understanding hypertextual relationships but, as the textual similarities (semantic, syntactic, stylistic) between original

and remake become 'weaker', the more important it becomes to recognise
that the structures of remaking 'are not in the text, but in a particular
reading of the text'.[34] In other words, the audience is encouraged to recognise the original and its remake in a variety of textual *and extra-textual*
ways. Accordingly, taxonomies of remakes do not only attend to textual
structures and the relative fidelity (sameness) or freedom (difference) of
the remaking, but also to the identification of the original, and whether the
remake is credited/uncredited or acknowledged/unacknowledged. The
first is an industrial definition of remaking that relates to the *economic value*
of the remake and its legally sanctioned use (usually in the form of a screen
credit) of a particular textualised source (a commercial property). The
latter, a critical definition of remaking, attends to the *cultural value* of the
remake by drawing attention to its reproduction of an earlier source (an
intellectual property) through such reception practices as promotion and
reviewing. These extra-textual markers stabilise the point of origin, limit-
ing the intertextual relay and securing the hypertextual relationship as
more than one of just general influence and convention.

These various textual (and other) relationships of adaptation and/as
remaking can be further developed and understood through extended case
studies. The first of these is the (historical) example of the remaking of
Akira Kurosawa's *Yojimbo* (*The Bodyguard*, 1961), the second film produced by Kurosawa Productions, and one of the most internationally
popular films in the Kurosawa canon. The dust jacket of the recent
Criterion Collection DVD (1999) draws attention to the remaking of
Yojimbo, describing it as follows:

> The incomparable Toshiro Mifune stars in Akira Kurosawa's visually stun-
> ning and darkly comic *Yojimbo* (*The Bodyguard*). In order to rid a village of
> corruption, masterless samurai Sanjuro turns a range war between two evil
> clans to his own advantage. Remade both as *A Fistful of Dollars* and, more
> recently, *Last Man Standing*, this exhilarating gangster-Western remains one
> of the most influential and entertaining genre-twisters ever produced.[35]

The description at once characterises *Yojimbo* as a groundbreaking *original*
that has generated further cross-cultural production (Italian and American
remakes) and also as a hybrid *chambara* or Japanese swordplay film, a movie
that injected a new realism into a staid genre: 'Kurosawa play[ed] with the
genre and the audience's expectations, filling the film [*Yojimbo*] with tough
yakuza who are cowards and a *ronin* [masterless samurai] who is uncouth
and unkempt'.[36] But Kurosawa effected the transformation by drawing
upon the conventions – the syntax – of two cornerstone American genres,

the Western and the gangster film: 'If we adopt the language of horse breeders to the genealogy of films, one might write *Yojimbo*, by *Shane* out of *Scarface*'.[37] Film maker John Sayles provides a similar description: 'an American-style individual – a guy named Sanjuro – enters [the town], and [*Yojimbo*] turns into a Western fairly easily'. But, Sayles adds, *Yojimbo* is also 'somewhat based on Dashiell Hammett's *Red Harvest*', a novel which tells a like story of a character (a private detective) who works for two opposing factions: 'all of a sudden there's this guy who keeps a personal code . . . but not necessarily a moral one'.[38]

Although not as critically acclaimed as some of Kurosawa's earlier work – for example, *Rashomon* (1950) and *The Seven Samurai* (1954) – *Yojimbo* was a commercial success in domestic and overseas markets and helped consolidate Kurosawa as an art-house *auteur*. *Yojimbo* earned around $1 million in Japanese rentals and was such a big success in American art-house theatres that it was made available to ('remade' for[39]) a wider mainstream market in a newly dubbed English-language version under the title, *Yojimbo: The Bodyguard*.[40] Stuart Galbraith notes the influence of Kurosawa's transformed *chambara*, stating that it not only spawned countless imitations in Japan but that 'its basic story and anti-hero concepts [were] *reworked* in a myriad of genres and countries'.[41] Best known among these is *A Fistful of Dollars* (*Per un pugno di dollari*, 1964) the film that effectively launched the careers of director Sergio Leone, composer Ennio Morricone and actor Clint Eastwood. According to Christopher Frayling, Leone saw *Yojimbo* late in 1963 and reasoned that since 'the original story of *Yojimbo* [came] from an American novel [*Red Harvest*] . . . it would be wonderful to take it back to where it originally came from'.[42] Fellow director Sergio Corbucci says that 'Leone spent much time "slaving away at a moviola machine and copying *Yojimbo*, changing only the setting and details of the dialogue"'.[43] Leone later admitted to having made a copy of the translated dialogue of the film but only 'in order to be sure not to repeat a single word. All I retained was the basic structure [syntax] of Kurosawa's film'.[44]

As in the case of many transformed or disguised remakes, the similarities between the two films are most evident at the syntactic level, where they repeat the archetypes (hero, villain, helper, etc.) and functions noted by Vladimir Propp in his structural account of folktales.[45] In *Yojimbo*/*A Fistful of Dollars*, a loner (samurai; gunfighter) wanders into an isolated town that has been ravaged by corruption and violence. The loner learns from an innkeeper (Gonji; Silvanito) that the depressed conditions in the town are due to the rivalry between two criminally-inclined, mercantile families and their gangs (led by Ushitora and Seibei; Rojo and Baxter).

Seeing an opportunity to profit from the situation, the loner offers his paid services first to one faction and then the next, playing one against the other in the hope that they will both be destroyed. The situation is complicated by the arrival of a merciless villain (Unosuke; Ramone) who is expert with a unique weapon (pistol; Winchester). The loner now sides with the dominant gang (Ushitora and Unosuke; Rojo and Ramon) but still manages to rescue a woman (Nui; Marisole) and her family that have been terrorised by that gang. Learning of the loner's double-cross, the gang captures and savagely beats him, and turns its attention to destroying its rival clan (Seibei; Baxter). The loner escapes with the help of the innkeeper, gradually recovers in an out-of-town refuge (temple; church), and then returns to exterminate the remaining gang. Dispatching the villain, the loner mutters a casual goodbye to the innkeeper and sets off for destinations unknown.

In addition to these structural parallels, many of the 'incidental details' of *Yojimbo* remain intact in *A Fistful of Dollars*,[46] but Leone 'undressed' the characters of Kurosawa's film, turning them into cowboys, 'to make them cross the ocean and to return to their place of origin'.[47] In doing so, Leone drew inspiration from a host of American Westerns. For instance, the iconography of George Stevens's classic *Shane* (1952) – which tells the story of a mysterious (Christ-like) figure who arrives from nowhere to help a struggling family – was 'particularly important'. But Leone also admitted to deriving ideas from such renowned Westerns as *Rio Bravo* (Howard Hawks, 1959), *The Man Who Shot Liberty Valence* (John Ford, 1962) and *Warlock* (Edward Dmytryk, 1959), the latter of which was a favourite of Leone's at the time.[48] More than this, just as Kurosawa had reworked the conventions of the *chambara* with a revolutionary approach to swordplay, music and sound effects,[49] Leone transformed the conditions of the European Western, introducing a new kind of realism and 'a hero who was negative, dirty, who looked like a human being, and who was totally at home with the violence which surrounded him'.[50] In doing so, Leone also introduced (what were later recognised as) hallmarks of his own directorial style: 'pervasive death imagery; breathtaking, rule-breaking use of the widescreen; a near-fetishist devotion to the close-up; . . . an unprecedented marriage of music and image; and, the relentless pace of mythic storytelling'.[51] As Frayling concludes, 'it is the flamboyance and the *rhetoric* of Leone's remaking of *Yojimbo* 'that support his argument that he was "translating" into Italian, rather than executing "a carbon-copy of *Yojimbo*" '.[52]

According to Frayling, Leone undertook his cultural remaking of *Yojimbo* with the express understanding that his Italian production company would purchase the necessary permissions from Toho (Kuro-sawa's distributor) to make it an authorised copy – a *credited* remake. But a 'nerve-racking moment' came three-quarters of the way through filming when one of the film's financiers advised that Leone, and everyone else associated with the film, 'should refrain under any circumstances from mentioning the word *Yojimbo*'.[53] For reasons that remain unclear, the rights were never secured, and upon seeing the film Kurosawa wrote to Leone saying: 'I have just had the chance to see your film. It is a very fine film, but it is my film. Since Japan is a signatory of the Berne Convention on international copyright, you must pay me'.[54] Toho and Kurosawa Productions subsequently filed a complaint with the International Federation of Film Producers to which Leone's lawyers responded by counter-claiming that Kurosawa had lifted the story, not from *Yojimbo* (or even *Red Harvest*), but from Carlo Goldoni's eighteenth-century play *Arlecchino servitore di due padrone* (*The Servant of Two Masters*).[55] The defence provided by this claim enabled Leone's lawyers to negotiate an out-of-court settlement, granting Toho exclusive distribution rights for the film in Japan, Taiwan and South Korea, plus 15 per cent of world-wide box-office receipts.[56]

A Fistful of Dollars went on to become an 'original' in its own right, the first of Leone's 'dollars-trilogy' (which included *For a Few Dollars More*, 1965; and *The Good, the Bad and the Ugly*, 1966). However, possibly due to the litigation, *Yojimbo* remained the principal point of reference, and in 1992 New Line Cinema began negotiating a credited remake of *Yojimbo*, purchasing remake rights to the Kurosawa work.[57] The film that resulted – Walter Hill's *Last Man Standing* (1996) – is first and foremost a Bruce Willis vehicle, but it also takes *Yojimbo* (even more than *A Fistful of Dollars*) back to its generic 'origins' bringing together the structure and the syntax of both Western and gangster pictures. *Last Man Standing* follows its precursors to tell the story of a loner, 'John Smith' (Bruce Willis), who enters a Prohibition-era border town which is divided between the local power of two gangs, one led by the Irishman Doyle, the other by the Italian Strozzi. As in the earlier films, the loner strikes a friendship with the local innkeeper, conspires to profit from the mutual destruction of the gangs, rescues a kidnapped woman from one faction and finally shoots it out with a formidable opponent (in this case, the villain Hickey, played by Christopher Walken). Additionally, Hill's film borrows some incidental detail, transforming, for instance, the harbingers of dread from the Kurosawa and Leone versions – a dog carrying a human hand down the street, a corpse riding a horse out of town – into a dead horse lying in the middle of a dusty Main Street.

Last Man Standing (Walter Hill, 1996). Courtesy New Line/
The Kobal Collection.

    As Kim Newman points out, transposing the story that Kurosawa set in
post-feudal Japan and Leone in the old West to the Prohibition-era border
town of Jericho, West Texas, brings *Last Man Standing* close in time and
location to the Personville setting of Hammett's *Red Harvest*. In fact,
Newman 'wonders why [Hill] didn't go the whole hog, buy the rights to
Red Harvest – unfilmed since a very loose 1930 adaptation, *Roadhouse
Nights* – and make a faithful film version of the original, rather than squir-
rel through a maze of intermediary mimicries'.[58] Newman stresses fidelity
to a single (credited) source over the remakings of *Yojimbo*, *A Fistful of
Dollars* and *Roadhouse Nights*, but at the same time notes that Hill's placement of 'urban gangsters in a left-over Wild West setting' makes *Last Man
Standing* 'an ironic evocation of . . . American cinema'.[59] In other words,
stylistically and thematically *Last Man Standing* sits comfortably alongside
Hill's earlier translations and evocations of the iconography of Hollywood
genres.[60] More than this, Newman points to Hill's preference, not for original titles, but 'pre-extant sources as outlines for his action films'. For
instance, *The Driver* (1978) pays homage to the films of Jean-Pierre
Melville, *Streets of Fire* (1984) is a Howard Hawks-type (rock and roll)
Western, and even Hill's 'straight' Western pictures – *The Long Riders*
(1980), *Geronimo: An American Legend* (1993), *Wild Bill* (1995) – 'return to
oft-told stories'.[61]

The above suggests that *Last Man Standing* can be called up as a credited, transformed remake of *Yojimbo*, but it indicates, too, the complexity of generic and cross-cultural remakings. While attention to the textual (syntactic) structures of these three films – *Yojimbo*, *A Fistful of Dollars* and *Last Man Standing* – reveals something of their likeness, an account of the historical, cultural and authorial 'filters' through which they are transformed tells something too about the *indigenisation* of these models.[62] That is, while international product (story, genre) might provide Kurosawa or Leone with an underlying form or narrative model, this is restructured in terms of local content, flavour, accent and social text.[63] More than this, rather than resulting in pale imitations of their prototypes these remakings can lead to new or revived indigenous forms (*chambara*, spaghetti Western) which are in turn (re-)exported as new (and 'original') cultural models. This transformative understanding of remaking is further evident in the next example, the adaptation and remaking of *Planet of the Apes*.

In the 1990s Twentieth-Century Fox began looking at ways of reviving its *Planet of the Apes* franchise. The property had been more or less dormant since the 1970s when the studio had extended the initial *Planet of the Apes* feature (Franklin J. Schaffner, 1967) through a number of sequels and television programmes. The first film in the series was derived from Pierre Boulle's 1963 novel *La planète des singes*, initially translated into English as *Monkey Planet* and later (following the release of the feature film) republished as *Planet of the Apes*. Described as a combination of 'speculative science fiction [and] Swiftian social satire',[64] the novel begins with a couple on a leisurely cruise upon an interstellar vessel discovering a message in a bottle. The frame story makes way for the tale of twenty-sixth century French astronaut (and narrator) Ulysse Mérou who, accompanied by fellow explorers Professor Antelle and Arthur Levain, travel to the distant solar system of Betelgeuse. Leaving their craft in orbit, the explorers land a pod on an Earth-like planet they name Sonor. They discover that the planet is inhabited by mute humans of low intelligence, and ruled by apes in a society (slightly) less technologically developed than the one on Earth. To their horror, they find that the apes harvest and conduct experiments on the humans: Mérou is captured and held in a research laboratory, Antelle is placed in a zoo where he loses his mind and Levain is killed in the hunt. Gradually Mérou, and his adopted human mate Nova, attract the attention of the kindly chimp researcher Dr Zira but only enrage the narrow-minded orang-utan Zaius. Mérou finally persuades an astonished Zira of his origins, learns the ape language and, following a presentation to the simian scientific council, is set free. Meanwhile, Zira's fiancé

Dr Cornelius discovers evidence in an archaeological dig that the planet was ruled by humans before it was usurped by their ape servants. This discovery causes unrest and endangers Mérou's safety. Zira and Cornelius arrange for a satellite to return Mérou, his adopted mate Nova and their child Sirius to the astronaut's still orbiting vessel. Mérou returns to Earth (several hundred years in Earth-time has lapsed since his departure) to find it technologically unchanged but now apparently ruled by apes. The novel concludes by returning to the frame story, where the couple – revealed to be chimpanzees – dismiss the prospect of intelligent humans as pure fantasy.

Adaptation rights for *Planet of the Apes* were purchased by producer Arthur P. Jacobs, who assigned Rod Serling (and later Michael Wilson) the task of writing a screenplay that brought together 'Boulle's literary philosophising [and] more cinematic pulp-science fiction imagery'.[65] Having secured the interest of actor Charlton Heston and director Franklin Schaffner, Jacobs eventually struck a deal with Twentieth-Century Fox for a $5 million screen adaptation. The completed film – coinciding not only with the release of *2001: A Space Odyssey* (Stanley Kubrick, 1968) and the *Star Trek* television series (NBC, 1966–69) but a burgeoning public interest in space travel – proved a commercial success, grossing around $25 million (and more upon subsequent reissue).[66] Schaffner's film, while retaining key plot elements and characters from the Boulle novel, wrought a number of significant transformations, both narrative and thematic. A type of free adaptation, *Planet of the Apes* replaces the explorers – Mérou, Antelle and Levain – with American astronauts Taylor (Charlton Heston), Dodge and Landon who travel some two thousand years into the future and crash land on what they believe to be an alien planet. As in the novel, they encounter a society (this one technologically far more primitive than their own) ruled by talking apes. From this point, Taylor's adventure roughly parallels that of Mérou: he is captured along with Nova, wins the confidence of Zira and Cornelius, incurs the anger of the elder Zaius and becomes aware that a human civilisation preceded that of the apes. The end, however, radically transforms all that has gone before. Instead of returning to Earth, Taylor and Nova (without child) escape to the desolate 'forbidden zone' where Taylor discovers evidence – in the form of a time ravaged Statue of Liberty buried to its chest in sand – that the ape society has evolved from an Earth devastated by a human propensity for war.

As Eric Greene points out in his extended analysis of the series, the ending of *Planet of the Apes* is but one – albeit the most famous – element in the series' ongoing presentation of 'apocalyptic images of cataclysmic race wars, nuclear destruction, struggles for dominance, [and] ecological and biological devastation'.[67] Set among American social and political events of the 1960s and 1970s (civil rights movement, Vietnam War protests) Schaffner's film, and the *Planet of the Apes* series on the whole, can be read as 'a liberal allegory of racial conflict',[68] but (as Greene hastens to add) the political statements were not 'platformed', and were never meant to overwhelm the commercial value of the film and its subsequent franchise.[69] Although the ending of *Planet of the Apes* seemed to leave little room for a sequel, the film's outstanding box-office returns prompted the producers to commission ideas for follow-ups, including (abandoned) treatments from Boulle and Serling.[70] The sequel, *Beneath the Planet of the Apes* (Ted Post, 1970), launched the franchise into the 1970s and was followed by three further features: *Escape from the Planet of the Apes* (1971), *Conquest of the Planet of the Apes* (1972), and *Battle for the Planet of the Apes* (1973). By the mid-1970s, the *Apes* cycle had developed a core following, and Paul Woods reports that 'from mid-1974 to late 1975 the market was flooded with *Apes* juvenilia and toys, including model kits and . . . action figures'.[71] With interest maintained by the release of all five feature films to television, the cycle was revived first as a television series (*Planet of the Apes*, 1974) and the following year as an animated series (*Return to the Planet of the Apes*, 1975). Greene and Woods document the exhaustive cultural production that maintained *Planet of the Apes* through the 1980s and into the 1990s, generating interest in, and speculation about, a remake. This included the reprint of Boulle's novel, the rerun of the *Apes* television series on the cable Sci-Fi channel, and the recycling of *Apes* iconography by visual and performance artists.[72] In its most popular reincarnation, *Planet of the Apes* was (closely) remade in an episode of *The Simpsons* ('A Fish called Selma') as an all-singing, all-dancing Broadway musical titled, 'Stop the Planet of the Apes I want to get off!'

The marketing and merchandising potential of a revived *Planet of the Apes* franchise saw Twentieth-Century Fox actively seeking to add a sixth feature film to the series. After several abandoned attempts through the 1990s to develop a new *Planet of the Apes* film,[73] Fox commissioned William Broyles to produce a screenplay unconstrained by the conceits of the previous drafts or earlier films in the series. Stating that Boulle's novel had been 'pretty much exhausted by the first movie', Broyles described his script – originally called 'The Visitor, episode one [of three] in the Chronicles of Aschlar' – as a 're-imagining' of the original series: 'it [is] a new movie . . . It's not a remake in any way, shape, or form. There are no characters that it shares with the original movie. There's no setting, and there's essentially no story'.[74] Understood as a *non*-remake, the completed film, *Planet of the Apes* (Tim Burton, 2001) tells the story of astronaut Leo Davidson (Mark Wahlberg) who crash lands on a world in which talking apes rule over an underclass of humans. Davidson's struggle for survival – assisted by Ari, daughter of an ape senator, and threatened by maniacal chimpanzee General Thade – also becomes a battle to liberate the enslaved human population. Drawing upon ancient and medieval history and accounts of pre-mechanised warfare, Broyles imagined Davidson as a Spartacus-type hero – in the original script, captured and placed in a gladiator camp – who ends up leading the oppressed humans in an epic battle against their captors.[75] Enough of this material survives in Burton's completed film for at least one commentator to describe it as 'a remake of Ridley Scott's *Gladiator* [2000], with monkey suits as well as centurion armour'.[76] More importantly, Broyles's decision to assign a wide range of behaviours to both humans *and* apes transforms the earnest attempts at racial allegory of (especially) the latter films of the *Apes* series into a concern for issues of 'species guilt'. Andrew O'Hehir says the film 'offers up a jittery catalogue of millennial anxieties, from the hazards of genetic engineering and the corrupting influence of technology to ecological catastrophe and weapons of mass destruction'.[77] More than this, Burton (backed with an estimated budget of $110 million) transformed the B-movie aesthetic of the *Planet of the Apes* series into a *B-movie blockbuster*: 'a wild concept coated in incongruous corporate gloss'.[78] As O'Hehir describes it, Burton's *Planet of the Apes*, along with *Shaft* (John Singleton, 2000) and *Rollerball* (John McTiernan, 2001), is part of a recent cycle in which 'a classic genre or exploitation film . . . is remade as a mass entertainment, inflated with a pompous sense of its own significance and loses the edge of anger or cynicism or paranoia that made it powerful in the first place'.[79] Michael Atkinson similarly writes: 'the miracle of the *Apes* films is that such complex textual issues dominate an otherwise preposterous manifestation of cheap trash culture'. This, he continues, is 'the gutsy, low-rent glory of authentic pulp. It's not a quality that can be recaptured in expensive remakes, no matter how strenuous the effort'.[80]

Despite its many differences, the reimagined *Planet of the Apes* still owes much to the Schaffner film (its reputation and progeny) and to Boulle's *La planète des singes*. For instance, Smith and Matthews state that 'the basic thrust of the plot, the arrival of a human space-traveller on a far distant Ape planet is taken from Boulle, but filters it through the first film adaptation'.[81] O'Hehir concurs pointing out that the Burton film not only 'rehashes' the basic premise of the original film and novel, but 'more generally [remembering that Boulle's hero was named Ulysse] the standard Odyssean saga of an adventurer far from home in a world turned upside

Planet of the Apes (Tim Burton, 2001). Courtesy 20th Century/
Zanuck Co./The Kobal Collection/Sam Emerson.

down'.[82] Perhaps most telling, though, is the way the new version handles
the original film's surprise ending in which Taylor realises in his discovery
of a bomb-blasted Statue of Liberty that the ape planet is actually a post-
apocalyptic Earth. The new film similarly concludes with a twist, but
rather than retrospectively codifying the alien world as Earth, Burton has
Davidson – like Ulysse Mérou – return (apparently) to Earth. In the novel,
Mérou lands back in Paris (the Eiffel Tower clearly visible) but to his
horror discovers that the welcoming party is led by a uniformed gorilla. No
direct explanation is offered but the assumption is that in the hundreds of
Earth years that have elapsed during Mérou's travels at light speed,
the Earth has reached a similar stage in its evolutionary cycle as the ape-
dominated Sonor. In the case of the Burton film, Davidson pilots his pod
through an electro-magnetic storm like the one that initially led him to the
planet of the apes. He crash lands in Washington, DC on the steps of the
Lincoln Memorial, only to find that the chiselled features of Abraham
Lincoln have been replaced by those of General Thade. He turns to find
that the emergency vehicles – police cars and fire trucks – that have scram-
bled to the crash-site are in fact driven by apes.

Reviews of *Planet of the Apes* consistently focused on the ending, variously describing it as 'spectacularly befuddling'[83] and a 'spellbinding

example of sheer creative desperation'.[84] Xan Brooks writes that the 'crazed final coda . . . makes little in the way of logical sense, and clashes conspicuously against the pedestrian narrative that precedes it',[85] and Smith and Matthews claim that the ending so confused audiences that some DVD editions were issued with a 'cardboard erratum slip' explaining the final plot point.[86] As (dis)ingenuous as the Broyles/Burton ending might be, these responses seem to miss the more obvious point: namely, that the remake of *Planet of the Apes* has a twist ending *because* the original does. That is, the 'monkey-puzzle of an ending',[87] might make little narrative sense, but it makes perfect *remake sense*. The *Planet of the Apes* series sketches a vast circuit of remakings – films, tele-series, comics, songs and Broadway musicals – but the ending of the Burton film underlines the cultural memory of the original ending and emphatically secures the authority and influence of the cult original.

The above (textual) accounts of remaking describe some of the changes – *filters of transformation* – effected on particular precursor texts, but the concept of remaking and how it has been transformed in its different historical contexts also requires examination. There would appear to be three principal moments in the transformation of the category of remaking, and in the relationship between the remake and its original. These are:

1. the early cinema before the establishment of the Hollywood mode of production (pre-1917);
2. the 'classical' Hollywood of the studio era (1917–60);
3. contemporary Hollywood cinema (post-1960).

Defined primarily in relation to a body of copyright law, the credited remake develops from being a counterpart to the early film practice of pirating (or 'duping') to become an economically driven staple of the Hollywood mode of representation. In the industrial context of the studio years, remakes typically follow a line of fidelity (sameness) in which the original narrative is linearly traced by a film that reinvents the property through revised genre conventions or different stars or new technologies. Through the 1960s and 1970s, the 'new American' cinema (visual artists such as Stan Brakhage, George Kuchar, Jack Smith), and the 'new Hollywood' cinema (maverick film makers like Dennis Hopper, Monte Hellman, Bob Rafelson) were searching for an alternative space free from the rigid hierarchies of the industrial mode of representation. Underpinned by developments in *auteur* criticism, remakes of this period typically filter the original property through individual styles to emphasise difference by focusing on particular sections or introducing new material.[88] Cazdyn states that such transformations are 'always conducted within the limitations of a particular historical situation', and that they are more obvious 'when discourses of "origins" are at their weakest'.[89] These shifts suggest a need to think the concept of remaking historically, an approach evident in the following brief discussion of the copyright and narrative practices of early cinema.

According to Thomas Elsaesser, the institutional development of early film was distinguished by at least two periods: the 'primitive' period from 1896 to 1907; and the period up to 1917, during which time the devices of the earlier period continued to exist alongside the newer strategies of the 'classical continuity' cinema.[90] Elsaesser states that the two 'most momentous' events of cinema's early history were:

1. the 'Nickelodeon boom', or the movement away from itinerant projection to the fixed siting of exhibition outlets;
2. the transition from single reel to multi-reel films, and the associated 'change this brought in the structure of the industry, the textual organisation of the film, and the commodity form of the product'.[91]

Additionally, as the early emphasis of competition and struggle for industry control shifted from attempts to monopolise the production, sale and/or leasing of exclusive or non-standardised equipment to the pursuit of dominance and standardisation in the sphere of manufacturing processes and film product, there was an associated tendency to regulate access to the market by 'controlling invention, and thereby prevent[ing] other producers from copying either patents or products'.[92] As Janet Staiger notes, the struggle for industrial control in the period to 1917 was not conducted so much through the manufacture of competitive products as through structural and legal practices: the working out of alliances and cross-licensing agreements ('combination') and the fighting of legal cases involving patent and copyright infringement ('litigation').[93] It is within this context of litigation, and specifically in relation to the establishment of proper procedures of film protection and copyright, that one can understand two early (and quite similar) types of 'film piracy' – *duping* and *remaking*.[94]

André Gaudreault states that, while the practice of copyrighting motion pictures in the United States began very early, the unprecedented nature of the new phenomenon – 'the "aggregation of photographs" that was the film strip' – put an existing body of copyright law under considerable strain.[95] As most films made prior to 1900 consisted of single shots, the initial response of companies and individuals was to register (at the Library of Congress) film products for copyright as single photographs, even though the composite nature of the film strip was recognised.[96] Accordingly, and in line with the aggressive commercial policies of the period, films of those competitors – especially overseas production companies – which had not taken the precaution of copyrighting their products were enthusiastically pirated or *duped* – that is, new prints for sale and distribution were produced from a *duplicate* negative which had been struck from a competitor's positive projection print. Charles Musser points out that there was considerable reduction in picture quality, but that the duper was able to provide audiences with 'dramatic headliners'[97] and enjoy the rewards of film sales without paying either for high negative production costs or any royalties to the original producer.[98] Gaudreault gives the famous example of Georges Méliès' *Voyage dans la lune* (1902), duped and widely distributed in the US without Méliès ever being able to collect proceeds.[99] And Musser notes that 1903 catalogues of the Edison Manufacturing Company featured dupes of foreign productions, including Méliès' *Joan of Arc*, *Robinson Crusoe* and *Gulliver's Travels*, Pathé Frères' *Ali Baba and the Forty Thieves*, and British pictures from G. A. Smith, James Williamson and the Charles Urban Trading Company.[100]

The clarification of copyright law through the resolution of a number of vexatious court cases that had hindered the American film industry (especially in the period 1901–03), coupled with the establishment of European producers as competitors in the US market, eventually had the effect of curtailing the strategy of duping.[101] This encouraged local film companies to produce more ambitious work, often with American locations and subject matter. For example, in spring 1903, Edison's Kinetograph Department embarked upon a large-scale production of Harriet Beecher Stowe's anti-slavery novel *Uncle Tom's Cabin*. Musser says that without the former profitable option of mechanically reproducing (or duping) the film, the rival Lubin Company simply waited until the Edison picture was released and made its own 'meticulous imitation' of its narrative unfolding – a direct *remake*.[102] While the remaking of a popular film was not a new phenomenon – Lubin's *An Affair of Honor* (1901) remade a Biograph film of the same name,[103] and Edison's own Kinetograph Department had intermittently pursued the practice with films such as *Black Diamond Express* (1896), a remake of Biograph's popular *Empire State Express*[104] – the more limited opportunities for duping a competitor's productions saw a decided increase in the number of film remakes. Driven by the protection of investment and financial gain, the Edison Company in turn pursued this 'ethical equivalent' to duping,[105] remaking Biograph's two biggest hits of 1904: *Personal*, which Edison retitled *How a French Nobleman Got a Wife Through the New York Herald Personal Columns* (1904), and *The Escaped Lunatic*, which became *Maniac Chase* (1904).[106]

Within a few years, greater industry cooperation was facilitated by the formation of the Motion Pictures Patents Company (MPPC, 1908). This 'trust' not only enabled its cartel – which included major American film producers (Edison, Biograph, Armat, Vitagraph) and the American representatives of several European companies (Pathé, Méliès, Gaumont, Eclipse) – to control access to raw film stock, levels of rental income and routes of film distribution, but introduced a self-regulating policy, both improving interiors of film theatres and imposing censorship upon film content.[107] Furthermore, the stable business climate and growth of the exhibition sector encouraged the MPPC (and its distribution arm, the General Film Company) to promote 'the drive towards standardisation in the industry, thereby not only cutting down on costly duplication in the technological sphere, but greatly increasing and accelerating the circulation of the product film'.[108] While not quite spanning a decade, the MPPC (eventually brought down by an anti-trust suit, 1912–15) is credited for both introducing to the film industry an organisation of pooling agreements and trusts which had distinguished American business since before the turn of the century,[109] and encouraging a dynamic of standardisation that would characterise the emerging Hollywood studio system. Moreover, while this emphasis upon uniformity and the promotion of *standardisation* enabled companies to develop similar business methods, Staiger notes that an economic imperative of competition compelled the emerging studios to style their films so as to promote innovation or product *differentiation*.[110]

One of the principal mechanisms by which a standard for filmmaking was reached in the industrial mode of representation that characterised the Hollywood studio system was the employment of advertising discourse.[111] Citing advertisements from Edison catalogues (for films such as *Life of an American Fireman*, 1903, and *Uncle Tom's Cabin*) and fan magazine materials (which begin circulation around 1910), Staiger notes the familiarity of appeals to what have become consistently promoted industry qualities: 'novelty, specific popular genres, brand names, "realism", authenticity, spectacle, [and] stars'.[112] Moreover, while these qualities both 'reinforced standard requirements for a film by stressing a certain set of characteristics in a certain way' and 'outlined the boundaries for variation', concurrent advertising appeals to principles of *innovation* and *novelty* allowed companies to differentiate their product as a grounds for both 'competition and repeated consumption'.[113] This emphasis upon product differentiation is consistent with the (above mentioned) abandonment of strategies of 'piracy' in favour of investment in 'more original' productions. Nevertheless, the repetition of an innovation – the impulse to reduce risks and maximise profit – leads to the establishment of *cycles* – a technique, a style, a series – within classical stylistic practice.[114] Accordingly, the early (pre-1907) practices of *recycling* did not disappear so much as go underground, to re-emerge in the form of the regulated differences of early genres (the chase film, the railroad genre, the crime film) and serials and series such as *Perils of Pauline* (1914) and *Bronco Billy* (1907–16). Moreover, as film copyright law became more precisely defined and as narratives became increasingly self-sufficient, remake piracy was displaced by a classical Hollywood remake practice which legitimated or disguised repetition through careful strategies of (A- and B-level) production, promotion and distribution. For example, Warner Brothers' boxing picture *Kid Galahad* (Michael Curtiz, 1937) was remade with a circus background as *The Wagons Roll at Night* (Ray Enright, 1941). But when remade again (Warner's back catalogue by this time leased to television networks) as the Elvis Presley vehicle *Kid Galahad* (Phil Karlson, 1962), the 1937 version was renamed *The Battling Bellhop* so that its television screenings would not conflict with the Elvis remake.[115]

The shift to multi-reel films, and the associated development of classical continuity cinema (1908–17), also occasioned a change in the intertextual referentiality between the story film and its source text.[116] Early film practice had assumed either audience competency in the popular stories and current events filmed, or supplemented such knowledge with exhibitor's provision of additional cues (a musical accompaniment, sound effects, an oral commentary). As this gave way to longer self-contained narratives and the development of continuity cinema, the focus for the construction of a story shifted from intertextual knowledges to *intratextual* repetitions, such as Bellourian 'alternation',[117] Bordwellian 'functional redundancy',[118] and (in a more complex way) generic conventions and star personae. Accordingly, the intertextual referentiality between a film adaptation and its literary property (novel, play, poem) and a film remake and its 'original' became increasingly *extratextual* – located in reviews, advertising, fiction tie-ins and other promotional materials. The situation changes again with the introduction of television and (later) new information storage technologies (VCR, laser disc, DVD), and an associated rise in film literacy through the abundance of television screens, publications and other visual media. This not only leads to renewed concerns over 'duping' in the form of video and Internet piracy, but also to a 'postmodern' situation in which extratextuality is complemented by a knowing type of intertextuality that becomes (in remakes like *Planet of the Apes*) 'a deliberate, built-in feature of the aesthetic effect'.[119] Finally this is supported by a contemporary situation in which more information circulates in advance of film screenings than ever before (see Chapter 5). These ongoing shifts suggest that – like adaptation theory – textual accounts of remaking need to be placed in a *contextual history*, in 'a sociology [of remaking] that takes into account the commercial apparatus, the audience, and the . . . [broader] culture industry'.[120]

Notes

1. Andrew, 'Adaptation', p. 28.
2. Ibid., p. 29.
3. Ibid.
4. Naremore, 'Introduction', p. 9.
5. Ibid., p. 1; see also Corrigan, 'Which Shakespeare to Love?', p. 160.
6. Eberwein, 'Remakes and Cultural Studies', p. 15.
7. See Andrew, 'Adaptation', pp. 32–4; and Ray, 'Film and Literature', pp. 121–3.
8. Somigli, 'The Superhero with a Thousand Faces', p. 284.
9. Stern, '*Emma* in Los Angeles', p. 226.
10. Cazdyn, *The Flash of Capital*, p. 95.
11. Grindstaff, 'A Pygmalion Tale Retold', p. 140.
12. Cazdyn, *The Flash of Capital*, p. 95, emphasis added.
13. Ibid.
14. Ibid., p. 117.
15. Stam, 'Beyond Fidelity', p. 62.
16. Ibid., p. 64.
17. Ibid., p. 66.
18. Ibid., p. 68.
19. Ibid., p. 66.
20. Cazdyn, *The Flash of Capital*, p. 117.
21. Stam, 'Beyond Fidelity', p. 66.
22. Ray, 'Film and Literature', p. 127.
23. Eberwein, 'Remakes and Cultural Studies', p. 15.
24. Stam, 'Beyond Fidelity', p. 68.
25. Ibid., pp. 68–9.
26. Cazdyn, *The Flash of Capital*, p. 89.
27. Altman, 'A Semantic/Syntactic Approach to Film Genre', pp. 26–40. See also Gabbard, 'The Ethnic Oedipus', pp. 95–114.
28. Michaels, '*Nosferatu*', p. 240.
29. Stern, '*Emma* in Los Angeles', p. 226.
30. McHoul and O'Regan, 'Towards a Paralogics of Textual Technologies', p. 21.
31. Altman, *Film/Genre*, p. 90.

32. Levy, 'Nice'n'Easy', p. 14.
33. Harris, 'Rev. of *The Truth About Charlie*', p. 61.
34. Altman, *Film/Genre*, p. 91.
35. http://www.criterionco.com/asp/.
36. Galbraith, *The Emperor and the Wolf*, p. 302.
37. Sesonske, '*Yojimbo*'.
38. Sayles, 'Walking Alone', p. 22.
39. The metaphor of translation (described earlier) is again apposite for it under-lines the ways in which multi-language versions (common in the early 1930s) and dubbed (and subtitled) versions of films constitute another type of remaking.
40. Galbraith, *The Emperor and the Wolf*, pp. 309–10.
41. Ibid., p. 302, emphasis added.
42. Frayling, *Sergio Leone*, p. 119.
43. Ibid., pp. 124–5.
44. Quoted in ibid., p. 125.
45. Propp, *Morphology of the Folktale*.
46. See Cumbow, *Once Upon a Time*, pp. 3–4.
47. Frayling, *Sergio Leone*, p. 125.
48. Ibid., p. 127.
49. Galbraith, *The Emperor and the Wolf*, p. 302.
50. Frayling, *Sergio Leone*, p. 126.
51. Cumbow, *Once Upon a Time*, p. 2.
52. Frayling, *Sergio Leone*, pp. 129–30.
53. Ibid., p. 147.
54. Quoted in ibid., p. 148.
55. Ibid.
56. Ibid., p. 149.
57. Galbraith, *The Emperor and the Wolf*, p. 311.
58. Newman, 'Rev. of *Last Man Standing*', p. 53.
59. Ibid.
60. Carroll, 'The Future of Allusion', p. 55.
61. Newman, 'Rev. of *Last Man Standing*', p. 53.
62. O'Regan, 'Negotiating Cultural Transfers', p. 214.
63. Ibid., p. 218.
64. Greene, *Planet of the Apes as American Myth*, p. 2.
65. Woods, 'Origins of the Species', p. 20.
66. See Phillips and Garcia, 'The Original Series'; and Winogura, 'Dialogues on Apes, Apes, and More Apes'.
67. Greene, *Planet of the Apes as American Myth*, p. 7.
68. Ibid., p. 1.
69. Ibid., p. 30.
70. Russo and Landsman, '*Planet of the Apes* Revisited', p. 43.
71. Woods, 'The Planet Goes Ape', p. 123.

72. Greene, *Planet of the Apes as American Myth*, pp. 146–87; and Woods, 'The Planet Goes Ape', pp. 123–36.
73. Plesset, 'Unfilmed Scripts', pp. 26–7.
74. Broyles, 'Time and Destiny', pp. 40 and 42.
75. Ibid., p. 42.
76. O'Hehir, 'Gorilla Warfare', p. 13.
77. Ibid.
78. Brooks, 'Rev. of *Planet of the Apes*', p. 56.
79. O'Hehir, 'Gorilla Warfare', p. 13.
80. Atkinson, 'Son of Apes', p. 66.
81. Smith and Matthews, *Tim Burton*, p. 229.
82. O'Hehir, 'Gorilla Warfare', p. 13.
83. Paatsch, 'A-Grade Apes', p. 38.
84. Schembri, 'Embrace the Big, Bad, Dopey Ape', p. 9.
85. Brooks, 'Rev. of *Planet of the Apes*', p. 56.
86. Smith and Matthews, *Tim Burton*, p. 245.
87. Brooks, 'Rev. of *Planet of the Apes*', p. 56.
88. Cazdyn, *The Flash of Capital*, p. 91.
89. Ibid., pp. 118 and 124.
90. Elsaesser, 'The Institution Cinema', p. 154.
91. Ibid., pp. 154–5.
92. Ibid., p. 157.
93. Staiger, 'Combination and Litigation', p. 47.
94. For a more detailed discussion of the dupe in early cinema see Forrest, 'The "Personal" Touch', pp. 89–126.
95. Gaudreault, 'The Infringement of Copyright Laws and Its Effects', p. 3.
96. Ibid., p. 4.
97. Musser, *Before the Nickelodeon*, p. 274.
98. Ibid., p. 495, n. 44. See also Gaudreault, 'The Infringement of Copyright Laws and Its Effects', pp. 2–5.
99. Gaudreault, 'The Infringement of Copyright Laws and Its Effects', p. 5.
100. Musser, *Before the Nickelodeon*, p. 238.
101. Ibid., pp. 277–8.
102. Ibid., p. 245.
103. Musser, *The Emergence of Cinema*, p. 329.
104. Ibid., p. 164.
105. Ibid., p. 389.
106. Musser, *Before the Nickelodeon*, pp. 280–1. See also Forrest, 'The "Personal" Touch', pp. 89–126.
107. Staiger, 'Combination and Litigation', p. 47.
108. Elsaesser, 'The Institution Cinema', p. 158.
109. Gunning, 'Weaving a Narrative', p. 13.
110. Staiger, 'The Hollywood Mode of Production', p. 97. See also Staiger, 'Mass-produced Photoplays', p. 102.

111. Staiger, 'The Hollywood Mode of Production', pp. 97–102.
112. Ibid., pp. 98–101.
113. Ibid., pp. 101 and 109.
114. Ibid., pp. 110–11. See also Balio, *Grand Design*, pp. 101–3.
115. Sennett, *Warner Brothers Presents*, p. 234.
116. Musser, *Before the Nickelodeon*, p. 340. See also Staiger, 'Rethinking "Primitive" Cinema', pp. 101–23.
117. Bellour, *The Analysis of Film*, especially pp. 262–77.
118. Bordwell, *Narration in the Fiction Film*, pp. 156–66.
119. Jameson, 'Postmodernism, or The Cultural Logic of Late Capitalism', p. 67.
120. Naremore, 'Introduction', p. 10.

CHAPTER 4

Genres

In *More Than Night*, James Naremore describes the category of *film noir* not as a set of narrative or stylistic features, but as a *discursive formation*: 'film noir belongs to the history of ideas as much as to the history of cinema . . . It has less to do with a group of artefacts than with a discourse'.[1] In the first instance, American *film noir* is a *critical genre*, 'a belated reading of classic Hollywood that was popularised by cinéastes of the French New Wave, [and later] appropriated by reviewers, academics, and film makers, and then recycled on television'.[2] Naremore describes a first, 'historical' age of *film noir*, enabled by the postwar arrival of Hollywood film into Paris, and a French predisposition to view the *film noir* as an 'existential allegory of the white male condition'.[3] In the late 1950s, French *auteur* film makers such as Jean-Luc Godard and François Truffaut took *film noir* as a pretext for reinventing cinema as a mode of self-expression. In the United States, the expansion of *film noir* was assisted by factors such as the importation of the French *politique des auteurs*, the upsurge of repertory theatre short seasons, the contribution of broadcast television to film literacy and the expansion of film courses in American universities. Along with shifts in Hollywood production methods and commercial infrastructure, these factors led to a delayed new wave of American film makers whose early films were influenced by the *nouvelle vague* and were 'somewhat noirish in tone'.[4] By the late 1960s, the critical appraisal of *noir* had motivated something of a revival, but *film noir* did not become an *industrial genre* until revisionist and neo-expressionist productions – such as *Chinatown* (Roman Polanski, 1974) and *Taxi Driver* (Martin Scorsese, 1974) – helped generate a cycle of *noir* remakings. 'At this point', Naremore concludes, '[film] noir had fully entered the English language, and it formed a rich discursive category that the entertainment industry could expand and adapt [*remake*] in countless ways'.[5]

Like the category of *film noir*, the concept of *remaking* is never simply a quality of texts, but is the secondary result of broader discursive activity. As described in the introductory chapter, film remaking is both enabled and limited by a series of historically specific institutional factors, such as copyright law and authorship, reviewing and media literacy, which are essential to the existence and maintenance – to the discursivisation – of the film remake. In the 1970s, the critical interest in *film noir* and the increasing development of a *noir* canon led to a number of direct remakes of classic *noirs*. *Murder, My Sweet* (Edward Dmytryk, 1944) was remade as *Farewell, My Lovely* (Dick Richards, 1975), *They Live by Night* (Nicholas Ray, 1948) as *Thieves Like Us* (Robert Altman, 1974), and *The Big Sleep* (Howard Hawks, 1946) was remade under the same title (Michael Winner, 1978). The cycle continued into the 1980s, with classic *noirs* like *Double Indemnity* (Billy Wilder, 1944), *The Postman Always Rings Twice* (Tay Garnett, 1946), *Out of the Past* (Jacques Tourneur, 1947), *The Big Clock* (John Farrow, 1948), and *D.O.A.* (Rudolph Maté, 1949) all providing material for remakes. More *noir* followed in the 1990s (and beyond), with *Gun Crazy* (Joseph H. Lewis, 1950) remade as *Guncrazy* (Tamra Davis, 1992), *Criss Cross* (Robert Siodmak, 1949) as *The Underneath* (Steven Soderbergh, 1995), and *Kiss of Death* (Henry Hathaway, 1947) and *Night and the City* (Jules Dassin, 1950) were remade with the same titles (Barbet Schroeder, 1995; Irwin Winkler, 1992). This chapter does not seek to provide an exhaustive overview of these (and other) remakings,[6] but mainly takes an interest in a cycle of *noir* remakes of the 1980s, namely: *Body Heat* (Lawrence Kasdan, 1981), *The Postman Always Rings Twice* (Bob Rafelson, 1981), *Against All Odds* (Taylor Hackford, 1984), *No Way Out* (Roger Donaldson, 1987) and *D.O.A.* (Rocky Morton and Annabel Jankel, 1988). In particular, this chapter looks at the role these remakes play in the commercial development of neo-*noir*, situated as they are between the revisionist (modern) *noirs* of the 1970s and the more formulaic (postmodern) neo-*noirs* of the 1990s.[7] Additionally, it is argued that these *noir* remakes depend not only on the repetition of existing textual structures but also upon audience knowledge of previous texts (the *noir* canon) and an understanding of the *broader generic structure* of *film noir*.

Two *noir* remakes from the 1980s – *The Postman Always Rings Twice* and *Body Heat* – provide an understanding of the critical discourses and industrial contexts attending neo-*noir*. Both appear at the beginning of the 1980s, but where *The Postman Always Rings Twice* looks back to the thematic and stylistic revisionism of 1970s *noirs* *Body Heat* looks ahead to the more formulaic and commodified *noir* of the mid-1980s and beyond.

Generally speaking, *The Postman Always Rings Twice* can be related to the
revival and transformation of *noir* in films such as *Chinatown* (1974),
Roman Polanski's revisionist private-eye movie; *The Long Goodbye* (1973),
Robert Altman's adaptation of the 1954 Raymond Chandler novel; and
Thieves Like Us (1974), Altman's period remake of the classic *They Live by
Night* (1948). More particularly, *The Postman* is a *direct and acknowledged*
remake of the 1946 MGM production of *The Postman Always Rings Twice*,
directed by Tay Garnett. Thomas Leitch describes *The Postman* as a 'true
remake' in so far as it establishes a relationship between itself, the earlier
film it remakes and the 'property' – James M. Cain's 1934 novel – upon
which both films are based.[8] This triangular notion of remaking operates
by 'ascribing value' to Cain's original literary text and then 'protecting' that
value by invoking Garnett's 1946 adaptation as a failed attempt to realise
the essential characteristics (or intrinsic value) of the original property.[9]
Leitch argues that the rhetorical strategy of Rafelson's *Postman* depends
on a distinction between 'positive and negative textual markers':

> richness, originality, and the imperial power of the classic on the one hand,
> and artifice, datedness, and repression of important material on the other . . .
> In this way the [*Postman*] remake is able to valorise Cain's original text,
> toward which it adopts an attitude of hushed reverence, while ascribing any
> dated qualities in need of revision to [the earlier MGM] version.[10]

The original property, James M. Cain's *The Postman Always Rings Twice*,
has been described as a 'quintessentially American' novel.[11] Along with
(then) contemporary authors, such as Dashiell Hammett, W. R. Burnett,
Horace McCoy, Cornell Woolrich and Raymond Chandler, Cain belonged
to a school of American writers of 'tough guy' or 'hard-boiled' mysteries
and crime novels of the 1930s and 1940s.[12] Writing about Cain and his
fellow 'poets of tabloid murder', critic Edmund Wilson described Cain as
a novelist intent upon making explicit all the things that had been excluded
from classic Hollywood by the Catholic Legion of Decency: 'sex, debauch-
ery, unpunished crime, [and] sacrilege against the Church'.[13] Between
1934 and 1976 Cain wrote some eighteen novels and although several of
these were adapted to film, Cain's work is best remembered as the source
for a cycle of 1940s *film noirs*: *Double Indemnity* (Billy Wilder, 1944),
Mildred Pierce (Michael Curtiz, 1945) and *The Postman Always Rings Twice*
(1946). Although the last to be adapted in this cycle, *The Postman* was
Cain's first novel, an immediate best-seller and an explicitly erotic work
that was banned in some parts of the United States. In Europe, the novel
quickly became the source of (at least) two continental versions: *Le Dernier
Tournant* (*The Last Turning*, Pierre Chenal, 1939) and *Ossessione* (Luchino

Visconti, 1942).[14] However, in Hollywood, the novel's explicitly erotic content saw a decade-long delay in its filming. When it finally appeared in 1946, the limitations imposed by the Production Code of the 1940s, together with the glossy production values that prevailed at MGM and the star presence of Lana Turner in the lead role of Cora, all contributed to a 'whitewashed' adaptation of the novel.[15] Richard Schickel provides a consensus view when he describes the MGM adaptation of *The Postman* as a 'rather cold, sanitised (and miscast) version', and a film that 'never did get the knack of noir'.[16]

Tay Garnett's version of *The Postman* closely follows the narrative invention of Cain's novel to tell the story of drifter Frank Chambers (John Garfield) who stops at a roadside café, accepting the elderly owner Nick Smith's (Cecil Kellaway's) offer of a job upon catching a glimpse of the latter's young wife, Cora. Frank and Cora soon begin a torrid affair and resolve to run away, but Cora is drawn back by the financial security of marriage and the business. As their frustration mounts, the couple decide to kill Nick, but their attempt at murder is thwarted by an electrical accident that merely results in an injury to Nick. Frank leaves the café, but is inevitably drawn back and, when Nick announces that he is considering selling the business, the couple make a second attempt on his life, this time bludgeoning Nick and staging a car accident to cover the crime. Nick is killed, and Frank inadvertently injured, in the accident, but District Attorney Sackett, convinced of Frank and Cora's guilt, manages to extract a complaint from Frank against Cora. This evidence, due to the efforts of Cora's defence council Keats, turns out to be inadmissible, and Cora is released on a suspended sentence. She turns her attention to using Nick's insurance money to upgrade the café and, although resentful of Frank's action, marries him in order to silence local gossip. Eventually, having weathered a blackmail attempt and Frank's brief affair with Madge, Frank and Cora (now pregnant) are reconciled. Just as they are looking forward to a new life, Cora is killed in a car accident and Frank, falsely convicted of her murder, is sentenced to death.

Despite the similarities, the 1946 version of *The Postman* did effect a number of transformations on Cain's adulterous murder story, expunging not only the novel's scandalous depiction of aggressive sexuality but also its ethnicity (the Greek husband, Nick Papadakis, became Nick Smith; the Jewish lawyer Katz was renamed Keats). At the same time, the film remained in a number of (narrative and thematic) ways surprisingly close to the detail of Cain's novel. In addition to the narrative plotting described above, it retained, for instance, *The Postman*'s sense of foreboding by translating Frank's first-person delivery into a characteristically *noir* voice-over narration. For example, the first sentence of the novel – 'They threw me off the hay truck about noon'[17] – was transformed into Frank's opening voice-over: 'It was on a side road outside of Los Angeles. I was hitchhiking from San Francisco down to San Diego, I guess. A half-hour earlier I thumbed a ride'. In the novel, this mood of predetermination is further communicated through several doublings, and reinforced more generally by Cain's oft-quoted statement of a desire to *repeat* across a body of work some '[terrifying] wish that comes true'.[18] These repetitions find perfect expression in the *rhyming effects* that characterise and contribute to the classical narrative style of the Hollywood studio film. At the global level (of action and event) the textual repetitions of Garnett's *Postman* include: two accidents with a lorry; two attempts (the latter successful) to kill Nick; two attempts to leave the café; and the two trials for murder. At the local level (of dialogue and motif) the doublings cover: the two notes in the cash register; the echoes at the lake; the name of the roadside diner ('Twin Oaks'); and, most eloquently, the lipstick roll (described below) that announces Cora's arrival in and departure from Frank's life. In a final repetition, Garnett (and screenwriters Harry Ruskin and Niven Busch) made the decision to have Frank spell out the metaphor of 'the postman' (which only features in the title of Cain's novel) to the sympathetic Sackett in the death cell. Each of these repetitions communicates the mood of *noir*ish foreboding and fatality conveyed by Cain's novel: 'So I'm in the death house now, writing the last of this'.[19]

The place of Cain's *Postman* and (to a lesser extent) Garnett's film version in the literary and film canon ensured that Rafelson's remake was discussed and evaluated in relation to both texts. The 1981 release of *The Postman* prompted a reprint of Cain's novel, and pre-publicity for the film focused on its being a 'corrective' to MGM's watered-down 1946 adaptation, a film described by one critic as 'less noir than purplish melodrama'.[20] Rafelson insisted that 'they [MGM] never made the [Cain] book . . . The book was really a neglected minor classic'.[21] Rafelson's claim to some greater fidelity centred in particular upon the 1981 *Postman*'s ability (in a post-Production Code Hollywood) to depict the notorious sex scenes of Cain's novel. A representative passage reads as follows:

Except for the shape, she [Cora] wasn't any raving beauty, but she had a sulky look to her, and her lips stuck out in a way that made me want to mash them in for her . . . I took her in my arms and mashed my mouth up against hers . . . I bit her. I sunk my teeth into her lips so deep I could feel the blood spurt into my mouth. It was running down her neck when I carried her upstairs.[22]

The 1946 version developed a strategy of (Freudian and institutional) censorship to deal with the *problem* of Cora's 'dangerous sexuality'. In the latter part of the film's opening segment, Nick leaves Frank alone in the diner where Cora announces her presence by (deliberately) dropping her lipstick to the floor. An eye-line match traces the lipstick roll, first to a shot of Cora's bare legs, and then to a long shot of her standing in the doorway, immaculately dressed in brilliant white shorts, halter top and turban. The lipstick – seen here to function as 'a fetish which brings together Cora's feminine mystique [her allure and potency] and Frank's fatal obsession'[23] – is returned to in the scene of Cora's death. At the end of the film, the car carrying Frank and Cora crashes through a guard-rail and Frank is thrown clear of the wreck. Turning back to attend to Cora, Frank's eye-line motivates a point-of-view close-up shot of Cora's hand holding the lipstick that she has been applying just before the crash. The camera cuts back to a medium close-up of the incredulous Frank before returning, in response to his exclamation of 'Cora', to a shot of the lipstick falling from her hand. In this final scene, as in Cora's initial appearance, the lipstick (in some sense) *is* Cora.

The Postman remake abandons the device of lipstick fetish and develops instead (from the novel) the feline metaphor of sexuality that begins with descriptions of Cora as 'cougar' and 'hell cat'[24] and persists throughout the story. This is present in a limited way in the 1946 version, but the Production Code – which expressly forbade the use of the term 'alley cat' (applied to a woman)[25] – would have curtailed its being drawn out in any detail. In Rafelson's film the metaphor is taken up in a variety of ways: through the narrative element of the domestic cat that thwarts the first murder attempt, the naming of the lawyer 'Katz', the wild-cat trainer Madge (Anjelica Huston) and (in another repetition) the 'return' of the house cat through Madge's gift of the puma: 'And the cat came back! It stepped on the fuse box and got killed, but here it [was] back'.[26] More obviously, the pre-release publicity for Rafelson's version focused on two scenes of 'orgasmic . . . sex and violence'[27] omitted from the earlier film version: the violent coupling of Frank (Jack Nicholson) and Cora (Jessica Lange) in the kitchen and their mutual arousal while messing each other up at the scene of Nick's accident-murder.[28] These scenes were expected to bring to Rafelson's film an authenticity and *attitude* from the novel that oscillated between religious rapture – 'I kissed her. Her eyes were shining up at me like two blue stars. It was like being in church' – and sadistic contempt – 'I was alone with her for a minute, and swung my fist up against her leg so hard it nearly knocked her over'.[29] The promise that *The Postman* remake would deliver on those elements left out of the 1946 version was

The Postman Always Rings Twice (Bob Rafelson, 1981). Courtesy
Paramount/The Kobal Collection.

further reinforced by a report in *Variety* that Rafelson was going to shoot
the film, on a closed set, as an X-certificate (the equivalent of NC-17) and
then cut it to an R-rating for its theatrical showing.[30]

Upon *The Postman*'s release, David Thomson stated that the
'restored' scenes were 'among the least hindered views of sex the cinema
[had] ever provided',[31] but critics such as Pauline Kael complained that
the 'detached, meditative tone' of Rafelson's film was at odds with the

'sleazy primitivism' of Cain's writing.[32] The perceived failure of Rafelson to bring to his adaptation the carnality and impulsiveness of Cain's novel appears to relate to a second (conflicting) claim to authenticity, namely the 1981 *Postman*'s careful reconstruction of the novel's setting in Depression-era southern California. Rafelson said that he 'thought it was owed to Cain for somebody to make it [*The Postman*] in the period he wrote it. I felt the story itself was *part* of the Depression'.[33] Rafelson went to the trouble of having the Twin Oaks setting built from scratch, choosing for the house a type of California architecture that was popular around 1915, specifically in order to avoid the Art Deco style featured in 1970s recreations of the 1930s. In maintaining that he 'didn't want everyone to be in awe of the period',[34] Rafelson attempted to distance *The Postman* from what was perceived as the comfortable nostalgia of a recent cycle of neo-*noirs* such as *Chinatown* (1974), *Thieves Like Us* (1974) and *Farewell, My Lovely* (1975). These were films that seemed to satisfy the *auteur* predilections of their (*nouvelle vague* inspired) directors *and* at the same time meet the financial interests of corporate Hollywood, films that 'both determined and reproduced the period's simultaneous impulses toward irony and nostalgia'.[35] In an endeavour to avoid the self-knowing memorialisation of the classic *film noir*, but at the same time meticulously recreate the story's period setting, Rafelson's earnest treatment of *The Postman* failed to capture the novel's tough-guy manner. As Kael put it: 'The words that would describe this movie [detached, meditative, studied] are at the opposite pole from how anyone would describe the book'.[36]

Rafelson's 'hushed reverence' toward Cain's story not only respects the latter's claim to being 'the granddaddy of hot tabloid novels',[37] but retrospectively (and somewhat unexpectedly) affirms the place of Garnett's version as a classic in the *noir* canon. More than this, Rafelson's *Postman* enters into the broader critical discourse of classic *film noir* (and its 1970s remakings). For instance, Thomson aligns it with the *l'amour fou* of Nicolas Ray's *They Live By Night*,[38] and Richard Combs suggests that Rafelson may have taken the opening of *The Postman* from Edgar G. Ulmer's *Detour* (1945), 'the poor man's (or more downbeat, or simply more hysterical) *Postman*'.[39] More importantly, the 1981 *Postman* can be related to Richard Martin's suggestion that 'film noir in the hands of the post-classical Hollywood film makers became both an object of generic revisionism and a tool for [the] . . . political investigation of American society'.[40] Noël Carroll argues that Hollywood genre films in the 1970s (and beyond) are marked by two tendencies, one founded on *dissonance* (difference) and the other on *harmony* (sameness). In the first case, a film maker *reworks* an established genre in order to generate expression through the challenging of the conventions and values associated with that genre. In the second, a film maker *memorialises* a past genre, lovingly recreating it through imitation and careful reconstruction.[41] Although there are substantial *stylistic* differences between them, films such as *The Long Goodbye* and *Chinatown* (and the two British remakes of classic *noirs*, *Farewell, My Lovely* and *The Big Sleep*), developed their 'ironic tone through [a] systematic contrast with the *moral* universe of 1940s private-eye films'.[42]

In Carroll's account of Hollywood allusionism, this ironic and/or nostalgic reworking of genre was the legacy of American *auteurism* and the 'unprecedented awareness' of film history that developed among film makers and audiences in the 1960s and 1970s.[43] *The Postman* doesn't approach the level of stylistic dissonance evident in Altman's *The Long Goodbye*, but it does extend the moral convictions and thematic preoccupations of Rafelson as (producer-director) *auteur* of the New Hollywood. Rafelson is best known for his work on low-budget BBS Productions (the company he formed in the 1970s with Bert Schneider and Steve Blauner) such as *Five Easy Pieces* (1970), *The King of Marvin Gardens* (1972) and *Stay Hungry* (1976). All three starred Jack Nicholson and Rafelson developed the idea of remaking *The Postman* after being dismissed as director of the Fox production, *Brubaker* (completed by Stuart Rosenberg, 1980). Given the opportunity to work again for a smaller production company (Lorimar) and with long time collaborator Nicholson, Rafelson's version of *The Postman* is seen as an extension of the *fatalism* running through his earlier work.[44] Rafelson takes the rough-house style of Cain's novella, 'retain[s] the plot but revise[s] the rhythm ... producing one of the formally most audacious of American mainstream movies [of the 1980s]'.[45] In this *auteurist* interpretation, *The Postman Always Rings Twice* is read – alongside Rafelson's earlier allegories of America – as a mix of 'carnality and capitalism': 'The precariousness of Frank and Cora's alliance becomes the heart of the film, and a shadowy metaphor for the pursuit of happiness and the American Dream, like the partnerships of love and profit in [*The King of*] *Marvin Gardens* and *Stay Hungry*'.[46]

The Postman's contemporaneous *noir*, Lawrence Kasdan's *Body Heat* (1981), deals with the same themes – sex and money ('carnality and capitalism') – but *reinvents* the classic *noir* visual style for the 1980s. *Body Heat* is widely recognised as a remake of *Double Indemnity*, Billy Wilder's 1944 adaptation (co-written with Raymond Chandler) of James M. Cain's 1943 novel. Leitch categorises *Body Heat*, alongside *The Postman*, as a 'true remake' – a film that establishes a triangular relationship between itself, Wilder's film and Cain's novel – even though it does not credit the book as its source. *Body Heat* can be described as a *disguised* or *unacknowledged* remake, a film that repeats fundamental narrative units from the Cain novel (and Wilder adaptation) but alters the details of its title, setting, period, character names and the like. In the absence of a screen credit acknowledging the original property, the remake becomes a theoretical construct or function of the film's production and reception. Important here is Cain's reputation, and the early 1980s revival of interest in Cain's work,[47] but more significant is *Double Indemnity*'s privileged place in the *noir* canon. For instance, Naremore writes: 'few would deny that *Double Indemnity* is a definitive film noir and one of the most influential movies in Hollywood history . . . [It] was an unorthodox film, challenging nearly a decade of Production Code resistance to . . . Cain's fiction'.[48] Frank Krutnik similarly declares that *Double Indemnity* was 'historically significant in the development of the 1940s erotic crime thriller, establishing through its rendering of the Cain tale a model for the narrative . . . structures of subsequent [*film noirs*]'.[49] Recently, Brian De Palma (whose homages to Alfred Hitchcock are discussed in Chapter 2) has paid tribute to *film noir*, by opening *Femme Fatale* (2002) with the title character, Laure Ash (Rebecca Romijn-Stamos), reflected in a hotel room television screen as she watches the Barbara Stanwyck archetype in *Double Indemnity*. These accounts of *Double Indemnity*'s reputation and place in film history help explain why critics such as Leitch directly compare *Body Heat* to Wilder's adaptation, but fail to note that *Double Indemnity* had already been more directly remade as a lesser-known movie for television, directed by Jack Smight in 1973.

Double Indemnity begins with Walter Neff (Fred MacMurray), bleeding from a bullet wound, staggering into his office in the Pacific Insurance Building. Neff speaks into his dictaphone and his story of 'an unholy love and an almost perfect crime' unfolds in flashback. Neff is an insurance salesman who becomes involved with the beautiful and dangerous Phyllis Dietrichson (Barbara Stanwyck). Phyllis convinces Walter not only to help her take out a $100,000 life insurance policy on her husband, but also to help her murder him. Together they stage Dietrichson's accidental death in order to qualify for the 'double indemnity', but things go wrong when Neff's boss, Barton Keyes (Edward G. Robinson), begins to suspect murder. Neff strikes up a friendship with Phyllis's step-daughter Lola, who believes that Phyllis has taken up with her (Lola's) former boyfriend Nino Zachetti. Thinking he has been double-crossed, Neff hatches a plan to kill Phyllis and frame Zachetti. In a confrontation in the darkened, Dietrichson living room, Walter kills Phyllis, but not before she fatally wounds him. At the

Body Heat (Lawrence Kasdan, 1981). Courtesy Ladd Company/Warner
Bros/The Kobal Collection.

end, the story returns to the present where the dying Walter is comforted
by the fatherly Keyes. *Body Heat* takes up this narrative framework and
reworks it into the story of Ned Racine (William Hurt), a naive and
corruptible Florida lawyer who is seduced by Matty (Kathleen Turner),
wife of ruthless businessman Edmund Walker (Richard Crenna), whom
they subsequently decide to kill by staging an 'accidental' fire. Murder is

suspected, and Ned is warned by his friend and fellow attorney Peter Lowenstein (Ted Danson) to stay away from Matty. Ned subsequently discovers that Matty has used him in order to manipulate Walker's will so that she is sole beneficiary. Now prepared to kill Matty, Ned arranges to meet her, but she is apparently killed in an explosion at her boathouse and Ned is arrested for the Walker murder. Imprisoned, Ned realises that Matty has in fact switched identities with a former high-school friend and has escaped with the insurance money to some foreign island.

Although Wilder's *Double Indemnity* is often taken as the 'original' against which Kasdan's *noir* remake is evaluated, *Body Heat* can more broadly be seen as a remaking of Cain's *oeuvre* (or at least those works by which he is best remembered). Schickel goes so far as to argue that *Double Indemnity* was a case of *auto*-citation, 'created by [Cain] in full knowledge that he was doing his own homage to [*The*] *Postman*':

> Both tell essentially the same story: an all too compliant male is enthralled by a strong and scheming woman. With her motivating it and with him taking care of details, the adulterous couple execute a perfect murder of the woman's husband. Then, when they are virtually in the clear, fate (or irony) swipes them with its big blundering paw and they receive their just desserts – but for the wrong reasons.[50]

Such a connection enables one to recognise (in *Body Heat*) *noir* elements – such as the hard-boiled dialogue and depiction of naked (and graphic) animal lust – that are common to both *The Postman* and *Double Indemnity*. For instance, *Body Heat* is remembered for dialogue such as Ned's 'You shouldn't wear that body', and Matty's 'You're not too smart, are you? I like that in a man'. However, at an even higher level of generality, it can be argued that *Body Heat* simultaneously refers to and remakes the *noir* genre to which its intertexts belong. David Chute understands this when he states that *Body Heat* refers to 'just about every major film and novel in the hard-boiled and film noir genres'.[51] Chute acknowledges that the 'archetypal "love kills" story line and the characters' doomed intensity' is borrowed from Cain, but he also finds in *Body Heat* elements of Chandler's novella *Red Wind*, Howard Hawks's *The Big Sleep* (1946) and Robert Aldrich's *Kiss Me Deadly* (1955).[52] *Body Heat* director Lawrence Kasdan similarly cites various sources of inspiration: '*Double Indemnity* yes, *The Postman* not so much. Cain's writing was important . . . [but so too were] movies like *Out of the Past* and *Murder, My Sweet*. Also *The Killing* [Stanley Kubrick, 1956]'.[53]

While critical accounts of Rafelson's acknowledged remake of *The Postman* were often limited to a discussion of its (greater or lesser) fidelity to the spirit of Cain's novel, *Body Heat*'s disguised remaking of Cain and/or Wilder enabled it to be related to a broader category of *noir* fiction and film. While this led a critic like Kael to dismiss *Body Heat* as 'a catalogue of noir clichés',[54] others saw it as 'a self-consciously knowing update of an archetypal film noir plot . . . with every element cranked up to overdrive and overkill'.[55] These opinions suggest that *Body Heat* (like *The Postman*) might be related to the revisionist and nostalgic tendencies of neo-*noirs* from the 1970s. Steve Jenkins, for instance, makes a connection between it and *Chinatown*, drawing out an analogous Oedipal pattern that sees the father figures of Edmund Walker and Noah Cross (John Huston) as an 'embodiment of material power and corruption'.[56] Martin takes this further, locating the theme of patriarchal immorality in the socio-economic context of 1980s America, specifically in 'the promotion of individualism, selfishness, and greed [that was] underpinned by Reaganomics'.[57] In the case of a film like *Body Heat*, this 'greed, both economic and sexual, . . . results in an extended personal nightmare from which there is . . . no escape [*no way out*]'.[58] This is furthered through the character of Matty who, like her husband (Walker), will do 'whatever's necessary', realising her (murderous) scheme through the entrapment of Ned Racine. While *Body Heat* does not offer up the same damning critique of capitalism as Polanski's *Chinatown*, the figure of the politically corrupt and morally reprehensible patriarch launches itself forward into mid-1980s *noir* remakes such as *Against All Odds* and *No Way Out*, while the murderous (spider) woman is taken up in such films as Rafelson's *Black Widow* (1987) and *The Last Seduction* (John Dahl, 1994).

A further connection between *Chinatown* and *Body Heat* can be found in the suggestion that the latter's anachronistic dialogue and ambiguous costumes and setting make it (metonymically) a *nostalgia film*. Fredric Jameson states that 'everything in [*Body Heat*] conspires to blur [its] immediate contemporary reference and to make it possible to receive this . . . as nostalgia work – as a narrative set in some indefinable nostalgic past'.[59] One could argue, though, that *Body Heat* does not recreate a (pseudo) period setting but rather *reinvents* the *film noir*, plundering a *critical* genre to promulgate a stylised, *industrial* cycle of neo-*noir*. In this respect the immediate precursor to *Body Heat* is not *Chinatown* or *The Postman Always Rings Twice*, but Martin Scorsese's *Taxi Driver* (1974). Naremore argues that '*Taxi Driver* is memorable not only for its [dense and mysterious] blacks but also for its neon, steam, and smoke'.[60] Augmented by lurid colour (and enabled by developments in high-speed colour negative film stock[61]), the blacks of *Taxi Driver* become a 'mannerism in all types of post-1970s noir'.[62] A film like *Body Heat* extends this approach, employing desaturated visuals 'to heighten the atmosphere of sex and violence, but also to evoke the monochromatic tradition of high-contrast, black-and-white thrillers'.[63] *Body Heat* is a film that combines dark (and shadow) and heat (and colour) to contribute to the sleek commodification of a highly stylised late-1980s (and 1990s) '*noir* look'.

At the beginning of the 1980s, *Body Heat* re-presented *film noir* to an increasingly knowing and cine-literate audience, and set the agenda for later 1980s remakes of classic *noirs*. Chute described *Body Heat* as 'one of the most accomplished American movies in years, and perhaps the most stunning debut movie ever'.[64] Unlike *The Postman*, which arrived with exemplary credentials – Rafelson (director), Nicholson (actor), David Mamet (writer), Sven Nykvist (cinematographer) – *Body Heat* was a first feature for its writer-director Kasdan and a defining film for actors William Hurt, Kathleen Turner and Mickey Rourke. More importantly, *Body Heat* anticipated the high-tech visual style and production design of the so-called 'high concept' film of the 1980s.[65] At the level of composition, *Body Heat* adapted the visual style of classic *noir* to compose its high contrast and sometimes minimal colour scheme. At the level of plot, it worked with a set of generic archetypes, enabling a more economical story line and schematic characterisations. In addition to this, *Body Heat* (rudimentarily) exhibited the importance that the high concept film was to place in such elements as pre-sold properties, genres, stars and music: it was in the tradition of James M. Cain and *film noir*, it traded on William Hurt's star potential (earned in *Altered States*, 1980), and it introduced the character of Teddy Lewis (Mickey Rourke) through the lip-synching of the Bob Seger hit, 'Feel Like a Number'. Finally, *Body Heat*'s forthright sex scenes anticipated such neo-*noirs* as *Against All Odds* and *No Way Out*, and the 'steamy' sexual encounters (of later high-concept films) such as *Angel Heart* (Alan Parker, 1987), *Sea of Love* (Harold Becker, 1989) and *Basic Instinct* (Paul Verhoeven, 1992).

In the mid-1980s, *Body Heat* provided a kind of 'rudimentary working prototype'[66] for medium to high-profile *noir* remakings such as *Against All Odds* (Taylor Hackford, 1984) and *No Way Out* (Roger Donaldson, 1987). Like *Body Heat*, both films were *indirect* (or transformed) remakes in that they altered not only the title of their original properties but also characters, settings and narrative units. *Against All Odds* took up the barest narrative outline from *Out of the Past* – one man is dispatched by another to Mexico to locate a beautiful woman who has gone missing – and reinvented this as a romantic thriller for the 1980s. In a similar way, *No Way Out* retained (from *The Big Clock*) only a basic narrative framework – a man conducts a murder investigation, *on himself* – but relocated the action from a bustling, 1940s New York media empire to a pre-glasnost, 1980s Washington Department of Defense. Both remakes differ, however, from *Body Heat* in at least two respects. First, each of the films clearly *acknowledges* its *noir* sources. The credits of *Against All Odds* declare that it is 'based on the film *Out of the Past* written by Daniel Mainwaring' (adapted from his 1946 novel – penned under the pseudonym of Geoffrey Holmes – *Build My Gallows High*). And the titles of *No Way Out* announce that it is 'based on the novel *The Big Clock* by Kenneth Fearing' (filmed under the same title in 1948). Second, whereas *Body Heat* is a self-conscious re-creation of *noir*, *Against All Odds* and *No Way Out* are films that wear their knowledge of *noir* with a 'light touch'.[67] These are films that eschew any overtly *noir* *mise-en-scène* to embrace instead *noir* thematic elements and the generic conventions of the 1980s Hollywood thriller. While the *noir* originals provide a loose model (and ready point of reference), the absence of a *noir* style means that the identification of these films as *noir* remakings has as much to do with their critical reception as with any specific textual borrowings, narrative or visual.

Acknowledged copyright and a well-established *noir* canon saw *Against All Odds* and *No Way Out* consistently identified as *transformed* remakes of classic *noirs*. Headlined by *Variety* as a 'sexy remake [that] just misses',[68] *Against All Odds* struggled in the shadow of its precursor: 'as subjects for remakes go, *Out of the Past* [is] a hard act to follow, since the original is such a paradigmatic [*noir*] work'.[69] Foster Hirsch similarly describes *Against All Odds* as a 'shamefully misbegotten remake', one that refuses the challenge of capturing the 'pulp poetry' of Jeff Bailey's (Robert Mitchum's) voice-over or recreating the formidable presence of Kathie's (Jane Greer's) *femme fatale*.[70] Although not entirely misplaced, these kinds of comments fail to recognise the specific ways in which *Against All Odds* – like *Body Heat* before it – *transformed* classic *noir* via some of the commercial imperatives of 1980s Hollywood. In the first instance, *Against All Odds* traded on the popular success of Taylor Hackford's previous feature, *An Officer and a Gentleman* (1982), and on the profiles of its upcoming stars: Jeff Bridges, James Woods and Rachel Ward. Second, *Against All Odds* might well have translated the 'hard sun and undulating shadows' and 'erotic fever' of *Out of the Past*[71] into ' "exotic" locations' and 'dutifully sweat-drenched sex scenes',[72] but this can be understood as a high-concept promotion of a 'California-*noir*' lifestyle of the type found in contemporaneous *noirs* like *The Morning After* (Sidney Lumet, 1986) remake of *The Blue Gardenia* (Fritz Lang, 1953). For instance, the image of Terry (Jeff Bridges) and Jessie (Rachel Ward) entwined on a tropical beach (reproduced for the *Against All Odds* promotional poster, print advertising and soundtrack album) shaped the film's narrative *and* commercial identity. Finally, Phil Collins's song (and music video) 'Against All Odds (Take a Look at Me Now)' brought together the film's picturesque locations and star profiles in a cross-promotional strategy that most clearly characterised the high-concept film of the 1980s.

The remakers of *The Big Clock* gave it a similar treatment, but (probably due to the more modest reputation of its original) *No Way Out*'s critical reception was more favourable than that of *Against All Odds*. *Variety* headlined *No Way Out* as a 'top notch remake with [a] sure fire thriller formula',[73] and Hirsch notes that in 'reclaiming noir as a Reagan-era star vehicle, [*No Way Out*] achieves a rare degree of independence while still satisfying genre requirements'.[74] While *No Way Out* retains and revises some of the details of the original – notably Louise Patterson's (Elsa Lanchester's) inspired abstract painting of the suspected murderer, which is updated to an endlessly protracted computer rendering – the remake is constructed as a labyrinthine thriller for the 1980s. *No Way Out* is primarily designed to showcase the talent of Kevin Costner, fresh off his successful role as Elliot Ness in *The Untouchables* (Brian De Palma, 1987), but also that of his co-actors, Gene Hackman and Sean Young. While the fashion look of the film might now appear as 'anachronistic' as that of *Body Heat*, *No Way Out* is determinedly voguish in its costuming (especially Costner and Young's outfits), and also in the interiors of Young's Georgetown apartment and the sounds of Maurice Jarre's electronic musical score. In addition (and as in *Against All Odds* and *Body Heat* before it) the sex scenes are forthright, and Costner and Young's first sexual tryst takes place in the back of a limousine to the (then) popular beat of Rod Stewart's 'Da Ya Think I'm Sexy?' All of this suggests that, for its contemporary audience, *No Way Out* appealed as much to the broad generic conventions of the glossy Hollywood thriller (and date-movie) as to any specific *noir* precursor.

Toward the end of the 1980s, *D.O.A.* (Rocky Morton and Annabel Jankel, 1988) extended the remaking strategies of earlier 1980s neo-*noirs* and anticipated the consolidation of *noir* as a commercial genre for the 1990s. Rudolph Maté's 1950 film *D.O.A.* had been previously remade in the late 1960s as *Color Me Dead* (aka. *D.O.A. II*, Eddie Davis, 1970). This little known and rarely seen version of *D.O.A.* was part of a three-package feature film deal – the other two films being *It Takes All Kinds* (1969) and *That Lady from Peking* (1970) – that Australian producer-entrepreneur Reg Goldsworthy had negotiated with US television director Eddie Davis. Crediting only the original screenwriters – Russell Rouse and Clarence Greene – the Davis version closely follows the dialogue and plot of Maté's film, but transforms the material through its EastmanColor photography, Australian locations (notably Sydney and the Gold Coast) and the use of (American) television actors: Tom Tryon in the Frank Bigelow role, Carolyn Jones as his girlfriend Paula Gibson and Rick Jason in the equivalent of the Majak role originated by Luther Adler. Discarding the flashback structure of the original, the film begins with an atmospheric night-sequence filmed through the windscreen of a car on the Sydney Harbour Bridge, but soon settles into a routine (if convoluted) thriller with Tryon attempting to track down his killers. *Color Me Dead* was released theatrically in Australia (March 1970) but sold direct to cable television in the United States. Situated midway between its classic 1950 original and its neo-*noir* remaking in 1988, *Color Me Dead* has more in common with television *noirs* such as *Dragnet* (NBC, 1951–59), *Naked City* (ABC, 1958–63) and *The Fugitive* (ABC, 1963–67) than with its direct precursor. Moreover, the television aesthetic and US release pattern of *Color Me Dead* adds weight to Todd Erikson's suggestion that, through the 1960s, the *noir* sensibility 'remained dormant . . . being kept alive [mainly] through television series that paid homage to it'.[75]

In contrast to *Color Me Dead*'s 'direct' remaking of Maté's film, the 1988 'update' might be described as a *non*-remake. Morton and Jankel's version retains the original title and gives Russell Rouse and Clarence Greene a story-writing credit (along with screenwriter Charles Edward Pogue), but this *D.O.A.* remake transforms the original property beyond recognition. The basic narrative line becomes, in the remake, little more than a high-concept story pitch for initialising the project and then marketing the product to the public: 'Someone poisoned Dexter Cornell. He's got to find out why. He's got to find out now. In twenty-fours hours he'll be Dead On Arrival'. In a similar way, the title 'D.O.A.' functions as a saleable generic marker of, and literal shorthand for, neo-*noir* and a readily identifiable (and transferable) logo for the promotion of the film. Following the trajectory signalled by *Body Heat*, *D.O.A.* announces itself as a high-tech *noir*, complete with a black-and-white prologue (brimming with shadows and tilted compositions) in which Cornell (Dennis Quaid) staggers into a police station to report that a murder has been committed and that Cornell *himself* is the victim (see more on this below). The remake takes this basic set-up from the original and then spins it into a convoluted trail of bigamy and murder, infidelity and suicide. *D.O.A.* was consistently dismissed for being a 'fantasia of classic noir motifs strained through an MTV filter'.[76] Tom Milne, for instance, says that the revision of the Rouse and Greene story is 'tarted up in a hideous pop-promo rash of distortions, computer tricks, and artsy irrelevancies'.[77] *D.O.A.*

anticipates in its excessive reworking of its source a 1990s interest in the readily consumable 'stylistic, iconographic, and narrative markers of classic film noir'.[78] Despite its title, *D.O.A.* is less a direct remake of a *noir* classic than a generic *noir* remaking: 'a sight-and-sound neo-noir spectacle'.[79]

The four-minute opening sequence of *D.O.A.* reads like a pop-primer on the visual codes of *film noir*. The sequence begins with melancholic music and a series of shaky hand-held shots of heavy rain washing over a dark city street and its gutters. A shadowy figure makes its way through the rain and, with the appearance of the film's title, the music shifts to a driving rock beat. There follows a close-up of the character's feet (men's shoes) stepping more purposefully through the puddles, and then shots of lights spelling out 'Merry Xmas' and the façade of a police precinct building. A wide, ground-level shot of the character making his way up the steps of the police station is followed by a close-up of his hand on the banister, revealing traces of blood. In a replication of the title sequence of the Maté version, tracking shots (shaky and tightly framed) now follow the character down the station corridors to a desk where he stumbles, knocking an ornamental Christmas tree to the floor. The desk sergeant says 'Jeez, buddy you look dead'. The man asks to see a detective about a murder. In reply to the sergeant's question 'who was murdered?' the man (lifting his face for the first time to reveal top-billed star Quaid) replies 'I was'. The music ends here and the final part of the segment (its last minute) begins with two ceiling shots, the second (showing a slowly rotating fan) tilting down to reveal the man, identified here as Cornell, in a shadowy interview room. A detective reveals that Cornell is (or will be) the sixth murder victim, and (gesturing to the clerk setting up video-equipment to record his statement) Cornell says 'when Cecil B. over there is ready, I'll tell you all about it'. The following shot is taken from a position behind the top-loading video cassette deck. As the clerk pushes the videotape down into the player, the camera tracks down disguising a cut that (in what is the opening shot of the next segment) reveals a chalkboard. The camera tracks to the right as the word 'COLOR' is written on the board, effecting the 'trick' transition to colour photography and to the beginning of the flashback which shows Cornell, a college English professor, in class.

Morton and Jankel's 'MTV remaking' of *D.O.A.* supports Martin's suggestion that the visual style of classic *noir* has been taken up and commodified not only by contemporary film makers, but also by television programmers and creators of music videos.[80] Following the early lead of *Body Heat*, *noir* remakes of the middle to late 1980s – *Against All Odds*, *No Way Out*, *D.O.A.* – chart the movement of *film noir* from its being primarily a *critical* genre to its emergence as an *industrial* genre and marketing category: 'a major signifier of sleekly commodified artistic ambition'.[81] In Naremore's assessment, an established *noir* canon means that any attempt to reproduce the low-budget past of pulp fiction and *film noir* now involves a self-conscious allusiveness: 'contemporary noirs . . . oscillate between elaborately designed, star-filled productions . . . and art movies'.[82] Examples of 'direct' *noir* remakes of the 1990s include *Guncrazy* and *The Underneath* (mentioned above), and *The Getaway* (Roger Donaldson, 1994; Sam Peckinpah, 1972) and *Payback* (Brian Helgeland, 1999; *Point Blank*, John Boorman, 1967). In a different way, Joel and Ethan Coen have revisited the trinity of Cain, Hammett and Chandler across a series of hardboiled homages. Their first feature, *Blood Simple* (1983), updates Cain for the Reaganite 1980s; *Miller's Crossing* (1990) adapts Hammett, specifically *Red Harvest* and *The Glass Key*; and *The Big Lebowski* (1998) follows Chandler, in particular Altman's version of *The Long Goodbye* (1973). Most recently, the Coen brothers have returned to the Cain universe and the exact visual style of *noir* to fashion the laconic 'anti-*noir*' of *The Man Who Wasn't There* (2001). Across these various reworkings, the *noir* sensibility is *transformed* through such factors as the conditions of regional (independent) filmmaking, political climate, ethnographic detail and *auteurist* inclination. Moreover (and as described in Chapter 6) the 'idea' of *film noir* is sustained through specific discursive formations, in particular a fully realised *noir* canon and its attendant practices: the dissemination of *noir* across a mediascape of film, television, photography and fashion, the discussion and citation of *noirs* in popular and academic film criticism, the selective release and re-release of *noirs* to theatrical and video distribution windows, and (in circular fashion) the decision of neo-*noir* filmmakers – notably Luc Besson, Quentin Tarantino and John Woo – to evoke earlier works and recreate cinema history. Beyond matters of narrative style and visual traits, beyond questions of originality and fidelity, an understanding of *film noir* and its 1980s remakings (and beyond) resides primarily in the determination of a discursive structure, in issues of cultural history and memory. As in classic *noir*, it is a question of how the past continues to inform – *has a firm hold of* – the present.

Notes

1. Naremore, *More Than Night*, p. 11.
2. Ibid., p. 10.
3. Ibid., p. 26.
4. Ibid., pp. 32–3.

5. Ibid., p. 37.
6. For an account of *noir* remakes see Hirsch, *Detours and Lost Highways*, pp. 23–65.
7. For accounts of neo-*noir* see Silver and Ward, *Film Noir*, pp. 398–442; and Erickson, 'Kill Me Again', pp. 307–29.
8. Leitch, 'Twice-Told Tales', p. 145.
9. Ibid., p. 147.
10. Ibid., pp. 145–6.
11. Yakir, 'The Postman's Words', p. 21.
12. Schickel, *Double Indemnity*, p. 16.
13. Quoted in ibid., p. 20.
14. Yakir, ' "The Postman" Rings Six Times', pp. 18–20.
15. Porfirio, 'Whatever Happened to the *Film Noir*?', pp. 102–11. See also Biesen, 'Raising Cain with the Censors, Again', pp. 41–8.
16. Schickel, *Double Indemnity*, p. 24.
17. Cain, *The Postman Always Rings Twice*, p. 7.
18. Cain, preface to *The Butterfly* (1947), quoted in Krutnik, 'Desire, Transgression and James M. Cain', p. 32.
19. Cain, *The Postman Always Rings Twice*, p. 123.
20. Combs, 'Rev. of *The Postman Always Rings Twice*', p. 96.
21. Quoted in Thomson, 'Raising Cain', p. 28.
22. Cain, *The Postman Always Rings Twice*, pp. 8 and 15.
23. Porfirio, 'Whatever Happened to the *Film Noir*?', p. 104.
24. Cain, *The Postman Always Rings Twice*, pp. 16 and 19.
25. See the Production Code of the MPPDA reprinted in Jowett, *Film: The Democratic Art*, pp. 468–72.
26. Cain, *The Postman Always Rings Twice*, p. 113.
27. Milne, 'Rev. of *The Postman Always Rings Twice*', p. 100.
28. Combs, 'Rev. of *The Postman Always Rings Twice*', p. 95.
29. Cain, *The Postman Always Rings Twice*, pp. 21 and 16.
30. Har., 'Rev. of *The Postman Always Rings Twice*', p. 133.
31. Thomson, 'Raising Cain', pp. 27–8.
32. Kael, *Taking It All In*, pp. 179 and 182.
33. Quoted in Thomson, 'Raising Cain', p. 28.
34. Ibid.
35. Ray, *A Certain Tendency of the Hollywood Cinema*, p. 267.
36. Kael, *Taking It All In*, p. 179.
37. Ibid., p. 178.
38. Thomson, 'Raising Cain', p. 25.
39. Combs, 'Rev. of *Detour*', p. 146.
40. Martin, *Mean Streets and Raging Bulls*, p. 25.
41. Carroll, 'The Future of Allusion', pp. 55–64.
42. Ibid., p. 61, emphasis added.
43. Ibid., p. 54.

44. Thomson, 'Raising Cain', p. 30.
45. Combs, 'Rev. of *The Postman Always Rings Twice*', p. 96.
46. Ibid.
47. See Krutnik, 'Desire, Transgression and James M. Cain', p. 31.
48. Naremore, *More Than Night*, pp. 81–2.
49. Krutnik, 'Desire, Transgression and James M. Cain', p. 38.
50. Schickel, *Double Indemnity*, pp. 21–2.
51. Chute, 'Tropic of Kasdan', p. 49.
52. Ibid.
53. Quoted in ibid., p. 54.
54. Kael, *Taking It All In*, p. 255.
55. Jenkins, 'Rev. of *Body Heat*', p. 4.
56. Ibid.
57. Martin, *Mean Streets and Raging Bulls*, p. 53.
58. Ibid.
59. Jameson, 'Postmodernism and Consumer Society', p. 117.
60. Naremore, *More Than Night*, p. 192.
61. Erickson, 'Kill Me Again', pp. 314–16.
62. Naremore, *More Than Night*, p. 192.
63. Ibid.
64. Chute, 'Tropic of Kasdan', p. 49.
65. See Wyatt, *High Concept*.
66. Martin, *Mean Streets and Raging Bulls*, p. 29.
67. Hirsch, *Detours and Lost Highways*, p. 33.
68. Har., 'Rev. of *Against All Odds*', p. 24.
69. Pulleine, 'Rev. of *Against All Odds*', p. 171.
70. Hirsch, *Detours and Lost Highways*, pp. 40–3.
71. Ibid., p. 41.
72. Pulleine, 'Rev. of *Against All Odds*', p. 171.
73. Lor., 'Rev. of *No Way Out*', p. 12.
74. Hirsch, *Detours and Lost Highways*, p. 33.
75. Erickson, 'Kill Me Again', p. 311.
76. Hirsch, *Detours and Lost Highways*, p. 54. See also Lor., 'Rev. of *D.O.A.*', p. 14.
77. Milne, 'Rev. of *D.O.A.*', p. 78.
78. Martin, *Mean Streets and Raging Bulls*, p. 118.
79. Hirsch, *Detours and Lost Highways*, p. 55.
80. Martin, *Mean Streets and Raging Bulls*, p. 29.
81. Naremore, *More Than Night*, p. 10.
82. Ibid., p. 160.

Part III Remaking as Critical Category

CHAPTER 5

Audiences

In an essay on the adaptation of Herman Melville's *Billy Budd, Sailor* (as Claire Denis's *Beau Travail*, 1999), Catherine Grant points out that 'the most important act that films and their surrounding discourses need to perform in order to communicate . . . their status as adaptations is to (make their audiences) *recall* the adapted work, or the cultural memory of it'.[1] This process of recollection is, of course, realised through texts and is inseparable from them, but alongside *textual* descriptions it is necessary to analyse those textual *activators*[2] – the various *extra*-textual modes and means – which enable the recognition of adaptations and their sources. In the case of remaking, the ability to identify and cross reference a remake similarly comes about not only through prior knowledge of previous texts and intertextual comparisons, but also from the extra-textual discourses surrounding the viewing experience. As in the case of film genre, it is necessary to acknowledge the *multi-dimensional* nature of remaking, not only textual structures but contextual determinants, such factors as 'the importance of audience knowledge and audience expectation', and of 'industry [discourses] and film reviewers'.[3] Additionally, because remaking can refer to more general structures of intertextuality (quotation, allusion, adaptation), the *identification* of a film remake is not restricted to the recognition of textual patterns of similarity, but can be achieved through classifying statements and 'common cultural consensus'.[4] This serves to shift attention from the texts of remaking to an interest in audience activity and institutional contexts, raising such critical questions as: 'How [is] "a common cultural consensus" . . . established? What agencies and institutions are involved? What is the role of the film industry? [and] What is the role of film critics [and] film reviewers?'[5]

The understanding that remaking needs to be treated not simply as a quality of film texts, but as a 'complex *situation*'[6] requires that attention be directed toward those 'factors that impinge on audience expectations, the construction of . . . corpuses, [and] processes of labelling and naming'.[7] Steve Neale pursues these issues with reference to film genre, following John Ellis to describe a film's *narrative image* as 'an idea of a film [that] is widely circulated and promoted', and which identifies the text for uptake and consumption.[8] Contributing to such images are: (1) institutionalised public discourses (press, radio, television); (2) unofficial 'everyday' discourses (word of mouth, peer reviews, the Internet); and (3) film industry discourses (publicity, marketing, exhibition).[9] More particularly, a film's narrative image can be related to the category of transtextuality that Gérard Genette describes as *paratextuality*: 'those liminal devices and conventions, both within the [text] (*peritext*) and outside it (*epitext*), that mediate the [text] to the reader'.[10] In the case of film remakes, these devices would include such peritextual materials as titles and subtitles, dedications and epigraphs, and epitextual elements such as production notes and diaries, authorial correspondence and interviews, and authorised promotional materials, including trailers, posters, soundtracks, press-kits, official websites and the like. Genette attempts to limit this category, admitting only those paratexts that the authors (writers, directors) or their associates (producers, distributors) accept responsibility for. But paratextuality might be expanded to describe 'all [of] the accessory messages and commentaries that come to surround the text and at times become virtually indistinguishable from it'.[11] This chapter considers the vital role that these paratexts play first in communicating a film's status as remake, and also in invoking an intertextual framework within which to comprehend and evaluate the new film.

Some remakes are based on highly recognisable properties. These might be films that have reached a wide audience (*King Kong*, *The Parent Trap*), or hold some canonical standing (*Psycho*, *Lolita*), or enjoy a cult following (*The Texas Chainsaw Massacre*, *Shaft*). Such remakes announce their status through their naming, with the title of the original property being 'the first, and most obvious, marker of an intertextual relationship with their "source"'.[12] Indeed, in some recent, high-concept remakings – *Planet of the Apes*, *The Italian Job*, *Dawn of the Dead* – the title may be among the few elements retained from the original, usually in order to provoke interest and 'to take advantage of a pre-existing market'.[13] But just as many remakes are derived from little known or rarely seen films (*Meet the Parents*, *Traffic*), and many others (*The Truth About Charlie*, *Wicker Park*) alter the titles of their sources, disguising their origins but also signalling the kinds of transformations – aesthetic, generic, ideological – operative in the remaking.[14] For instance, in a double movement, the title *City of Angels*

(Brad Silberling, 1998) retains a thematic similarity – an angel 'falls' to earth – to its original, *Wings of Desire* (*Der Himmel über Berlin*, Wim Wenders, 1987) while signalling its cultural and geographic relocation to the city of Los Angeles. In another case, the title *Tortilla Soup* (Maria Ripoll, 2001) takes Ang Lee's story of an ageing gourmet cook and his three daughters (*Eat Drink Man Woman* [*Yin shi nan nu*], 1994) and adjusts it to the 'tastes' of its Latino-American family (and presumed market). And finally, *Treasure Planet* (John Musker and Ron Clements, 2002) signals the updating and generic recasting of Robert Louis Stevenson's 1883 classic *Treasure Island* as a space adventure-fantasy. Perhaps more importantly, and regardless of whether the remake retains or alters the title of its source, a film's remake status – at least in a legal-industrial sense – is secured by a second peritextual marker: an on-screen credit. Such a marker can be either a complete credit (original title *and* screenwriters) or one that lists only the original writers. In either case, this credit not only maintains economic and intellectual property rights, but is essential to the identification of a (single) original source. For instance, the end credit of *Last Man Standing* (1996) – 'based on a screenplay by Ryuzo Kikushima and Akira Kurosawa' – secures the film not as a remake of similarly plotted texts – Sergio Leone's *A Fistful of Dollars* (1964) or Dashiell Hammett's novel *Red Harvest* – but locates its origin in Akira Kurosawa's *Yojimbo* (1961).

The process of identification begun with the peritextual markers of titles and credits is extended and amplified through the adjacent, epitextual zones of industry promotion and marketing, distribution and exhibition. In the case of adaptations, it is not uncommon for a film to *directly* advertise itself – ground its credentials and value – in a classic or popular literary (or other) textualised source. For instance, the trailer for *Cold Mountain* (Anthony Minghella, 2003) announces that it is 'based on the National Book Award-winning novel by Charles Frazier', and a title card in the trailer for *The Human Stain* (Robert Benton, 2003) advises that it is 'based on the novel by Pulitzer Prize winning author Philip Roth'. Although it is unusual for a remake – especially in its *theatrical* release – to draw attention to its source in this way, it is not entirely unheard of in ancillary markets. For example, the video cassette package for Warner Brothers' third version of W. R. Burnett's novel *High Sierra* describes the remake – *I Died a Thousand Times* (Stuart Heisler, 1955) – as 'one of the lushest and most expensively mounted gangster epics of the 50s', but also admits that it is 'based on *High Sierra*, the 1941 classic that made Humphrey Bogart a star'.[15] In another example, *King Kong* (John Guillermin, 1976) seeks to locate its appeal, and status as modern 'classic', in its updating of the 1933 RKO original:

The Big Apple is again besieged by the monstrous King Kong. Jeff Bridges and Jessica Lange star in this ambitious remake of the 1933 original, which adds a great deal of camp and good fun to the story. Again, the gargantuan ape battles attacking aircraft high above the streets of New York, this time plunging from the top of the World Trade Center to his death amidst thousands of horrified onlookers. *King Kong* won an Oscar for special effects, and the horror and the thrills are brought anew to another generation in this classic and classy production.[16]

More commonly, press releases identify a film as a remake and frame publicity discourse around its remake status.[17] For example, the Buena Vista International press kit for the Disney remake of *Mighty Joe Young* (Ron Underwood, 1998) announces that the 'ambitious update of the classic film', *Mighty Joe Young* (Ernest B. Schoedsack, 1949), had its origins in discussions between Disney Studios and RKO Pictures (home of the original film), and in a shared 'admiration for the RKO treasure and . . . enthusiastic desire to update the much-loved classic for a present-day audience'. The press notes at once underline the status of the original, its enduring themes and the opportunity it provided for filmmakers to create a new (original), quality entertainment. The press kit quotes director Ron Underwood: 'I fondly remember the original film, and wanted to capture the same magic that I felt watching it . . . This movie uniquely fit my interest and my love for the big American movie. It possesses so much humanity and emotion'. Producer Tom Jacobson similarly says of the remake: 'What a great opportunity! I loved the original movie [and] I knew it would be challenging and exciting creatively to make, and would be a unique and special movie-going experience – the type of entertainment which transports you to another world'. These views are more widely disseminated through the review materials subsequently generated by the production company press packs (more on this below). In the case of *Mighty Joe Young*'s Australian theatrical release these press materials formed the basis of a centre-page lift-out in *The Sunday Age* newspaper. One side featured a colour poster of 'Joe' with co-star Charlize Theron (who plays Jill Young); the reverse side consisted of a Cinemedia Screen Education 'study guide'. Alongside promotional stills, the guide drew attention to the historical background of the film, not only its status as remake, but its lineage from *King Kong* (1933) through to other ape films such as the *King Kong* remake (1976) and *Gorillas in the Mist* (Michael Apted, 1988).[18]

The type of production company materials – synopses, filmographies for cast and crew, technical details, publicity stills – once made available only to members of the media, have more recently become widely distributed on official websites, and have been extended to include trailers and various promotional downloads (wallpapers, screen savers and the like). More specifically, under the heading of 'production notes', filmmakers – producers, writers, directors – will typically express their interest in, and motivation for, remaking an original film (underlining its classic status and enduring qualities) and then go on to describe the various ways in which they have transformed that property for a contemporary audience. The following excerpts are recent examples of promotional discourse taken from official websites (emphasis has been added):

Meet Joe Black (Martin Brest, 1998):
Meet Joe Black is the culmination of two decades of gestation on the part of director/producer Martin Brest and was inspired by a character from the 1920s stage play adapted for the screen in 1934 as *Death Takes A Holiday* [Mitchell Leisen]. 'I first saw the original film over 20 years ago,' Brest says, 'and it intrigued me; haunted me, really. *There was a suggestion in the old movie of what might be a great story, but it was a story that had yet to be discovered.* We had to start from scratch because *rather than do a remake* I wanted to explore an element that sparked my interest.'[19]

Sweet November (Pat O'Connor, 2001):
Producer Deborah Aal first saw the original *Sweet November* [Robert Ellis Miller, 1968] in 1969, and was so deeply affected by its emotional impact that the story stayed with her. 'Long before I ever thought of the possibility of making movies, it was one of the films I most wanted to see remade,' says Aal. '*I knew there was a way of contemporising the story without losing what was so wonderful about the original.* The story is very much about the enduring and abiding strength of the human heart.'[20]

Vanilla Sky (Cameron Crowe, 2001):
Alejandro Amenábar's 1997 Spanish romantic thriller, *Abre Los Ojos*, became the catalyst for *Vanilla Sky*. Producer Paula Wagner says the film appealed to her, Tom Cruise and Cameron Crowe, and it offered an opportunity for them to work together again: . . . 'To us, *Vanilla Sky* is the equivalent of doing a cover to a great song. *We pay homage to the film, but we also hope to bring our own nuances and interpretations to it.*' [. . .] Crowe adds that he also wanted to take a deeper look into the meaning of love and sex in the new millennium . . . '*Abre Los Ojos* inspired me to make my own statement. *It was like a perfect kind of Petri dish to explore all this stuff. Hopefully we've created a cool dialogue with Amenábar's original movie.*'[21]

Insomnia (Christopher Nolan, 2002):
Originally presented in the 1997 Norwegian film *Insomnia* [Erik Skjoldbjaerg] this premise and the protagonist's unique predicament [a veteran cop struggles to find respite from the relentless Midnight Sun and his own distorted judgement] intrigued producers Paul Junger Witt and

Ed McDonnell, who began developing an American version of the story with screenwriter Hillary Seitz. 'Like Christopher Nolan, *we loved the original film*,' Witt says, '*but we viewed it as so culturally specific that we knew our version would not be a traditional remake or a literal translation.*'[22]

The Italian Job (F. Gary Gray, 2003):
This updated version of *The Italian Job* pays homage to the first film [*The Italian Job*, Peter Collinson, 1969] *but in no way tries to replicate it*. Director F. Gary Gray and producer Donald De Line both contend that today's audiences will be enjoying *a very different film full of all new and very clever twists*. 'I liked a lot of things about the original,' says Gray. 'It had great style and unforgettable performances. *But the film that we've made is for modern audiences, with updated technology.*'[23]

Dawn of the Dead (Zack Snyder, 2004):
A long time fan of horror films and the 'not-quite-dead' sub-genre, producer Eric Newman remembers, 'Growing up, I had always loved those movies, but *Dawn of the Dead* was my favourite. There were always other zombie movies around, but *Dawn* felt to me like the one movie that stood out from the rest. I feel that the genre has not received the attention it deserves in this generation.' [. . .]

'*This is a re-envisioning of a classic*. There was not, is not, a valid reason to "remake" *Dawn of the Dead*. That's not what we set out to do, not what any of us wanted. There are some amazing updates on some great films – I love Kaufman's *Invasion of the Body Snatchers*, Carpenter's *The Thing*, Cronenberg's *The Fly*. They're great movies that add to rather than diminish the original films. *We really saw this as a chance to continue the zombie genre for a new audience*,' offers Newman. [. . .]

[Director Zack] Snyder echoes the producers when he explains, 'I had no desire to remake the picture. A remake, to me, is you take the script and you shoot it again. And that can be cool, but you don't mess with it. A re-filming of the original version was so not needed. *Reinterpretation is what we wanted to do. Re-envision it.* We put some steroids into it. I don't want to have this film compared to any other – our *Dawn* is its own thing with its own personality, voice and experience.'[24]

These statements typically operate first by ascribing *value* to the earlier text (why remake a film if it doesn't have something to recommend it to begin with?) and then suggesting the various filters – technological (*The Italian Job*), cultural (*Insomnia*), personal (*Sweet November*), existential (*Meet Joe Black*), authorial (*Vanilla Sky*) – enlisted in its transfiguration. The most elaborate of the above statements is that which attends the remaking of *Dawn of the Dead*. The original *Dawn of the Dead* (1979) was the middle film of George A. Romero's infamous trilogy that began with the low-budget, black-and-white horror of *Night of the Living Dead* (1968) and culminated in *Day of the Dead* (1985). The cycle has proven to be hugely influential. Referenced in dozens of films, Romero's *Dead* trilogy has also spawned remakes (*Night of the Living Dead*, Tom Savini, 1990), spoofs (*The Return of the Living Dead*, Dan O'Bannon, 1985) and spin-offs (*Resident Evil*, Paul Anderson, 2002). Most recently the trilogy has provided material for *Shawn of the Dead* (Edgar Wright, 2004) and (in the wake of the *Dawn of the Dead* remake) Romero has undertaken a fourth feature, *Land of the Dead* (2005). Among this group of films Romero's *Dawn of the Dead* has earned itself a substantial reputation, not only for the visceral jolts of its raw and excessive gore but also for what is seen as its commentary on consumer culture. In the film, the living dead (zombies) are irresistibly attracted to a suburban shopping mall where a small group of survivors takes refuge. As one character puts it, the dead are drawn to the mall because they dimly remember that 'this was an important place in their lives'. The press kit comments (by director Zack Snyder and producer Eric Newman) for the new version attest to a desire to retain the *aura* of the cult classic, while reviving or resurrecting the (dead) franchise as a digitally boosted, big-budget genre movie. Moreover (and this is at least implicit in the other press kit extracts, too), it sets up a contrast between (the repetition of) the classical 'remake' and (the innovation) of the modern 'update' or *re-envisioning*. In this way, the comments not only advertise and provoke the viewer to see a particular film (as) remake, but contribute to the larger discourse of contemporary remaking.

The attention that these materials draw to the processes (and category) of remaking is sometimes expanded and elaborated upon in special extras packages that feature on many DVD releases. For instance, the DVD for *The Italian Job* remake replicates and extends the press kit materials (cited above) by way of a number of 'making of' short documentary items. One of these, 'Pedal to the Metal: the Making of *The Italian Job*', begins with director F. Gary Gray announcing that 'because it [*The Italian Job*] was inspired by another movie I wanted to watch the first movie first. So I rented the original *Italian Job* and I watched it and I loved it'. Producer Donald De Line follows, saying '*The Italian Job* is a remake of a movie that Paramount made in 1968'. Some brief scenes from the original film follow, before executive producer James Dyer moves in to stress the originality of the new undertaking: 'This movie [Gray's version] is a little different. *It's not a remake whatsoever*, but it does use similar tools to tell the story: heist, armoured truck, gold, Mini-Coopers'. As in the case of the website production notes, the strategy is to combine a focus on the original with an emphasis on the transmutations that have been effected to accommodate a contemporary audience. A second documentary, 'Putting the Words on the Page for *The Italian Job*', takes up exactly this line, stressing the fact that the 1960s version is a point of departure rather than replication. Co-writers Donna Powers and Wayne Powers state: 'We wanted to respect that [original] movie and almost leave it as its own beast, and . . . the remake be our own [while] at the same time maintain[ing] some of the icons of the [first] film: the Minis [and] the chase in the tunnel'. Gray follows up, adding 'I read the [Powers] script and I loved it. It was totally different, though. *I thought it was going to be a remake but it was really just . . . inspired by the original.* It wasn't the same story nor the same script'.[25]

The DVD for the *Solaris* remake (Steven Soderbergh, 2002) adopts a similar approach, at once identifying the original picture and distancing the remake from it. In doing this the DVD extras exploit a familiar strategy whereby the ins and outs of the remake (and remake practice in general) are evaded by calling up the new version as a fresh 'adaptation' of the original literary source.[26] Andrei Tarkovsky's earlier 1972 version follows the basic outline of Stanislaw Lem's 1961 science fiction novel to tell the story of psychologist Kris Kelvin, who is sent to a space station orbiting Solaris, a planet whose surface consists of a sentient ocean. The planet reacts to the scientists probing its surface by sending 'visitors' – living beings created from their innermost fears and desires – to the station. Kris's visitor is his wife Hari (Rheya in the novel and remake) whom he has mourned since her suicide. Despite retaining the structure and some of the dialogue of Lem's novel, Tarkovsky's film (as commentators have noted) is less interested in the novel's scientific speculation and psychological insights than in developing questions of family and morality.[27] Early reports indicated that Soderbergh's version would steer closer to the themes of the novel. But reviewers noted that the remake transformed the source material (even more than Tarkovsky's version), abandoning its broad philosophical questions to focus on the love story: the relationship between Kris and Rheya, and (in a reprise of Hitchcock's *Vertigo*, 1958) their opportunity for a 'second chance'.[28] The 'making of' extras on the 20th Century Fox DVD support this type of interpretation. For instance, in an episode titled 'Inside *Solaris*', producer James Cameron states: 'this [picture] isn't really a remake of the Tarkovsky film. It's a *different* adaptation of the underlying novel by Stanislaw Lem'. In another, '*Solaris*: Behind the Planet', Soderbergh similarly intones: 'my interest in *Solaris* was really driven by the ideas at the centre of the book'. Curiously enough, the screenplay that is reproduced in the extras package states that the film is 'based on the novel by Stanislaw Lem *and* the screenplay by Friedrich Gorentstein and Andrei

Tarkovsky'. But throughout the documentary extras Soderbergh consistently pushes away from the Tarkovsky film to the earlier source, underlining his interest in a 'great love story' and his own unique (*auteur*) vision: 'it [the novel] just seemed to be about everything I'm interested in personally'.[29]

In addition to the above production notes and DVD extras, comparison between remakes and originals is sometimes encouraged by the recycling of original artwork in advertising and promotion. This is the case in the packaging for the DVD editions of the feature film, *Insomnia*. The Norwegian film version, which opened theatrically on just two screens in the US (May 1998), earned a total of around $200,000, compared to its remake which opened on 2,610 screens (May 2002) for total box-office earnings of around $67 million.[30] The American remake adheres to the basic template of the original, while accommodating Hollywood genre elements and transferring the action from the never-ending daylight of the Scandinavian summer to that of the Alaskan wilderness.[31] Additionally, it recasts Al Pacino in the role created by Stellan Skarsgard, drawing on Pacino's wired-cop persona from *Serpico* (Sidney Lumet, 1973), *Sea of Love* (Harold Becker, 1989) and *Heat* (Michael Mann, 1995) to create a character at once more sympathetic and more tragic. In 2003 the Umbrella Entertainment group released the Norwegian original to DVD using the identity of the US remake to lift its profile. The reverse side of the DVD jacket reads: '*Insomnia* is a brilliantly crafted and compelling thriller. Dark and creepy with excellent performances throughout, it is a must-see for anyone who enjoyed the Pacino/Williams re-make'. More than this, the (seemingly paradoxical) invitation to *rediscover* the appeal of the remake (*in the original*) is communicated instantly through the replication of artwork from the promotion of the US remake. The DVD jackets for both versions feature a basic colour scheme in shades of white, blue and red. In both instances, the title 'Insomnia' appears in large blue letters (accented with horizontal bars) and other wording is in smaller red letters. The US version (Buena Vista Home Entertainment, 2003) places the title between stills (in widescreen ratio) of stars Al Pacino (top) and Robin Williams and Hilary Swank (bottom). Above the picture of Pacino is lettering identifying the film's pictured stars (Pacino, Williams and Swank). The Norwegian version places the title at the top, and separates its two widescreen windows (which feature composite stills from the film) with a smaller red caption that reads 'the original version'. In this case, it is not the 'prestige' of the European original that bestows (aesthetic) value of the remake, but the reputation (generic, economic) of the new version that invites comparison with the source.

In addition to these various production practices, a further important factor in the recognition of remakes is their placement in a particular exhibition (or delivery) context. In the case of video/DVD, the recognition and comparison of remakes and originals is encouraged by the (often) simultaneous release (and re-release) of different film versions in the home video distribution window, and their adjacent display in video stores. *Insomnia* provides one example, and others include Paramount's concurrent release of both versions of *The Italian Job* to DVD in October 2003, and the DVD release for *The Truth About Charlie* (Jonathan Demme, 2002) which included a bonus disc carrying the original, *Charade* (Stanley Donen, 1963). As pointed out in the introductory chapter, remakes and originals often enjoy a symbiotic (rather than competitive) relationship in the contemporary media marketplace. In a related instance, the Criterion Collection website provides a list of some twenty-three titles – including *Insomnia* and *Charade* – which 'inspired subsequent remakes or reimaginations'.[32] Television networks can play a similar role – at once cross-promoting their own programmes and drawing attention to remakes – by broadcasting films to coincide with new releases. For instance, the Australian theatrical release of the *Shaft* remake (John Singleton, 2000) in October 2000 saw the Seven Network broadcast all three *Shaft* features from the 1970s on consecutive weekends: *Shaft* (Gordon Parks, 1971) on 22 October, *Shaft's Big Score* (Gordon Parks, 1972) on 29 October and *Shaft in Africa* (John Guillerman, 1973) on 5 November.

Similar strategies can be found theatrically in repertory, festival and cinematheque programming. Although the selection of films in these contexts usually draws attention to continuities through categories such as authorship, genre and production cycles, there are cases where films are brought together in order to demonstrate influence and direct remaking. One such example was the National Film Theatre's (UK) February and March 1990 scheduling of several remake pairs under the heading 'Make mine a double'. These included *High Noon/Outland* (Fred Zinnemann, 1952; Peter Hyams, 1981), *Invasion of the Body Snatchers* (Don Siegel, 1956; Philip Kaufman, 1978), *Batman* (Leslie H. Martinson, 1966; Tim Burton, 1989) and remakes of the classic *noirs: Double Indemnity* (Billy Wilder, 1944), *The Postman Always Rings Twice* (Tay Garnett, 1946), *Out of the Past* (Jacques Tourneur, 1947) and *The Big Clock* (John Farrow, 1948). A more recent example is the 2003 *Remembrance* cinema programme at the Australian Centre for the Moving Image (Melbourne) which focused on works that possessed some 'historical recollection of cinema'. In this exhibition, *auteurism* plays a role in organising audience reception, drawing attention to the way remaking creates an opportunity for filmmakers to make classic texts their own, 'over-writing them with their own traceable signatures, perhaps reconfiguring them by incorporating references to other (rewritten) intertexts'.[33] The notes for this programme announce that 'film maker cinephiles' – such as Jean-Luc Godard, Martin Scorsese and Todd Haynes – express their love of films and filmmaking through 'the technical reconstruction of shots; the reconfiguration of narrative; the reprising of gestures, characters, performance; and by reusing excerpts or musical refrains'.[34] Remake series gathered together for the *Remembrance* exhibition include: *Rio Bravo* (John Ford, 1959) and *Assault on Precinct 13* (John Carpenter, 1976); *The Searchers* (John Ford, 1952) and *Taxi Driver* (Martin Scorsese, 1976); *Vertigo* (Alfred Hitchcock, 1958) and *Sunless* (Chris Marker, 1962); *Blow-Up* (Michelangelo Antonioni, 1966) and *The Conversation* (Francis Ford Coppola, 1974); *All That Heaven Allows* (Douglas Sirk, 1955), *Imitation of Life* (Douglas Sirk, 1959) and *Far From Heaven* (Todd Haynes, 2002). Significantly, not one of these is an industrial or credited remaking, but rather a remake identified and maintained by critical and exhibition practices that are cognisant of theories of film authorship. Todd Haynes' *Far From Heaven* – described in the *Remembrance* programme as a 'loving tribute to the cinema of Douglas Sirk' – provides a useful example.

Like Rainer Werner Fassbinder's 1974 film *Fear Eats the Soul* (*Angst essen Seele auf*), *Far From Heaven* is widely recognised as a tribute to the films of Douglas Sirk. More particularly, both films are uncredited but critically acknowledged (transformed) remakes of Sirk's 1956 melodrama *All That Heaven Allows*. Contributing to the critical discourse around the latter film was an appreciation of several Sirk pictures (including *Written on the Wind*, *Imitation of Life* and *All That Heaven Allows*) that Fassbinder wrote some three years before the release of *Fear Eats the Soul*. As Laura Mulvey points out in an early article on Sirk and melodrama,[35] it is 'impossible' to better Fassbinder's 'plot synopsis' of *All That Heaven Allows*:

Jane Wyman is a rich widow, and Rock Hudson is pruning her trees. In Jane's garden is a 'love tree', which only blooms where love is present, and so Jane's and Rock's chance encounter becomes a great love. But Rock is fifteen years younger than Jane, and Jane is completely integrated into the social life of an American small town. Rock is a primitive type, and Jane has a lot to lose – her girlfriends, the good reputation she owes to her deceased husband, her children. In the beginning Rock loves nature, and Jane at first doesn't love anything, because she has everything. That's a pretty shitty starting point for a great love. Her, him, and the world around them . . . Finally Jane tells Rock she's leaving him, because of the idiotic children and so on. Rock doesn't put up much of a fight – he has nature, after all. And Jane sits there on Christmas

Eve; the children are going to leave her, and have given her a television set . . .
Then later Jane goes back to Rock, because she keeps having headaches,
which happens to all of us if we don't fuck often enough. But when she's
back, it isn't a happy ending, even though they're together, the two of them.[36]

As Mulvey points out, *All That Heaven Allows* followed Sirk's success with
Magnificent Obsession and prompted Universal to give him the budgets and
creative freedom that enabled the development of his 'mature style'. *All
That Heaven Allows*, she writes, 'contains all the elements of characteristically Sirkian composition: light, shade, colour, and camera angles combine
with his trademark use of mirrors to break up the surface of the screen.
Here are all the components of the "melodramatic" style on which Sirk's
critical reputation is based'.[37] Impressed by Sirk's ability to make films that
combined the public appeal of melodrama with broad social criticism,
Fassbinder undertook his own remarkable cycle of transformed melodramas, including a remake of *All That Heaven Allows*. In *Fear Eats the
Soul*, Fassbinder amplifies the basic premise of Sirk's film, transposing its
1950s middle-class New England setting to 1970s working-class Munich,
to tell the story of a widowed sixty-year old charwoman (Emmi) who falls
in love with a Moroccan immigrant (Ali) who is thirty years her junior.
Despite differences in age, race and social standing, the two marry, but
Emmi is ostracised by her neighbours, co-workers and her three adult children. The couple's relationship comes close to breakdown before Emmi
and Ali are finally reconciled in a tenuously happy ending. Striving for a
balance between stylisation and realism, Fassbinder transposes the 'locale,
period and atmosphere' of Sirk's film[38] to examine the melodrama's themes
of 'tensions in the family, and between sex and generations'.[39] In the
process, Fassbinder not only extends and makes explicit these elements
(kept at some distance in Sirk's restrained original), but by introducing the
issue of race 'condenses' *All That Heaven Allows* and *Imitation of Life*,
Sirk's most engaged examination of racial tension.

Like *Fear Eats the Soul*, *Far From Heaven* is a tribute to Douglas Sirk
and his melodramas of the 1950s. Amy Taubin describes it as a 'reworking'
of *All That Heaven Allows*,[40] and Richard Falcon says that its 'wholesale
appropriation of Sirkian narrative, colour palette, *mise-en-scène* and acting
styles [makes] it a unique homage'.[41] Sharon Willis describes the opening
sequence of *Far From Heaven* as one that 'feels almost "traced", as if super-
imposing its frame on *All That Heaven Allows*'.[42] As she points out, both
films begin with a view of a clock tower framed by autumnal leaves, which
gives way to a high-angle establishing shot of a gleaming sky-blue and
white station wagon crossing a neat town square. In addition to this initial

'quotation', *Far From Heaven* more generally borrows from *All That Heaven Allows* a plot trajectory that sees a middle-class woman become involved with her gardener. But Haynes reframes the relationship as one of interracial intimacy, casting Julianne Moore as Cathy Whitaker, a married mother of two who turns to widowed African-American gardener Raymond (Dennis Haysbert) for comfort when she discovers that her husband Frank (Dennis Quaid) is a closeted homosexual. For Willis, these transformations constitute 'an almost electrifying network of condensation and displacement' whereby Haynes's film not only remakes *All That Heaven Allows*, but 'recasts *Written on the Wind*'s drama of heterosexual discontent' and the set-up of *Imitation of Life*, 'which stages its twin maternal melodramas within the framework of inter- and intraracial difference'.[43] This suggestion – that Haynes remakes not just one but *three* of Sirk's most memorable melodramas – is taken further by Mulvey (and others) who recognise in *Far From Heaven* elements of Max Ophuls's 1949 melodrama, *The Reckless Moment* (itself recently remade as *The Deep End*, Scott McGehee and David Siegel, 2001).[44] More than this, the piling of cross-race romance upon cross-class romance (together with the complicating issue of homosexuality) suggests that *Far From Heaven* is filtered through *Fear Eats the Soul*, which Haynes seems to acknowledge by 'replicating', in Cathy and Raymond's dance at the roadhouse, a scene in which Emmi and Ali dance in a dingy bar under the scrutiny of disapproving patrons.

Far From Heaven not only transposes the narrative tensions – sexual, racial and social – of Sirk's and other melodramas (those of Fassbinder, Ophuls and John Stahl[45]), but recreates 'a world where meaning is derived from *mise-en-scène* [and] artifice is the essence of expression'.[46] Haynes and cinematographer Edward Lachman strove to work within the same limitations as Sirk, using gels and over-exposures to produce a saturated Technicolor look, and optical (rather than digital) effects to achieve smooth transitions.[47] At one level, the carefully constructed *mise-en-scène* serves as a reminder 'that collective memory of the 1950s is [largely] a product of media imagery – of advertising, of lush, widescreen, highly coloured Hollywood movies, of early television and the sanitised family fare promoted then'.[48] But at another level, it demonstrates that *mise-en-scène* is as crucial to the remaking of Sirkian melodrama as any narrative line. This is nowhere better demonstrated than in Willis's careful analysis of Haynes's film. For instance, Willis draws attention to 'the primary importance of colour to the genre [of melodrama], as Sirk handles it', arguing that Cathy's signature lavender scarf is 'a key signifier in the film's metonymic and figural economies'.[49] In a scene in which three of Cathy's

Far from Heaven (Todd Haynes, 2002). Courtesy Killer Films/
The Kobal Collection.

friends have come for lunch, the lavender scarf stands out against the
women's outfits – ranging from warm reds through oranges to gold – that
otherwise are in harmony with the autumnal foliage: 'these colours blend
with the foliage around them and create an exaggerated replica of a
common Sirk effect: by keying a woman's clothing to the setting, Sirk
merges her into her environment'.[50] As Willis goes on to point out, the
'chromatic dissonance' of Cathy's scarf, here (and elsewhere in the film)
signals her transgression of the social order, in particular 'her daring
expedition with Raymond into the public sphere where *colour* [as in
Fassbinder's version] is also a central issue'.[51]

All That Heaven Allows not only remakes film history – revisiting the
narrative economy and moral structures of Sirkian *mise-en-scène* – but
(importantly, in assessing the significance of critical commentary in the
identification of remakes) recuperates some thirty years of feminist film
theory. When Fassbinder released his remake of *All That Heaven Allows*
it coincided with, and contributed to, a critical reassessment of Sirk's
work. Although Sirk's melodramas of the 1950s had proven popular with
contemporary audiences, they had been routinely dismissed by critics as
entertaining but trite 'women's pictures'. In the 1970s this perception
began to change, prompted by such events as the publication of Jon
Halliday's book-length interview with Sirk (1971)[52] and a retrospective at

the Edinburgh Film Festival (1972) that featured twenty Sirk films and an English translation of Fassbinder's essay-tribute ('Six Films by Douglas Sirk') in the festival programme.[53] From the early 1970s onward, essays in feminist film theory adopted Sirk as a special example, reclaiming his films to open up new perspectives on the family melodrama and insist upon the importance of issues of gender, domesticity and consumer culture.[54] Unlike Fassbinder's remake, Haynes's film revisits Sirk *through* the filter of successive phases of film theory, prompting Willis to note that '*Far From Heaven* is as much a homage to film theory, and in particular feminist film theory, as it is to Douglas Sirk'.[55] In addition to the interpretative optic of feminist writing on melodrama, Mulvey points out that gay critics and film makers (including Fassbinder and Haynes) 'see a camp subtext in [Sirk's eight] films with Rock Hudson, in which double entendre and ambiguous situations can be read as something other than what they seem'.[56] This is nowhere more evident than in Mark Rappaport's *Rock Hudson's Home Movies* (1992), an 'essay-film' that reframes sequences from some thirty of Hudson's films to expose subtexts and provide self-understanding for current gay cultural production. Understood in this context, those familiar with the Sirkian (sub)text might see *Far From Heaven* as 'filmed film criticism'.[57] The *Remembrance* programme does not bring *all* of these interests directly into focus, but facilitates and encourages a critical and authorial understanding of remaking.

Like genre, remakes are located in critical practice. As seen in the example of *Far from Heaven*, remaking can be 'usefully defined as a tool of critical explanation' and as a 'powerful and reasoned way of justifying the value we place or would place on a [text]'.[58] Because of the transtextual nature of remaking, this critical occasion or 'viewing moment of [the remake] becomes a junction between the textual evocation of the [original] and the spectator's memory of that [precursor]'.[59] As Dan Harries points out (with reference to parodic films), 'one's previous experience with the [original] is typically needed in order both to sufficiently generate expectations based on that [text] and to notice the discrepancies [*or transformations*] generated from the [original]'.[60] Harries acknowledges, though, that viewers will come to a film with varying degrees of knowledge and that even parodies (and sequels) which would seem to require a detailed intertextual knowledge of specific precursor texts are often naturalised according to generic experience and discourses surrounding the film viewing. What this means is that while it might be the case that a critical encounter is determined by a viewer's direct experience of a textual precursor, it is also true that one's memory of an original might derive not from an actual viewing but from a 'generally circulated cultural memory'.[61] Film criticism can contribute substantially to the memory and recollection of the earlier film, and to expectations surrounding the remake. Feature articles and detailed reviews in academic film journals and film-dedicated publications (such as *Sight and Sound* and *Film Comment*), assume that 'the reader has, will or should have seen the film' under consideration,[62] and 'set out in the example of their own critical practice a range of legitimate cultural activities to perform in the reception of [the remake]'.[63]

Contributing more broadly to the identification and evaluation of remakes are the (countless) journalistic reviews of film, video and DVD releases found in mass-circulation newspapers, current affairs and lifestyle magazines, music and home entertainment magazines, video store leaflets, local television guides, Internet user-comments and film-by-film reference guides such as *Leonard Maltin's Movie & Video Guide* and *Time Out Film Guide*. The following brief descriptions – drawn from the opening paragraphs of recent reviews in the US trade magazine *Variety* – demonstrate the way in which remaking can be understood as a 'classifying statement'.[64] These descriptions help determine the viewer's initial response to new (often unfamiliar) texts, and contribute to 'the priority we place on particular plot details, the meanings we ascribe to various textual features, the expectations we form about likely story developments, our predictions about its resolution, and our extrapolations about information not explicitly presented':[65]

> The Chinese-language *Eat Drink Man Woman* [has] an encore as an Hispanic-American family comedy [*Tortilla Soup*].[66]

> Largely listless and witless, this extensive reworking of the 1968 sci-fi favourite [*Planet of the Apes*] simply isn't very exciting or imaginative.[67]

> An all-star remake of the all-star original, *Ocean's Eleven* is a lark for everybody concerned, including the audience.[68]

> A middling Tom Cruise vehicle as far as the general public is concerned, *Vanilla Sky* will surprise buffs for being a virtual scene-by-scene remake of the 1997 Spanish feature *Open Your Eyes* (*Abre los ojos*).[69]

> A disgraced soccer star trains a motley bunch of convicts in *Mean Machine*, a British makeover of Robert Aldrich's 1974 *The Longest Yard* that's okay entertainment but nothing more.[70]

> Although Norman Jewison's stolidly grim and ultimately ludicrous 1975 original [*Rollerball*] was hardly a landmark of nightmarish sci-fi, it towers over this . . . picture that John McTiernan has remade.[71]

The central commercial elements of time travel, flashy effects, monster villains, star Guy Pearce and boomer nostalgia for the 1960 George Pal version [of *The Time Machine*] will probably spur solid [box-office] at home and abroad.[72]

This refitting [*Unfaithful*] of Claude Chabrol's 1968 classic *La femme infidele* is less concerned with suspense and dramatic fireworks than is the usual American 'erotic thriller'.[73]

The Good Thief . . . audaciously retool[s] Jean-Pierre Melville's 1955 French heist thriller-cum-character study *Bob le flambeur* as a cluttered, crowd pleasing multinational caper movie.[74]

The Ring is a stylish Hollywood remake of the Japanese horror sensation that unfortunately has little personality of its own.[75]

[Jonathan Demme] display[s] considerable chutzpah merely in choosing to remake as elegant and inimitable an entertainment as *Charade* [in] *The Truth About Charlie*.[76]

A sci-fi entry in name only, this second screen version of Stanislaw Lem's novel [*Solaris*] is technically superb and features a strong, serious performance by George Clooney.[77]

Proponents of the studios' recent penchant for remakes of beloved pics have strong defense in *The Italian Job . . .* This new *Job* [is] a generally better movie than the satisfying 1969 caper starring Michael Caine.[78]

The Texas Chainsaw Massacre is an initially promising, but quickly disappointing retread of Tobe Hooper and Kim Henkel's highly influential horror classic.[79]

Hell overflows – again – in *Dawn of the Dead*, a big-budget redo of George A. Romero's influential 1978 gorefest, . . . one of the best films (horror or otherwise) of the 70s.[80]

By definition, remakes rework an earlier film (or films), but viewers are not necessarily assumed to have, nor do they *require*, any familiarity with these prototexts. Remakes are generated by a variety of sources – some visible, others obscure. Audiences come to the new versions with varying degrees of knowledge and expectation: those who have never heard of the original, those who have heard of it but not seen it, those who have seen it but don't remember it, and those who have a detailed knowledge of it.[81] In recognition of the fact that audiences are multiple and diverse, each of the above reviews carries, in the first instance, a generic classification: *Tortilla Soup* is 'family comedy', *Ocean's Eleven* is 'lightweight caper', *Rollerball* is 'nightmarish sci-fi', *Unfaithful* is 'erotic thriller', and so on. Viewers who fail to recognise, or know little about, an original text may understand a new version (a remake) through its reinscription of generic elements, taking the genre as a whole (rather than a particular example of it) as the film's intertextual base. For instance, the producers of *The Texas Chainsaw Massacre* say that the idea of remaking the seminal slasher movie was in part motivated by research showing that 90 per cent of the film's anticipated core audience (eighteen to twenty-four year old males) knew the title of Tobe Hooper's original but had never seen it.[82] These audience members might take to the screening no more than a general description of the original – a group of teenagers is terrorised by a cannibal family led by the chainsaw-wielding Leatherface – and view the remake as part of a cycle of contemporary 'meat movies' that includes *Wrong Turn* (Rob Schmidt, 2002), *Cabin Fever* (Eli Roth, 2002) and Tobe Hooper's 2003 remake of *The Toolbox Murders* (Dennis Donnelly, 1978). Moreover, in addition to framing remakes as genre texts and/or drawing comparisons to specific generic intertexts presumed to be closer to the contemporary viewer's experience than some (temporally or geographically) distant original, film reviews will typically position the remake as a vehicle for a star performer or *auteur* filmmaker. In this case, the *Mr Deeds* remake (Steven Brill, 2002; *Mr Deeds Goes to Town*, Frank Capra, 1936) is first of all an 'Adam Sandler vehicle'; the Eddie Murphy version of *Doctor Dolittle* (Betty Thomas, 1998; Richard Fleischer, 1967) is best read alongside Murphy's remake of *The Nutty Professor* (Tom Shadyac, 1996; Jerry Lewis, 1963);[83] *You've Got Mail* (Nora Ephron, 1998; *The Shop Around the Corner*, Ernst Lubitsch, 1940) is foremost an opportunity to reunite stars Tom Hanks and Meg Ryan from *Sleepless in Seattle* (Nora Ephron, 1993);[84] and for *Ocean's Eleven* 'Soderbergh has assembled a cast list that reads like a Who's Who of *People* magazine's Sexiest Men Alive: George Clooney, Brad Pitt, Matt Damon, and Andy Garcia. And as the Girl there's the biggest star of them all, Julia Roberts'.[85] Similarly, *The Good Thief* provides room for director Neil Jordan to explore 'his ongoing themes of honour, identity and faith among fringe dwellers';[86] Steven Soderbergh takes *Solaris* in a 'more personal direction to make it something close to "Scenes From a Marriage in Outer Space" ';[87] and *Planet of the Apes* is 'a Tim Burton film', an occasion for the director of cult properties like *Batman* (1989), *Edward Scissorhands* (1990), *Ed Wood* (1994) and *Sleepy Hollow* (1999) to pursue his interest in 'bizarre reversals and the blurring of primitive and civilised behaviour'.[88]

In the above examples the general repetitions of generic patterns and exclusive stars (actors/directors) help frame the interpretative horizon

(narrative image) for those viewers with little experience with, or recollection of, a precursor text. But equally, the string of (remake) euphemisms that
attends the description of these films – *encore, reworking, refitting, retooling,
retread, redo, makeover, new version* – encourages some viewers to place the
remake within the generic category of 'remaking' and adopt (to some degree)
a transtextual reading of the film. This may have the effect of inviting
viewers to restrict attention to the comparison of particular elements or
details, or abandon broader generic or cultural analysis as a means of establishing the film's contemporary meaning and value.[89] For instance, an analysis of *The Truth About Charlie*, a film whose original's (*Charade*) reputation
is maintained principally for the way its lead players (Audrey Hepburn, Cary
Grant) inhabit their roles, typically leads to the assessment that the new
actors (Thandie Newton, Mark Wahlberg) can only approximate this 'inimitable screen charisma'.[90] In a similar way, reviewers of the *Dawn of the Dead*
remake bemoan the fact that Snyder uses the shopping mall as a location, but
not additionally (as Romero had) as an occasion to critique consumer culture
by drawing parallels between mall shoppers and zombies. This in turn leads
to reviewers devaluing such (worthwhile) features as the remake's high-
tension opening (used in its entirety as a trailer for the film) and the innovative end credit sequence – a video diary – that provides a capsule account of
the fate of the survivors. More generally, this contributes to the assessment
that (in its remakings) Hollywood has become 'more skilful' but 'less daring'
over the past twenty-five years.[91] And finally (in a different way), the remake
of *Planet of the Apes* consistently drew comments around Tim Burton's
reworking of the original's famous ending in which Taylor (Charlton
Heston) discovers the ruins of the Statue of Liberty. As described in
Chapter 3, the Burton ending – which befuddled many viewers – makes
perfect sense when 'reframed' as a remaking.

All of this suggests that review comments do not simply label or '*describe*
the knowledge' that films are remakes, but 'in a very practical sense . . .
determine that knowledge'.[92] As described above, a filmgoer who is unfamiliar with the title and detail of an original source (and its remakes) will
not recognise any specific intertextual cues, and yet (as Grant points out
with reference to 'free' adaptations):

> The likelihood of such an unknowing spectator seeing the film without first
> having been alerted to the film's status [as remake] by its intertextual relay is
> small. Even if spectators initially do not share . . . the generally circulated
> cultural memory of the film's intertext, their experience of viewing [the
> remake] will be shaped by the widely circulated discourses ascribing it to the
> subgenre of the [film remake].[93]

Alongside of other textual activators (paratextual elements), the film reviewer's identification of a film as remake thus encourages or even 'forces [viewers] to read in a different way'.[94] In other words, it occasions an interpretative shift, creating a horizon of expectations that at once enables and limits spectatorial response: opening up some meanings, closing down others. No textual or historical account of remaking can be complete without attention to these, and other, epitextual zones of remaking.

Notes

1. Grant, 'Recognising *Billy Budd* in *Beau Travail*', p. 57.
2. Jenkins, 'Reception Theory and Audience Research', p. 169.
3. Neale, *Genre and Hollywood*, p. 17. See also Harries, *Film Parody*, pp. 101–19.
4. Neale, *Genre and Hollywood*, p. 18.
5. Ibid.
6. Altman, *Film/Genre*, p. 84.
7. Neale, *Genre and Hollywood*, p. 31.
8. Ibid., p. 39. See Ellis, *Visible Fictions*, p. 30.
9. Neale, *Genre and Hollywood*, p. 39.
10. Macksey, 'Foreword', p. xviii.
11. Stam, 'Beyond Fidelity', p. 65.
12. Grant, 'Recognising *Billy Budd* in *Beau Travail*', p. 58.
13. Stam, 'Beyond Fidelity', p. 65.
14. Ibid.
15. VHS package, *I Died a Thousand Times*, Warner Home Video, 1991.
16. DVD jacket, *King Kong*, Paramount, Region 1 DVD, 1999.
17. Harries, *Film Parody*, p. 118.
18. *The Sunday Age*, 28 March 1999.
19. http://www.meetjoeblack.com/.
20. http://www.sweetnovember.net/index_noflash.html.
21. http://www.vanillasky.com/flash_site/index.html.
22. http://dontcloseyoureyes.warnerbros.com/.
23. http://www.italianjobmovie.com/flash/index.html.
24. http://www.dawnofthedeadmovie.net/.
25. *The Italian Job*, Paramount, Region 4 DVD, 2003.
26. See Romney, 'Future Soul', p. 14.
27. Johnson and Petrie, *The Films of Andrei Tarkovsky*, pp. 98–110.
28. See Johnson and Petrie, 'Ethical Exploration', pp. 17–18; and Taubin, 'Steven Soderbergh Follows Andrei Tarkovsky into Space', p. 22.
29. *Solaris*, 20th Century Fox, Region 4 DVD, 2003.
30. The Internet Movie Database, imdb.com
31. Wrathall, 'Rev. of *Insomnia*', pp. 62–4.
32. http://www.criterionco.com/asp/.

33. Grant, 'Recognising *Billy Budd* in *Beau Travail*', p. 58.
34. *Remembrance Cinema Program.*
35. Mulvey, 'Notes on Sirk and Melodrama', p. 56.
36. Fassbinder, 'Imitation of Life', p. 78.
37. Mulvey, '*All That Heaven Allows*'.
38. Reimer, 'Comparison of *All That Heaven Allows* and *Ali: Fear Eats the Soul*', p. 282.
39. Mulvey, 'Notes on Sirk and Melodrama', p. 54.
40. Taubin, 'In Every Dream Home', p. 22.
41. Falcon, 'Magnificent Obsession', p. 12.
42. Willis, 'The Politics of Disappointment', p. 131.
43. Ibid., p. 132.
44. Mulvey, 'Rev. of *Far From Heaven*', p. 41.
45. Pulleine, 'Stahl into Sirk', p. 236.
46. Hoberman, 'Sign of the Times'.
47. Silberg, 'A Scandal in Suburbia', p. 56.
48. Mulvey, 'Rev. of *Far From Heaven*', p. 40.
49. Willis, 'The Politics of Disappointment', pp. 148–9.
50. Ibid., p. 149.
51. Ibid., p. 150, emphasis added.
52. Halliday, *Sirk on Sirk.*
53. Rpt. as Fassbinder, 'Imitation of Life'.
54. Neale, *Genre and Hollywood*, p. 184.
55. Willis, 'The Politics of Disappointment', p. 134.
56. Mulvey, '*All That Heaven Allows*'.
57. Hoberman, 'Sign of the Times'.
58. Adena Rosmarin, quoted in Altman, *Film/Genre*, p. 85.
59. Harries, *Film Parody*, p. 108.
60. Ibid.
61. Grant, 'Recognising *Billy Budd* in *Beau Travail*', p. 57.
62. Morris, 'Indigestion: A Rhetoric of Reviewing', p. 118.
63. Grant, 'Recognising *Billy Budd* in *Beau Travail*', p. 70.
64. Rosmarin, quoted in Altman, *Film/Genre*, p. 85.
65. Jenkins, 'Reception Theory and Audience Research', pp. 170–1.
66. Eisner, 'Rev. of *Tortilla Soup*', p. 19.
67. McCarthy, 'Fox Wages Gorilla Warfare on B.O. with *Apes* Redo', p. 17.
68. McCarthy, 'Breezy *Ocean's* Could Make Splash in B.O. Pool', p. 33.
69. McCarthy, 'Rev. of *Vanilla Sky*', p. 32.
70. Elley, 'Rev. of *Mean Machine*', p. 22.
71. Koehler, 'Rev. of *Rollerball*', p. 41.
72. McCarthy, '*Time Machine* Hits Snag in Distant Future', p. 31.
73. McCarthy, 'Lyne's Cool *Unfaithful* May Warm Up Fox's B.O.', p. 41.
74. Cockrell, '*Good Thief*'s Good Bet', p. 28.
75. McCarthy, 'Remake of Japan Horror Pic Sounds a Tinny *Ring*', p. 21.

76. McCarthy, 'Stylish *Charade* Redo Pushes the *Truth*', p. 31.
77. McCarthy, 'Clooney's Star Shines in Soderbergh *Solaris*', p. 22.
78. Koehler, 'Jazzy *Job* Works as Classy Caper', p. 42.
79. Foundas, 'Rev. of *The Texas Chainsaw Massacre*', p. 41.
80. Foundas, 'Rev. of *Dawn of the Dead*', p. 39.
81. Leitch, 'Twice-Told Tales', pp. 139–40.
82. Foundas, 'Rev. of *The Texas Chainsaw Massacre*', p. 41.
83. O'Sullivan, 'Rev. of *Dr. Dolittle*', p. 38.
84. Maslin, 'hanks&ryan@romance.com', p. E.1:1.
85. Mitchell, 'For the New Rat Pack. It's a Ring-a-Ding Thing', p. E.1:1.
86. Cockrell, '*Good Thief*'s Good Bet', p. 28.
87. McCarthy, 'Clooney's Star Shines in Soderbergh *Solaris*', p. 22.
88. Desowitz, 'New Apes, New Planet, Old Story: Simians Still Rule', p. 2A.3.
89. Altman, *Film/Genre*, p. 95.
90. O'Hehir, 'Rev. of *The Truth About Charlie*'.
91. Ebert, 'Rev. of *Dawn of the Dead*'.
92. Grant, 'Recognising *Billy Budd* in *Beau Travail*', p. 69.
93. Ibid.
94. Horton and McDougal, 'Introduction', p. 2.

CHAPTER 6

Discourse

Peter Wollen describes the film canon – the great works of cinema – as something in 'constant flux . . . [with] marginal adjustments being made all the time . . . through a complex process of cultural negotiation among a motley set of cultural gate-keepers'.[1] Wollen lists four key agencies or projects that contribute to the process of canon formation. The first of these is the archives and cinematheques that 'decide which films to preserve and, through their film programming policy, which to screen'.[2] Wollen notes collections such as the 'National Treasures' list of American films decided annually by the Library of Congress (Washington, DC), and the selection of world cinema that makes up the '360° Pan' list of the 'Treasures from the National Archive' in London. (The latter includes several films discussed in this chapter: *Gun Crazy*, *Bob le flambeur*, *A bout de souffle*, *Pierrot le fou*, *Le Samouraï*, *Bonnie and Clyde*.) Second to the archive, Wollen places the role of academics and critics, singling out the *Sight and Sound* lists of 'Top Ten' films drawn up every decade (since the 1950s) which serve 'as a record and summation of international critical opinion' and influence public taste for the decade to come.[3] The next contributing agency is the part played by filmmakers, and includes their appreciation of 'the ambitiousness or originality of other people's projects, as well as filmmakers' wish to place their own work within a historical tradition or pay their debt to people who influenced them'.[4] In the latter instance, dues are paid through various modes and degrees of *remaking* – quotation, allusion, adaptation. Cinephile directors – from Jean-Luc Godard, through Martin Scorsese and Paul Schrader, to Quentin Tarantino – expatiate at length, in interviews and on camera, on the 'great films' and on their homages and tributes to film history. Critics in turn comment upon this 'intra-filmic network of influences . . . [making] the work of one filmmaker seem crucial in understanding the work of another, who in turn . . . and so on'.[5] This then feeds back into the audience to make up the fourth and final contributing project: namely, the role played by film-buffs and cultists, that 'special sub-group of spectators who feel especially enthusiastic about one genre, one director or even one favourite film'.[6] This agency is compounded by the fact that critics and filmmakers can emerge from the ranks of cultists. For instance, Jack Smith's ruinous remakings of exotic Hollywood adventure movies in films such as *Blonde Cobra* (Ken Jacobs, 1959–63) and *Flaming Creatures* (1963) are grounded in his cultist appreciation of a group of 'secret flix'.[7] The same can be said of the critics-turned-filmmakers at *Cahiers du cinéma*, in particular the reworking of Hollywood genres in films such as Jean-Luc Godard's *A bout de souffle* (*Breathless*, 1960) and François Truffaut's *Tirez sur le pianiste* (*Shoot the Piano Player*, 1960). Godard acknowledges just this when, in speaking of the early work of the *nouvelle vague*, he says:

> Our first films were all *films de cinéphile* – the work of film enthusiasts. One can make use of what one has already seen in the cinema to make deliberate references. This was true of me in particular . . . For some shots I referred to scenes I remembered from [Otto] Preminger, [George] Cukor, etc. And the character played by Jean Seberg [in *A bout de souffle*] was a continuation of her role in *Bonjour Tristesse* [1958]. I could have taken the last shot of Preminger's film and started after dissolving to a title, 'Three Years Later'.[8]

Godard's first feature, *A bout de souffle*, was – and continues to be – one of the most influential films of the *nouvelle vague* and a cornerstone of the film canon. In *A bout de souffle*, Godard's cinephilia manifested itself as a penchant for homage and quotation, invoking (in Michel and Patricia) the crazy love (*l'amour fou*) of classic *noirs*: *You Only Live Once* (1937), *They Live by Night* (1948) and *Gun Crazy* (1950). Five years later, Godard 'revisited' the outlaw couple in a kind of sequel, *Pierrot le fou* (1965), and *A bout de souffle* – its precursors and its progeny – have in turn been 're-made in USA' in films such as *Bonnie and Clyde* (1967) and *Breathless* (Jim McBride, 1983). This chapter looks at the role that a canonised body of film work plays in the motivation, recognition and understanding of the circuits of remaking sketched among these (and other) films. As Rick Altman's work on genre makes clear, our 'primary knowledge' of films and film remakes 'comes . . . from our culture's commitment to comment on and conserve cinema'.[9] As seen in Chapter 5, critics and reviewers discuss remakes in relation to their originals, but only in those cases where the earlier films continue to *circulate* through the efforts of cultural taste-keepers (aesthetes, educators) and the agency of archives and distributors. Although television (broadcast, cable) and information storage technologies (VHS, DVD) have contributed to the number of films memorialised in *personal archives*, it is nonetheless the case that only a small fraction of world cinema output is seen, let alone remembered, beyond its initial appearance. More than this, in addition to 'the visible face of the canon' – publications, archives, home-video libraries – there is also 'a largely invisible cultural structure that underpins it: *a tissue of quotations, linkages, assumptions and ultimately memories*'.[10] This chapter attests ultimately not only to the actual machinery of the canon, but also to the virtual 'recollection images' – or *mnemosigns*[11] – of its remaking.

In the late 1960s, the 'new Hollywood' produced *Bonnie and Clyde*, a film that became a 'cultural phenomenon': exciting a youthful generation of cinema-goers, revising cultural attitudes toward the depiction of violence, stimulating a trend toward 1930s' fashions and earning more than $22 million at the US domestic box-office (on an estimated budget of $2.5 million).[12] The film arose from a complex junction of historical and cultural forces, including:

1. the reality and myth of the outlaw couple, Bonnie Parker and Clyde Barrow, whose exploits in the early 1930s had received extensive media coverage in the South and mid-West;
2. an American genre tradition of gangster films, outlaw Westerns and road movies of the 1930s onward;
3. the reworking of selected examples from this group of films by French New Wave directors of the late 1950s and early 1960s;
4. a contemporary socio-cultural milieu, moulded by the assassination of John F. Kennedy and US involvement in the Vietnam War; and
5. the emergence of the 'new Hollywood' out of the collapse of the studio system, the disintegration of the Production Code and the film industry's increasing coming to terms with a diversified and globalised media landscape.

As Robert Ray points out, *Bonnie and Clyde* was a film whose appeal derived from its ostensible break with the classical Hollywood cinema (the 'old Hollywood'), a film that begins in imitation of Godard's *A bout de souffle* 'with a distorting succession of fragments, withholding the customary establishing shot until the sequence's tenth take'.[13]

In 1964, *Bonnie and Clyde* screenwriters, David Newman and Robert Benton, were working as editor and art director (respectively) for *Esquire* magazine in New York. Looking back on the development of the *Bonnie and Clyde* project they said: 'At that time . . . we were riding the crest of the new wave that had swept in on our minds, and the talk was Truffaut, Godard, De Broca, Bergman, Kurosawa, Antonioni, Fellini and all the other names that fell like a litany'.[14] Newman and Benton acknowledge not only these 'modernist' *auteurs* and the concurrent creation of a group of American *auteurs* – Alfred Hitchcock, John Ford, Howard Hawks, Orson Welles – but they specifically single out a particular film: 'our minds [had] most recently [been] blown by *Breathless*, [and] we addressed ourselves more and more . . . to the idea of actually doing something about it. And the first idea . . . was a movie about two Texas desperados named Bonnie Parker and Clyde Barrow'.[15] More particularly, the two writers situate the genesis of *Bonnie and Clyde* in three factors:

1. a kind of *Zeitgeist* (or spirit of the period) that they labelled, in their *Esquire* essay of the same title, 'the new sentimentality';
2. a new book by John Toland, titled *The Dillinger Days*, that provided a history of the notorious John Dillinger gang, with footnotes concerning Depression-era contemporaries Bonnie and Clyde;
3. an Alfred Hitchcock retrospective at the Museum of Modern Art which gave them an 'education in pure cinema'.[16]

Of Hitchcock's importance, Newman and Benton say: '*Bonnie and Clyde* is loaded with its influences [its debt to other films and filmmakers], and some may be more apparent than Hitchcock, but there wasn't a day spent in writing that didn't include at least one discussion on what *he* would have done'.[17]

Despite locating their motivation in the work of Godard and Hitchcock, Newman and Benton note that the 'heaviest influence' as they actually wrote the screenplay for *Bonnie and Clyde* was François Truffaut, especially two films: *Shoot the Piano Player* (1960), with its 'comedy and bleakness, gangsterism and humanity'; and *Jules et Jim* (1963), 'which managed to define the present as it evoked the past'.[18] Newman and Benton – at that time, unknown and untried screenwriters – took their enthusiasm for these two films to the extreme, attempting to interest Truffaut himself in directing the film. But first, the screenwriters immersed themselves in historical accounts drawn from various sources (ranging from old newspapers to true detective magazines) of the life and times of Bonnie and Clyde. They found that early 1930s America had seen, and enjoyed, the revival of crime and an outlaw style that had not been around since the days of the old West. The prohibition era and organised crime of the 1920s gave way to the Depression and with it came a different kind of criminal, one who was strange and exotic – a kind of *desperado*. Among the factors contributing to this shift (and ultimately influencing the structure of the completed film) were 1930s developments in mechanised transport. Fast cars and smooth interstate highways meant that 'a bandit could rob a bank in one state, drive like hell, and be two hundred miles away from the scene of the crime by night'.[19] Additionally, the proliferation of print and radio technologies ensured that the exploits of the Barrow gang were not only well known across the country, but (especially in Texas) were exaggerated and sensationalised in media reportage.[20] As Timothy Corrigan puts it, filtered through intense media scrutiny (and a 1960s sensibility), 'Bonnie and Clyde [become] road rebels as odd heroes whose travels are a media tour of meaningless violence . . . All experience becomes the mechanical reproduction of the road through a real or metaphoric windshield'.[21]

A month after Newman and Benton had finished the writing, François Truffaut arrived in New York with a copy of their script treatment (translated into French) and made suggestions for revising and transforming the scenario. As Matthew Bernstein points out, the script drafts that Newman and Benton had prepared up to that point 'already emulated the French new wave'. What is less well known is that Truffaut's input did not open 'the film up to more playful, disparate elements à la *Shoot the Piano Player*', but (if anything) gave the 'treatment stronger dramatic shape, [and] pushed the film toward a more conventional dramaturgy'.[22] As it turned out, Truffaut was unable to follow through with the film (having committed to the filming of an adaptation of Ray Bradbury's *Fahrenheit 451*), but he took the liberty of passing the project on to Jean-Luc Godard. Like Truffaut, Godard expressed interest, but as Newman and Benton describe it, the 'mercurial, impulsive, rash, brilliant' Godard was considered too much of a risk by the film's producers.[23] The project languished before (almost two years later) Truffaut brought it to the attention of actor Warren Beatty, who subsequently purchased the script (as executive producer), acquired the services of director Arthur Penn and later negotiated a production deal with Warner Brothers. On a final note, Newman and Benton say that Truffaut's one other significant contribution was the (*cinéphile*) suggestion of screening 'a few movies that seemed relevant'. 'One evening', say Newman and Benton, 'we found ourselves in a projection room looking at Joseph Lewis's *Gun Crazy*, a film based on the Bonnie and Clyde legend'.[24]

Along with *Bonnie and Clyde*, *You Only Live Once* (Fritz Lang, 1937) and *They Live by Night* (Nicholas Ray, 1949), *Gun Crazy* (1950) is now considered one of the four canonised or 'great renditions' of the Bonnie and Clyde tale.[25] The first of these, *You Only Live Once* appeared just a few years after Bonnie and Clyde's violent deaths (in 1934). Although it is not a 'direct' recreation of the Bonnie and Clyde story, it incorporates a number of features from their life and times to tell the tragic tale of small-time criminal Eddie Taylor (Henry Fonda) and his girl, Joan Graham (Sylvia Sidney), on the run from the law. *They Live by Night*, based on Edward Anderson's 1949 novel *Thieves Like Us*, is a similarly framed, sensitive rendering of the flight of two doomed criminal-lovers, 'Bowie' (Farley Granger) and 'Keechie' (Cathy O'Donnell). Where Robert Altman's 1974 remake, *Thieves Like Us*, is seen as a detached piece of genre revisionism, *They Live by Night* is 'notably warm-blooded, a romantic fable about two young lovers adrift in a world they did not create'.[26] By contrast, John Treherne documents the case of *Persons in Hiding* (Louis King, 1939), a film only loosely related to Bonnie and Clyde, but based on a book produced by Edgar J. Hoover to counter the kind of sympathetic portrayal of criminals found in films like *You Only Live Once*.[27] In this version, Dorothy Bronson (Patricia Morison) is a discontented hairdresser who teams up with small-time criminal Freddie Martin (J. Carrol Naish). Carlos Clarens describes the (now) rarely screened *Persons in Hiding* as a 'little B-film, with . . . B-film ambitions [that] could not quite suppress the romantic aspect of an outlaw couple . . . This was surely the way Americans thought about Bonnie and Clyde in the thirties – as picturesque but unglamorous second-raters'.[28]

   The first film to directly deal with the historical characters of Bonnie and Clyde was *The Bonnie Parker Story* (William Witney, 1958), a drive-in feature with television's Dorothy Provine playing Bonnie Parker (in the words of the film's tag-line) as a 'Cigar Smoking Hellcat of the Roaring Thirties'. But the film most often cited as a direct precursor to Penn's version is Joseph H. Lewis's classic *film noir*, *Gun Crazy*. Produced by entrepreneurs Frank and Maurice King and initially released in January 1950 as *Deadly is the Female*, *Gun Crazy* was re-released six months later under the title of its source material, a *Saturday Evening Post* short story by MacKinlay Kantor. Neglected for many years, *Gun Crazy* was redis-covered in 1967 (the release year of *Bonnie and Clyde*) and continued to maintain focus as critical interest grew in *film noir* and in Lewis as B-movie *auteur*.[29] In this tale of lovers-on-the-run, the main characters – Barton Tare (John Dall) and Annie Laurie Starr (Peggy Cummins) – are 'essen-tial, elemental, driven, diagrammatic beings . . . defined by their extreme emotional relation, and reaction, to guns'.[30] *Gun Crazy* now occupies a 'pivotal place in the distinguished company of the fugitive-couple nar-rative cycle' that leads to *Bonnie and Clyde*. But where other renditions – Lang's Depression-era *You Only Live Once* and Ray's moody *They Live*

By Night – see their protagonists as innocent victims, 'the King Brothers were clearly more interested in the greater commercial potential gained by centring the romantic narrative on rebellious characters who actively choose to be criminals'.[31] As Jim Kitses notes, 'it is . . . this radical shift in moral weight that gives [*Gun Crazy*] its hard edge, and thereafter informs *Bonnie and Clyde* and its own offspring'.[32] The cycle of films spawned by *Bonnie and Clyde* includes titles such as *Badlands* (Terrence Malick, 1973), *Sugarland Express* (Steven Spielberg, 1974) and *Thieves Like Us*,[33] and (later) *Guncrazy* (Tamra Davis, 1992), *Natural Born Killers* (Oliver Stone, 1994) and Jim McBride's *Breathless* remake (1983).

Like *Bonnie and Clyde*, *Gun Crazy* has been described as a 'quintessentially *American* film'.[34] This is not only because of its rendering of American film genres – Hollywood romance, crime picture, road movie, *film noir* – but also for the fact that 'in noir, *all of America is gun-crazy*, the inevitable dark-side effect of a ferociously aggressive patriarchal capitalism fuelled by a violent national history and ideology'.[35] More than this, Kitses states that 'the up-and-down emotional world of *Gun Crazy*, its roller-coaster trajectory, [is] expressed through the dominant motifs . . . of speed and circularity that organise the film'.[36] Like the later *Bonnie and Clyde*, 'the high-speed getaways, together with the scenes of the couple in transit, shape *Gun Crazy* as a road movie, the constant movement and furious action a graphic expression of their nomadic life together and its illicit pursuit of happiness'.[37] The centrality of the automobile in *Gun Crazy* is especially compelling in the three-and-a-half minute, sequence-shot that famously documents the couple's Hampton Building and Loan robbery from a fixed position in the back seat of their stolen Cadillac. Even more impressive, though, is the scene (a turning point in the film's narrative) following the robbery at the Armour meat-packing plant in Albuquerque. As they have previously arranged, Bart and Laurie end up in separate getaway cars and start off in opposite directions along the same road. But a short way along they simultaneously brake, wheel their cars around, and meet each other in the middle of the two-lane road. Kitses describes the 180-degree turns of Bart and Laurie's cars as 'a triumph of *mise-en-scène*, [a] moment [that] wittily marks the summit of the couple's passionate commitment to each other in vehicular terms'. 'What', asks Kitses, 'could be more American?'[38]

It is these scenes of movement and action in *Gun Crazy* that not only offer the audience a dynamic, *emotional* experience, but express 'a way of life, a *modus operandi*, ultimately a philosophical system'.[39] As Kitses notes, we see in the film's energy 'the model in action, and of action, that so attracted Godard and his *nouvelle vague* compatriots to the American cinema and its genres'.[40] It is important to remember too that when journalist Françoise Giroud coined the phrase 'nouvelle vague' for weekly news magazine *L'Express* in 1957 she was describing a youth phenomenon – a *movement*.[41] Emerging from this moment, the young iconoclast Godard, seemed to recognise in American cars and movies shared qualities – 'movement, image, mechanisation' – for the 'transformation in [outmoded] European consumption patterns and cultural habits'.[42] Along with the notion of *l'amour fou* – a theme that enabled Godard to describe his own relationship with the cinema as both lover *and* satirist[43] – it is this *vitality* that 'drives' the representations of *A bout de souffle* and the later *Pierrot le fou*.[44] For instance, of an early, stylised sequence from *Pierrot le fou* that shows 'outlaw couple' Ferdinand and Marianne in a car with coloured (studio) lights sweeping over the windscreen, Godard said:

> When you drive in Paris at night, what do you see? Red, green, yellow lights. I wanted to show these elements but without necessarily placing them as they are in reality. Rather . . . I wanted to recreate a *sensation* through the elements which constitute it.[45]

In the earlier *A bout de souffle*, this dynamism is inscribed at the very outset in the (transgressive) spatial and graphic continuity – the jump cuts and mismatched shots – of Michel behind the wheel of a stolen 1950 Oldsmobile convertible on the Nationale 7 highway. In Godard's brand of Americanism, the cinema and automobile become 'a vehicle . . . [for] introspection and transformation'.[46]

Of his debut feature *A bout de souffle*, Godard said 'What I wanted was to take a conventional story and *remake, but differently*, everything the cinema had done'.[47] Throughout the 1950s, Godard and fellow *cinéphile* critics at *Cahiers du cinéma* – notably Claude Chabrol, Jacques Rivette, Eric Rohmer and François Truffaut – had re-*written* the American cinema, advancing a theory of film authorship (*la politique des auteurs*) and employing the principles of *mise-en-scène* criticism in their re-evaluation of genre-based, Hollywood studio films. Their brand of *auteur* criticism involved not just the detection of *individual style*, but (more controversially) was developed in relation to the work of American filmmakers – such as Samuel Fuller, Alfred Hitchcock and Howard Hawks – who were working in the controlled environment of the Hollywood studio system. For the *Cahiers* critics, the best Hollywood directors would exhibit, over a period of time, a recognisable stylistic and thematic personality. But because these filmmakers often had little control over subject matter, script and dialogue, all evidence of this personal signature had to be found in the *mise-en-scène*, in 'the visual orchestration of the story, the rhythm of the action, the plasticity and dynamism of the image'.[48] By the end of the 1950s, the *Cahiers* critics had put their theory into practice, *reinventing* the cinema as a mode of self-expression in films such as *The 400 Blows (Les quatre cents coups*, François Truffaut, 1958), *Les cousins* (Claude Chabrol, 1959) and *Hiroshima mon amour* (Alain Resnais, 1959). One of the last of the group to embark on a feature film, Godard described *A bout de souffle* as the culmination of a 'decade's worth of making movies in my head'.[49]

Godard shot *A bout de souffle* across the summer of 1959 on location in Paris and Marseilles for the cost of around 40 million francs (about half the average budget for the period).[50] Developed from a scenario by Truffaut (with Godard taking responsibility for the dialogue), *A bout de souffle* reworks the conventions – in particular the motifs of pursuit and entrapment – of the quintessential American B-movie *film noir*. The basic story – that of a fugitive on the run – follows the misadventures of a petty car thief, Michel Poiccard (played by Jean-Paul Belmondo). After killing a motorcycle policeman, Michel makes for Paris where he looks up a former girlfriend, an American student, Patricia Franchini (Jean Seberg). Michel convinces Patricia to flee with him to Italy, but she changes her mind and reports him to the authorities. Finally, as a result of Patricia's betrayal, Michel is shot by the police. Though the plot is unremarkable, *Breathless* captures the vitality – the movement and energy – of American *film noir* through the stylistic innovation of its *mise-en-scène*. Godard, and cinematographer Raoul Coutard, rejected the machinery of studio production and shadowy look of classic *noir* for documentary-style location shooting, including the use of hand-held cameras and natural light. In the editing room, Godard constructed an elliptical, fragmented narrative. He violated the codes of classical continuity and dramaturgy, contrasting the rapid editing and jump cuts of the film's opening sequence (on the Nationale 7 highway) to the use of lengthy tracking shots, evident in Michel and Patricia's walk along the Champs-Elysées.[51]

Beginning with a dedication to the Hollywood B-movie studio, Monogram Pictures, *A bout de souffle* adopts a self-conscious attitude to its reworking of *film noir* and American B-movies generally. Godard says he set out to make 'an ordinary gangster film',[52] and Dudley Andrew points out that 'Godard packed his film with direct and glancing citations to this genre'.[53] These references included allusions to such films as *The Harder They Fall* (Mark Robson, 1956), *Ten Seconds to Hell* (Robert Aldrich, 1959), *Whirlpool* (Otto Preminger, 1949) and *The Enforcer* (Bretaigne Windust, 1951), and Michel models himself – through the imitation of a particular gesture – after *noir* tough-guy, Humphrey Bogart. The two come together in a short (six-shot) sequence of Michel outside a movie theatre displaying a poster for *The Harder They Fall*. Michel mutters 'Bogey', and there follows a shot/reverse-shot sequence of Michel 'identifying' with (a lobby card of) Bogart. Godard himself readily pointed out some of the more obscure references, stating (for instance) that Patricia's look at Michel through a rolled-up poster, and dissolve to a kiss is a direct quotation from Samuel Fuller's *Forty Guns* (1957).[54] Godard reviewed the Fuller Western for *Cahiers du cinéma* two years earlier and had described in detail the scene recreated in *A bout de souffle*:

> Gene Barry is courting ravishing young Eve Brent . . . Eve sells guns. Jokingly, Gene aims at her. The camera takes his place and we see Eve through the barrel of the gun. Track forward until she is framed in close-up by the mouth of the barrel. Next shot: they are in a kiss.[55]

In addition to these 'direct citations', *A bout de souffle* is characterised by its 'general "*film noir* tone"'.[56] For example, Andrew states that Michel's plan to flee to Italy with Patricia 'recalls the "escape over the border" dreams of so many forties' anti-heroes, like the fated couple of *Gun Crazy*'.[57] Additionally, Andrew suggests that the celebrated sequence-shot that depicts Bart and Laurie's hold-up of Hampton Building and Loan 'may well have inspired' Godard, and that Michel's anecdote about a guy who pulls a robbery in order to impress his girl 'seems to rewrite *Gun Crazy*, for that couple too goes deeper into crime as their love grows'.[58] Michel not only invokes the 'driven heroes' of Raoul Walsh films like *High Sierra* (1941) and its remake *Colorado Territory* (1949), but *A bout de souffle*'s 'dramatic flow unmistakably recalls a whole battery of films, all of whose doomed and passionate couples [in the words of the *Ten Seconds to Hell* poster "quoted" by Godard] "live dangerously until to the end"'.[59] This assessment is consistent with James Naremore's assertion that, as *auteur* critic-come-filmmaker, Godard held a (surrealist-like) disposition toward *l'amour fou*:

> The auteurists adored such movies as *Vertigo, You Only Live Once, Rebel Without a Cause, They Live By Night, Gun Crazy*, and *Letter from an Unknown Woman* – all of which were concerned with compulsive lovers who flouted bourgeois morality and consumed themselves with passion. As film makers [the New Wave] enshrined this theme in their work: for example in Godard's *Breathless* and *Pierrot le fou*.[60]

According to Andrew, Godard uses the intertextual references of *A bout de souffle* in at least two ways. The first (stronger use) 'deepens the aesthetic and philosophical thrust of [the film] by linking it to low-art *film noir*. The second (weaker use) involves a kind of inter-art intertextuality, quoting elite works – by William Faulkner, Dylan Thomas, Paul Klee and others – 'to vary the tone of his scenes, [and] to keep his drama within a live and lively cultural space'.[61] By contrast, Jefferson Kline argues that *all* of Godard's intertexts – high and low, literary and cinematic – are congruent 'to the dominant (American) philosophical thrust of the film'.[62] Kline finds in Thomas's *Portrait of the Artist as a Young Dog* (referenced in the extended sequence in Patricia's apartment) and Maurice Sach's *Abracadabra* (which turns up in the final scene between Michel and Patricia) passages that 'portray the American B cinema as a model for their characters' fantasies and behaviour'.[63] This in turn suggests a linkage with *A bout de souffle*'s third major literary intertext, Faulkner's *The Wild Palms*. Kline writes:

> *The Wild Palms*, like so many other of the American B movie models [that] Godard's characters [follow], recounts another ill-starred romance . . . Patricia's quotation 'Between grief and nothing I will take grief' . . . reads like a Sartrean passage of existential choice . . . In refusing grief Michel appears to betray Faulkner, but ironically, in choosing death be enters into a double bind: his is exactly the path chosen by all the heroes he emulates. Almost in spite of himself he ends up being *essentially* American.[64]

Godard's Americanism spins out through one further intertext: film maker Jean-Pierre Melville, whose 'erudite passion for American detective movies was already legendary'.[65] Melville is often called up as a forerunner of the French New Wave, having concisely described the movement (and his own work) as an artisanal system of production. 'The new cinema', he said, 'is natural location, non-synchronised shooting, fast film stock, small crew and . . . [the innovative photography] of Henri Decae'.[66] Moreover, like Godard's early period of film work, Melville's *cinéphilia* was concerned substantially with American film, and he is said to have 'exercised a very strong influence on Truffaut's and Godard's discovery of the "little masters of the 'B' pictures"'.[67] In the mid-1950s, Melville had begun a cycle of gangster films or French *policiers*: *Bob le flambeur* (1956), *Deux hommes dans Manhattan* (1959) and *L'Aîné des Ferchaux* (1963). The first of these – *Bob le flambeur* – tells the story of Bob (Roger Duchesne), an ageing but still influential gangster and gambler (*flambeur*) down on his luck who plans one last robbery before retiring. Drawing upon what Melville considered the 'perfect' American heist movie, *The Asphalt Jungle* (John Huston, 1950), *Bob le flambeur* brings together a naturalistic interest in Parisian location shooting and a mythical concern for the professional Hollywood gangster. This 'dual project' is evident in the film's opening:

> On the one hand, the fashion in which Bob is placed on the streets of Montmartre and Pigalle is almost neo-realist in feel. On the other, the repetition of [Bob's] name, the excessive musical accompaniment, the reiterated silhouetting, the sardonic narcissism, all point to Melville's self-conscious citation of a Hollywood archetype.[68]

A bout de souffle made even more explicit its debt to American cinema and paid tribute to Melville in at least two ways. First, Godard cast Melville himself as the writer Parvulesco interviewed at Orly airport by Patricia. Melville appears in the film wearing his signature Ray-Bans and American-style hat, and claims that he modelled the character of Parvulesco on Russian-born American novelist Vladimir Nabokov: 'I had seen Nabokov in a televised interview, and being like him, subtle, pretentious, pedantic, a bit cynical, naïve, etc., I based the character on him'.[69] Second, Godard's debt to Melville – and more specifically to *Bob le flambeur* – is inscribed textually in *A bout de souffle*'s use of 'location shooting, rough editing and in its hero, Michel Poiccard'.[70] More particularly, in an early scene, Michel's contact at the Inter-American Travel Agency, Tolmatchoff, is questioned by the police. They say: 'Remember when you tipped us off to your friend Bob? You're going to repeat that performance'. The reference here, to the character Bob, is widely recognised as being to 'none other than Michel's prototype, a small-time gangster with plenty of style, the star of Melville's precocious [*Bob le flambeur*]'.[71]

Melville's best known films – *Bob le flambeur* and *Le Samouraï* (1967) – have more recently been revisited – remade – as *The Good Thief* (Neil Jordan, 2002) and *Ghost Dog: The Way of the Samurai* (Jim Jarmusch, 1999), respectively. The first of these, a credited remake of *Bob le flambeur*, transposes the action from Paris to present-day Nice to tell the story of down-on-his-luck American gambler Bob Montagne (Nick Nolte). Bob lays plans for a decoy heist of a Monte Carlo casino so that his accomplices can actually rob a nearby vault of its priceless paintings. His team bungles the job, but Bob – in the casino at the time of the robbery – finally hits a lucky streak and wins a fortune. Ginette Vincendeau states that *The Good Thief* 'demands' to be seen in relation to its original, not only because the Melville film 'has attained cult status among a certain band of cinephiles', but also because *The Good Thief* is 'centrally concerned with issues of doubling, fakes, [and] dual nationalities'.[72] Originally titled 'double down' (a blackjack term), Neil Jordan says of *The Good Thief*: 'I was asked to do a remake of Melville's film, but there didn't seem to be any cogent reason to redo it. So I thought if I doubled up the plot I'd be able to come up with a different movie that would have some reference to the original but wouldn't be utter plagiarism'.[73] The relationship between the two films is, however, more complicated because (as previously described) the 'identity' of *Bob le flambeur* is itself grounded in Melville's passion for American film culture. *Bob le flambeur* remakes the American gangster movie, 'acclimatis[ing] it through a set of cultural filters into a "French" product: the pace of filming (stillness, contemplation, *temps morts* [*sic*]), the actors, language (the idiomatic slang of the *Série Noire*) and location'.[74] Jordan's film 'doubles' Melville, but also performs a similar gesture of exchange, taking a basic template and transforming it through the twin filters of the (international) heist movie (other recent examples include John Frankenheimer's *Ronin* (1998), and remakes of *The Italian Job* and *Ocean's Eleven*), and international star cast: Nick Nolte, but also Gérard Darmon, Tchéky Karyo, Emir Kusturica and others.

Another reinvention of Melville's work can be found in Jim Jarmusch's *Ghost Dog: The Way of the Samurai*, an (uncredited) remaking of *Le Samouraï*. Melville's most famous film, *Le Samouraï*, tells the story of Jef Costello (Alain Delon), a lone contract killer who lives by a strict personal and professional code akin to that of the masterless samurai, or *ronin*. But as in Melville's other work, *Le Samouraï* is also a tracing of American culture, in this case 'a "remake" of Frank Tuttle's *This Gun for Hire* (1942) and as based on a novel by Joan MacLeod called *The Ronin*'.[75] Vincendeau says that, like Melville's earlier creation Bob, 'Jef has been perceived as a walking "quote" – with his name, occupation, trench-coat and felt hat – of the classic American noir gangster'.[76] And, as in the case of *The Good Thief*, Jarmusch takes the outline of Melville's film and 'multiplies' the citations, filtering the ancient code of the samurai through Italian mobster and black urban culture. Furthermore, like Melville's Jef Costello, the Ghost Dog (Forest Whitaker) is a 'mythic profile',[77] a reclusive assassin who tends to his birds (Jef keeps a bullfinch, Ghost Dog a roost of pigeons) and adheres to a samurai-like code of honour. More than this, where Melville's film begins with a (*faux*) quotation from the *Book of Bushido* ('There is no greater solitude than that of the Samurai, unless perhaps it be that of the tiger in the jungle'),[78] *Ghost Dog* starts with (and quotes throughout by way of extended inter-titles) Tsunetomo Yamamoto's *Hagakure: The Book of the Samurai*. Additionally, Jarmusch references Melville's mannerist style. For instance, early in *Le Samouraï* there is a celebrated passage in which Jef steals a 1967 Citroën DS by systematically trying out a set of keys in the ignition until (the fifth) one takes. Jarmusch reworks the minimalism of this scene, with the Ghost Dog calmly running a number of sequences through an electronic coding device to enter and start up the targeted vehicle.

Jonathan Rosenbaum describes Jarmusch as an 'international sampler', a connoisseur of intercultural essentials.[79] As this suggests, *Ghost Dog*'s reworking of the Melville prototype is channelled not only through Jarmusch's own mannerist (and minimalist) aesthetic, but through the appropriation of a host of culturally disparate artefacts such as hip-hop, animated cartoons and gangster movies. For instance, members of the mob are seen watching a chronological progression of cartoons, from *Betty Boop* through *Felix the Cat* and *Woody Woodpecker* to *Itchy and Scratchy*, which (like the excepts from *Hagakure*) seem to foreshadow the action. At one point, Ghost Dog looks through a window to see one of the gang's minders amused by a television cartoon that shows a character attach his automatic rifle to a tap mounted on an external wall. He pumps rounds of ammunition up the plumbing to unleash a literal shower of bullets over a second character sitting in a bathtub. After dispatching the bodyguard, Ghost Dog enters the basement to the house (it belongs to crime-boss Sonny Valerio) where he unscrews the drain pipe for the bathroom above, and shoots Valerio in the forehead when he leans over the basin. This would seem a straightforward (internal) repetition of the previous sequence but the quotation is again 'doubled' in that it also references a similar episode in Seijin Suzuki's *Branded to Kill* (1967). Jarmusch extends his 'personal thanks' to Suzuki (Melville, Yamamoto and others) in *Ghost Dog*'s credit sequence. He additionally made a point of showing the veteran Japanese B-movie director his completed film of which Suzuki playfully remarked: 'I see you've taken some things from me, and when I make my next film I'm going to take some things from you'.[80]

Given the interest in cooptation described above it is perhaps not surprising that Hollywood would eventually return to and directly remake Godard's *A bout de souffle* (see below), but not before Godard had performed his own limited remaking of his first feature in *Pierrot le fou* (1965). Based on Lionel White's novel *Obsession*, *Pierrot le fou* tells the story (as Godard describes it) of the 'last romantic couple'.[81] According to Kline, Godard follows the outline of White's novel which involves a man who, like the character of Pierrot-Ferdinand (Jean-Paul Belmondo again), leaves his wife to run off with the babysitter (in this case, Odile-Marianne played by Anna Karina). Kline states that a number of details – Pierrot and Marianne's flight and the scenes of underworld involvement, murder and betrayal – 'all stem directly from White's plot'.[82] At the same time, a number of similarities can be drawn between *Pierrot le fou* and *A bout de souffle*:

> In both films a protagonist, played by Jean-Paul Belmondo, falls in love with a woman he knows only casually, runs off with her, moving from stolen car to stolen car, hoping to get to Italy . . . In each, the hero and his moll temporarily hole up in a protected space from which she proceeds to betray him . . . Both films end with the violent death of the male protagonist, in both cases a death 'chosen' by that character.[83]

Significantly, too, each film incorporates an interview with a director-mentor. In *A bout de souffle* it is Jean-Pierre Melville as Parvulesco; in *Pierrot le fou* it is Samuel Fuller who appears (as himself) in an early scene to deliver his definition of movies (and description of the film that is about to unfold): '[cinema is] a battleground. Love. Hate. Action. Violence. Death. In one word . . . Emotion'. Kline argues that other intertexts – works by Aragon, Balzac and Céline – are ultimately used to screen out both *A bout de souffle* and White's *Obsession* to depict a radically 'different epistemological topos'.[84] Nevertheless, the fact that *Pierrot le fou* functions (in some sense) as a 'double' of *A bout de souffle* is made clear (at the beginning of the later film) when Marianne and Pierrot reveal that this (last romantic) couple has 'met before' – in October 1959 – the exact time that *A bout de souffle* was being assembled.[85]

In July 1978 American independent film maker Jim McBride approached screenwriter L. M. Kit Carson with the idea that they collaborate on a credited 'redo' of Godard's *A bout de souffle*, updated and relocated to present-day Los Angeles. McBride and Carson had worked together on *David Holzman's Diary* (Jim McBride, 1967) and the unfinished adaptation of Walker Percy's 1961 novel *The Moviegoer*.[86] As for many emerging American film makers of the 1960s and 1970s, *A bout de souffle* had been a 'root movie experience', and McBride and Carson saw the idea of a *Breathless* remake as a 'fitting reckless payback to Godard'.[87] An initial script was developed and the remake rights secured from Godard well before the end of 1978, but the project was not green-lighted until Richard Gere – an emerging star with hits such as *American Gigolo* (Paul Schrader, 1980) and *An Officer and a Gentleman* (Taylor Hackford, 1982) – was signed for the lead role some three years later. In June 1982, McBride, Carson and Gere met to streamline the script and intensify the main characters ahead of an August–September shoot. Part of the process included a screening of films such as *Killer's Kiss* (Stanley Kubrick, 1955), *High*

Gun Crazy (Joseph H. Lewis, 1950). Courtesy United Artists/The Kobal Collection.

Breathless (Jim McBride, 1983). Courtesy Orion/The Kobal Collection.

Sierra and *Gun Crazy*. Of this revisiting of (some) key intertexts for *A bout de souffle*, Carson said: 'Godard took chunks of American movies and reinvented them . . . I realise [that what] we're doing [is] a *double remake*'.[88]

Pamela Falkenberg (similarly) describes *A bout de souffle* as 'a simultaneous and double rewriting: the rewriting of the French commercial cinema (conceived of as a transformation) through the rewriting of the Hollywood commercial cinema (conceived of as reproduction)'. *Breathless* is in turn seen as an 'inverse rewriting': 'the rewriting of the commercial Hollywood cinema (conceived of as transformation) through the rewriting of the French art cinema (conceived of as reproduction)'.[89] And more recently Carolyn Durham has argued that a further set of inversions accrue around the remake's reversal of national and sexual identity.[90] These exchanges and inversions can be described as follows. *A bout de souffle* begins in Marseilles with small-time gangster Michel Poiccard stealing an American car, an Oldsmobile. On his way to Paris to see an accomplice (Tolmatchoff) about money, he shoots and kills a motorcycle cop. This sets in motion a classic *noir* story of pursuit and entrapment. In Paris, Michel looks up Patricia, an American student and aspiring journalist with whom he has had a brief relationship. Michel holes up in Patricia's (small) apartment and, as the police net tightens, they lay plans to escape over the border (to Italy). But at the last minute Patricia changes her mind and reports Michel to the police. The film ends with Michel gunned down by the law. McBride's remake closely follows (but inverts) the contours of Godard's film. *Breathless* begins in Las Vegas with small-time thief Jesse Lujack stealing a European car, a Porsche. On his way to Los Angeles to see an accomplice (Tolmatchoff) about money, he shoots and kills a highway patrolman. This sets in motion a neo-*noir* story of pursuit and entrapment. In Los Angeles, Jesse looks up Monica Poiccard (Valérie Kaprisky), a French student and aspiring architect with whom he has had a brief relationship. Jesse holes up in Monica's (spacious) apartment and, as the police net tightens, they lay plans to escape over the border (to Mexico). But at the last minute Monica changes her mind and reports Jesse to the police. The film ends with Jesse (apparently) gunned down by the law.

Beyond these general repetitions *Breathless* assumes Godard's interest in self-conscious allusion to, and quotation of, American pop culture. For instance, in *A bout de souffle* Godard adopts Humphrey Bogart as an emblem of 1950s 'cool', posing Michel in front of a poster from *The Harder They Fall* and having him run his thumb across his lips in imitation of Bogart. Carson and McBride return (and update) the 'gesture', having Jesse identify not only with the 'original crazy boy of rock'n'roll', Jerry Lee Lewis, but because this didn't 'feel size enough', invoke also Marvel Comics' the

Silver Surfer. In another instance of inversion and doubling, Carson says 'we reverse Godard: he went cool, we go hot . . . That's our Bogart: Jerry Lee Lewis/The Silver Surfer . . . It's sci-fi and rock'n'roll, the two most important artefacts in [American] culture today'.[91] *Breathless* incorporates the Jerry Lee Lewis song 'Breathless' into its opening and closing sequences, and Jesse adopts the Silver Surfer's motto, 'Love is the power supreme'. In addition to this, numerous frame enlargements from *The Silver Surfer* comic books not only recall Godard's use of the iconography of Pop Art within the collage aesthetics of *Pierrot le fou*, but constitute a kind of 'internal remaking'. That is, Jesse's readings from *The Silver Surfer* (outside the casino, at the news-stand, in Monica's apartment) depict him as a character who *stays* to save those who do not necessarily want his help and confront those 'who are always after him, like the cops and the marines'. In this way, the Silver Surfer – 'a space-lost freak, looking for love' – reflects Jesse's (outlaw) character, and the story of the Surfer and his girlfriend, who are 'trapped in two different galaxies', anticipates the central action of *Breathless*.[92]

In another example, Godard's enthusiasm for American B-movies is acknowledged through the direct quotation of *A bout de souffle* prototype, *Gun Crazy*. This occurs toward the end of *Breathless*, when Jesse and Monica take refuge from the police in a movie theatre. They hide in the space behind the screen and begin to make love, with *Gun Crazy*'s Bart and Laurie projected (in reverse) behind them. As Durham notes:

> Monica and Jesse make love to the accompaniment and in imitation of the actors whose romance is projected in larger-than-life-size images on the screen behind . . . Monica's Hollywood double [Laurie] describes her ideal man in terms that clearly identify Jesse as his identical twin: 'I want a guy with spirit and guts, a guy who can laugh at anything or do anything, a guy who can [. . .] win the world for me'.[93]

Monica and Jesse embrace, and Monica repeats one of Laurie's lines – 'I don't want to be afraid of love or anything else' – to which Jesse replies, 'You don't have to be afraid of nothing'. The sequence ends with the camera tilting up over Jesse and Monica to close in on a shot (the beginning of the next segment in *Gun Crazy*) of a gumball machine shattered by a bullet. In both films, and especially in *Breathless* (occurring so near the end), this is played as a presage, an obvious marker that things will not end well.

For Lucy Mazdon, *Breathless*'s voracious appetite for quotation – 'the fragmentation and incorporation of both *A bout de souffle* (the simulation of a simulation) and . . . the "whole 'degraded' landscape of schlock and kitsch" ' – make it 'a textbook of postmodern style'.[94] Following Godard's own 'post-modernism', McBride (and those, like Quentin Tarantino, who follow) seem to recognise that 'the truth of any new cinema . . . is not established by looking at life in the streets or in a director's psyche, but by looking at other movies, at books, songs, and representations of all sorts'.[95] More than this, McBride understands that what makes *A bout de souffle* an enduring *original*, 'what can only be original, is the film's *energy*'.[96] In *Breathless*, this vitality is evident in the rampant 'sampling' of its soundtrack: rock'n'roll (Sam Cooke, Mink DeVille), African beats (King Sunny Ade), salsa (Joe 'King' Carrasco, Eddie Palmieri), surf (Link Wray and the Wraymen), ambient (Robert Fripp and Brian Eno, Philip Glass), and post-punk (Pretenders, X). More significantly (and as in *Gun Crazy*), this energy is expressed in vehicular terms, specifically in the sequence in which Jesse picks up Monica in a classic, 1957 Ford Thunderbird convertible (which he has just stolen from characters played by McBride's wife and son). The camera assumes a position just outside the driver's-side door to take in a close-up shot of Monica and Jesse. As they embrace and kiss, it scribes a 180-degree arc across the bonnet of the car (taking in a view of the couple through the windscreen) to come to rest on the opposite side of the car, just long enough for Monica to say 'I feel so brave with you'. Again they kiss, and the camera repeats the movement (in reverse) to return to its initial position, and Jesse's reply: 'Come on, let's just go, sugar. Let's just go [to Mexico]'. All of this is accompanied by the driving surf-guitar of Link Wray and the Wraymen's 'Jack the Ripper'. There follows then a sequence of seven shots. Jesse reverses the T-bird half way down the street, turns it in the opposite direction and takes it – at high speed – up and over a crest in the road. The movement of the car literally flying over the hill, renders in action the film's breathless-style and literalises Monica's earlier comment to Jesse: 'you're like one of those rides at Disneyland . . . Wow, you make me dizzy'.

Monica's words point not only to Jesse's 'breathless' character, but to Richard Gere's remarkable *somatic* performance: Gere runs, pumps and hustles his way through the entire film. This nervous energy begins outside a Las Vegas casino with Jesse stealing a Porsche, which he drives out across the Mojave Desert, headed for Los Angeles. Among the car's contents he finds a nickel-plated .45, and a number of audio cassettes (disco . . . Manilow . . .) which he discards before taking from his pocket the Killer's – Jerry Lee Lewis's – recording of 'Breathless'. Against the backdrop of a vivid ('postmodern') sunset and to the pounding beats of 'Breathless', Jesse proceeds to sing along and wildly gesticulate. Jesse later introduces Monica to Jerry Lee's music (in another wild drive), and he returns to the song 'Breathless' in the film's closing sequence. Following

Monica's call to the police, Jesse runs to meet his friend Tony Berrutti who implores Jesse to leave with him. (As the kid at the news-stand has earlier said of the Silver Surfer: 'only a jerk would stay when he could leave'.) Jesse refuses, and with police sirens wailing in the background, Berrutti tosses him a handgun which falls at Jesse's feet. Monica and the cops arrive: Jesse caught between them. Jesse performs one last wild rendition of 'Breathless', singing and dancing, pumping his arms defiantly at the police, reaching out longingly to Monica. She screams out his name and runs toward him. Jesse reaches down, picks up the gun and turns to face the police. The image freezes at the moment of his (inevitable) death, and to sounds of X's punk cover-version (*remake*) of 'Breathless'.

Some ten years after its release, *Breathless* made it into Quentin Tarantino's 'strictly unofficial' all-time list (anti-canon) of 'coolest movies', just behind his top three in *Rio Bravo* (Howard Hawks, 1959), *Taxi Driver* (Martin Scorsese, 1976) and *Blow Out* (Brian De Palma, 1981).[97] This is not surprising for *Breathless* is a film that anticipates Tarantino, not only for its pop-cultural references and inspired use of 'found' music, but also for the way that Gere's hyperactive characterisation of Jesse *infects* the motormouth persona of Tarantino. More than this, Tarantino – who acknowledges (in his top three films) both classic and first-wave American *auteurs* (Hawks, Scorsese and De Palma) – becomes himself foremost among the emerging video-generation or second-wave *auteurs* of the 1990s. In this capacity, Tarantino at once affirms and extends the canon, tracing a line from *Gun Crazy* through *A bout de souffle* to *Breathless*, and *authorising* his own arcane references and extended remakings.

Notes

1. Wollen, 'The Canon', p. 218.
2. Ibid., p. 219.
3. Ibid., pp. 221–2.
4. Ibid., p. 222.
5. Ibid., p. 223.
6. Ibid.
7. See Smith, 'The Perfect Filmic Appositeness of Maria Montez', pp. 28–36.
8. Godard, in Milne and Narboni, *Godard on Godard*, p. 173.
9. Altman, *Film/Genre*, p. 124.
10. Christie, 'The Rules of the Game', p. 26, emphasis added.
11. Deleuze, *Cinema 2*, pp. 44–67.
12. Friedman, *Bonnie and Clyde*, pp. 21–41. See also Friedman, *Arthur Penn's Bonnie and Clyde*, and Cawelti, *Focus on Bonnie and Clyde*.
13. Ray, *A Certain Tendency of the Hollywood Cinema*, p. 290.

14. Newman and Benton, 'Lightning in a Bottle', p. 13.

15. Ibid., pp. 13–14.

16. Ibid., p. 14.

17. Ibid., pp. 14–15.

18. Ibid., p. 15.

19. Ibid., p. 18.

20. Carson, ' "It's Never the Way I Knew Them" ', p. 44.

21. Corrigan, *A Cinema Without Walls*, p. 150.

22. Bernstein, 'Perfecting the New Gangster', p. 25.

23. Newman and Benton, 'Lightning in a Bottle', p. 23.

24. Ibid., p. 21.

25. Meisel, 'Joseph H. Lewis', p. 90. See also Cawelti, *Focus on Bonnie and Clyde*, p. 2.

26. Hirsch, *Detours and Lost Highways*, p. 34.

27. Treherne, *The Strange History of Bonnie and Clyde*, p. 227.

28. Quoted in ibid. pp. 228–9.

29. See, for instance, Kerr, 'My Name Is Joseph H. Lewis', and the retrospective of nine Lewis films in *Monthly Film Bulletin*, March and April 1980.

30. Martin, 'Violently Happy', p. 57.

31. Kitses, *Gun Crazy*, p. 14.

32. Ibid.

33. See Kinder, 'The Return of the Outlaw Couple', pp. 2–10.

34. Kitses, *Gun Crazy*, p. 10; and Penn, 'Song of the Open Road', p. 59.

35. Kitses, *Gun Crazy*, p. 34, emphasis added.

36. Ibid., p. 36.

37. Ibid., p. 43.

38. Ibid., p. 54.

39. Ibid., p. 64.

40. Ibid.

41. Marie, *The French New Wave*, p. 27.

42. Ross, *Fast Cars, Clean Bodies*, p. 38.

43. Naremore, 'Authorship and the Cultural Politics of Film Criticism', p. 17.

44. Bruno, 'Driven', p. 57.

45. Milne and Narboni, *Godard on Godard*, p. 234, emphasis added.

46. Bruno, 'Driven', p. 58.

47. Milne and Narboni, *Godard on Godard*, p. 173.

48. Elsasser [*sic*], 'Two Decades in Another Country', p. 211.

49. Quoted in Andrew, *'Breathless*: Old as New', p. 4.

50. Marie, ' "It Really Makes You Sick!" ', p. 158.

51. Ibid., pp. 158–73.

52. Milne and Narboni, *Godard on Godard*, p. 174.

53. Andrew, *'Breathless*: Old as New', p. 13.

54. Ibid., p. 17. See also Andrew, 'Notes on the Continuity Script', p. 149, n. 29; and Iampolski, *The Memory of Tiresias*, p. 31.

55. Milne and Narboni, *Godard on Godard*, p. 62.
56. Andrew, '*Breathless*: Old as New', p. 13.
57. Ibid., p. 14.
58. Ibid.
59. Ibid.
60. Naremore, 'Authorship and the Cultural Politics of Film Criticism', p. 17.
61. Andrew, '*Breathless*: Old as New', p. 17.
62. Kline, *Screening the Text*, p. 196.
63. Ibid., p. 198.
64. Ibid., pp. 199–200.
65. Marie, *The French New Wave*, p. 44.
66. Quoted in Vincendeau, *Jean-Pierre Melville*, p. 15.
67. Marie, *The French New Wave*, pp. 44–5.
68. Vincendeau, *Jean-Pierre Melville*, p. 111.
69. Quoted in ibid., p. 116.
70. Ibid.
71. Andrew, '*Breathless*: Old as New', p. 13.
72. Vincendeau, 'Gamblers Anonymous', p. 22.
73. Jordan, 'Double Down', p. 78.
74. Vincendeau, 'Gamblers Anonymous', p. 24.
75. Vincendeau, *Jean-Pierre Melville*, p. 175.
76. Ibid., p. 179.
77. Rosenbaum, 'International Sampler'.
78. See Nogueira, *Melville*, p. 129.
79. Rosenbaum, 'International Sampler'.
80. Quoted in ibid.
81. Milne and Narboni, *Godard on Godard*, p. 216.
82. Kline, *Screening the Text*, p. 203.
83. Ibid., p. 186.
84. Ibid., p. 204.
85. Williams, '*Pierrot* in Context', p. 50.
86. Hillier, *The New Hollywood*, p. 68.
87. Carson, '*Breathless* Diary', p. 34.
88. Ibid., p. 38.
89. Falkenberg, '"Hollywood" and the "Art Cinema" as a Bipolar Modeling System', p. 44.
90. Durham, *Double Takes*, pp. 49–69.
91. Carson, '*Breathless* Diary', p. 35.
92. Durham, *Double Takes*, p. 58.
93. Ibid., p. 65.
94. Mazdon, *Encore Hollywood*, pp. 85–7.
95. Andrew, '*Breathless*: Old as New', p. 19.
96. Ibid., p. 18, emphasis added.
97. Clarkson, *Quentin Tarantino*, pp. 297–300.

Conclusion: Remaking Everything

Quentin says: 'It [was] a film-geek thing to do'. A twenty-two-year-old film school graduate, with the 'cool-sounding name' of Mr White, entered *Who Do You Think You're Fooling?*, a short film comparing Quentin Tarantino's *Reservoir Dogs* (1992) and Ringo Lam's *City on Fire* (1987), in the 1995 New York Underground Film Festival.[1] The question of the similarities between the two films had already surfaced in the pages of *Empire* and *Film Threat* magazines, and Tarantino had defended his film in (what White describes as) the 'Great Poster Defense' at the 1994 festival at Cannes. Asked whether *Reservoir Dogs* and Ringo Lam's film – the story of an undercover cop who had infiltrated a band of thieves preparing to rob a jewellery store – were the same, Tarantino replied:

> I loved *City on Fire*. I got the poster framed in my house, so it's a great movie . . . I steal from every single movie made . . . If my work has anything it's because I'm taking from this and from that, piecing them together. If people don't like it, tough titty, don't go see it.[2]

'The Ringo Lam thing' was more widely reported in two books on the life and movies of Quentin Tarantino – Wensley Clarkson's *Quentin Tarantino: Shooting from the Hip* and Jami Bernard's *Quentin Tarantino: The Man and His Movies* (both 1995) – that appeared at a time when Tarantino had only as many films (as director) to his credit. Tarantino had exploded on to the filmmaking scene in October 1992 with the release of the *noir*-inflected *Reservoir Dogs*, and with the follow-up of his monumentally successful (and influential) *Pulp Fiction* two years later (October 1994) he became a *cause célèbre*. *Pulp Fiction* was accompanied by a media storm, provoking reviews, articles and interviews in such publications as *The Face* and *Grand Street*, and a print symposium in *Artforum*.[3] As

Peter Biskind noted, the French in particular embraced Tarantino, the cinephile's cinephile:

> The French loved *Reservoir Dogs* – it was like a smart bomb lasered into the core of their infatuation with the dark stars of American B movies. More, it flattered them with bows in the direction of Jean-Pierre Melville and Jean-Luc Godard . . . In the country that minted the *auteur* theory, Tarantino himself [had] nearly as much marquee value as his actors.[4]

The Bernard and Clarkson biographies further celebrated the new media icon, Tarantino. But in reporting the question of *Reservoir Dogs*' 'homage' to *City on Fire* they reveal an underlying conflict between what is, on the one hand, a portrait of Tarantino as a new and original American talent, a creator-*auteur* close to the real matter of life, and on the other, an account of a film geek-*metteur-en-scène*, a rip-off artist steeped in trash culture and second-hand material. Clarkson attempts to negotiate the tension between innovation and imitation by constructing an elaborate story-myth of origin: of an abandoned child-bride who drags her infant Quentin from the backwoods of Tennessee to the mean streets of Los Angeles. Consulting 'the person who knows Quentin best – his mother Connie Zastoupil' – and Tarantino's published screenplays (which 'tell so much of [Quentin's] life that they provided the thread . . . needed to sew the narrative together'[5]) Clarkson locates Tarantino's ongoing exploration of the themes of loyalty and betrayal in a succession of difficult father–son relationships.[6] Deserted before birth by his natural father, abandoned at age nine by his adoptive father and betrayed by Zastoupil's third husband (whose interest in Quentin was grounded in a desire to be near the Hollywood film industry), Tarantino invests in various father figures (Howard Hawks, Monte Hellman, Harvey Keitel) and fills his films with 'adoptive fathers and father surrogates'[7] – Mr White (Harvey Keitel) in *Reservoir Dogs*, Captain Koons (Christopher Walken) in *Pulp Fiction*, Elvis (Val Kilmer) in *True Romance*, Bill (David Carradine) in *Kill Bill, vol. 2* (2004). If this is an instance of some authentic, real-life experience finding its way into Tarantino's work, then Clarkson similarly describes Quentin as a streetwise youth whose stint as usher/bouncer at the Pussycat Porno Theater and time in the LA County Jail gave him 'authority [to write] about something he had experienced for himself, rather than seen on TV or at a movie theater'.[8]

At the same time, Clarkson sketches a portrait of the archetypal film geek. Raised on *Clutch Cargo* cartoons and Fruit Brute breakfast cereal (which find their way into *Pulp Fiction* and *Reservoir Dogs* respectively), the young Quentin divides his time between the Tarzana 6 Movie Theatre where, accompanied by his mother, he watches films like *Carnal Knowledge* (Mike Nichols, 1971) and *Deliverance* (John Boorman, 1972) and the Carson Twin which features kung-fu movies and 'naughty late-night Roger Corman double bills like *The Student Teachers* [1973] and *Night Call Nurses* [1973]'.[9] Graduating from school drop-out (Quentin loses interest in school after kindergarten) to some-time actor and screenwriter, Tarantino later enters 'movie geek paradise' when he takes a job at Video Archives in Manhattan Beach. Here Tarantino introduces patrons equally to the films of Eric Rohmer and 'Women in Prison' movies, but also 'earns his own PhD in cinema' through the (repeated) viewing of hundreds of films on video.[10] This encyclopaedic knowledge of film and devotion to popular culture which infuses his written work (the Madonna rap in *Reservoir Dogs*, the hamburger Royale spiel in *Pulp Fiction*, the Superman speech in *Kill Bill, vol. 2*) ultimately, however, marks Tarantino as someone far from the essence of life:

> Quentin knows everything about pop culture. But his greatest strength is his greatest weakness. He is only interested in pop culture . . . [The] problem people have with Quentin's work is that it speaks of other movies, instead of life. The big trick is to live a life and then make movies about that life.[11]

While Bernard's book is a little more critical (than Clarkson's) of the Tarantino hype, it nonetheless turns around a similar opposition of, on the one hand, 'movies about life' and, on the other, of 'movies about movies'. Bernard begins by stating, against 'those who claim Quentin lives his life through [the inauthentic world of] movies', that Tarantino is 'thoroughly connected and engaged with the [real] world'.[12] This idea is worked through principally in relation to Tarantino's strong disapproval (and bad-mouthing) of Oliver Stone's rewrite of the Tarantino screenplay for *Natural Born Killers* (1994). In response to Tarantino's suggestion that Stone should have turned the script for *Natural Born Killers* into a smaller film – *a movie* – Stone is reported to have said:

> I make movies, too. I love movies . . . [but] film should be about life experience. When I was in film school, a lot of the kids were doing technically brilliant films, but they based them on other movies. So it's important for movies to break through that barrier and try to be about your own felt experience . . . The question is, can [Tarantino] expand his world view beyond . . . the combination of violence and humour? Pop culture icons, references to Madonna and Michael Jackson – it's fun. But that's not what you can live on . . . You can make fun movies, or pulpy movies, but I don't know, is there really something being said?[13]

Here, Stone takes Tarantino's suggestion – that an established *film*maker do something small, something more authentic – and turns it on its head: authenticity is not determined by the scale of the production, but by the nature of the referent – 'real life' as opposed to 'other movies'. This is an interesting inversion, for elsewhere Tarantino is defined against a privileged film school-educated generation, the likes of Coppola, Spielberg and Lucas, but also Stone who went to NYU film school via Yale. Emphasising a more intuitive – that is, *authentic* – approach to filmmaking, Robert Rodriguez (Tarantino contemporary and collaborator on *Four Rooms*, 1994, and *From Dusk Till Dawn*, 1996) says:

> I look at Alex [Rockwell] and Quentin and Alison [Anders] and I'm sitting there, we couldn't afford film school. We couldn't get into film school. We were coming from different kinds of struggling families . . . [We] didn't have contacts . . . We just concentrated on the work, and people found us . . . And we can offer stuff that you don't usually see coming out of film schools, cause we didn't learn how to do it by listening to someone else, but by watching movies and coming up with our own plans and ideas.[14]

Like fellow director and former Video Archives buddy Roger Avary, Tarantino is considered part of a 'video store generation'.[15] Richard Pena, (former) director of the New York Film Festival, describes him as 'a second-generation movie brat whose range of influence now goes beyond old Hollywood and European [*auteur*] cinema to include Hong Kong and a lot of other references, including television [and popular culture]'.[16]

Pena's comment further complicates the question of originality and intertextual referentiality by indirectly introducing the issue of *extra*textuality. Cinema constantly remakes itself, but whether this is understood as homage, imitation or theft depends (as described throughout this book) upon historically specific technologies such as copyright law and authorship, film reviewing and exhibition practices. In discussing Tarantino's borrowings from other films, it is necessary to acknowledge that the (intertextual) referent is no more or less immediate than in the work of Hollywood's first new wave, for instance Paul Schrader's various updates of *The Searchers* in scripts and films such as *Taxi Driver*, *Rolling Thunder*, *Hardcore*, *Patty Hearst* and *Bringing Out the Dead*. The difference is that Schrader's references were grounded in the work of a celebrated American *auteur* and in *The Searchers*, one of the most highly canonised of Hollywood Westerns.[17] When comparisons were made between Jean-Pierre Melville's *Le Doulos* (1962) and *Reservoir Dogs* in a *Film Comment* interview,[18] Tarantino missed his opportunity to further authorise his borrowing and 'correct' the canon. This is something that Tarantino has actively done in more recent years, negotiating the re-release of *Blow Out* (Brian De Palma, 1981), finding distribution for *Chungking Express* (Wong Kar Wai, 1994) and introducing mainstream audiences to the work of Sonny Chiba and the Shaw Brothers in *Kill Bill, vol. 1* (2003). On top of this, Tarantino's film work is now the source of inspiration for the work of others, for example *Amores perros* (Alejandro González Iñárritu, 2000) and *Cidade de Deus* (*City of God*, Fernando Meirelles, 2002). All this is to say that Tarantino's 'remake' of *City on Fire* was considered 'theft' principally because it referred to a lesser-known Hong Kong film which (at the time) lay outside the established canon and didn't carry (until *after* White's critique) any extratextual authorisation. It seems likely that, if Tarantino had mobilised his own superfan persona (and 'great poster defense') earlier, or if a press release had bestowed upon *City on Fire* the authority of an emerging body of Hong Kong film (the work of John Woo, Stanley Kwan, Tsui Hark), then Mike White's *Who Do You Think You're Fooling?* would have been a film essay of elucidation rather than an exposition (exposé).

Ideas of originality and remaking – innovation and repetition, authenticity and imitation – continue to inform discourses around Tarantino's work. In fact, in the interviews that appeared at the time of the release of *Kill Bill, vol. 1*, Tarantino himself took up the terms of the earlier *Reservoir Dogs–City on Fire* debate to draw a (complicated) distinction between 'two universes'. The first 'has all the fun of a movie-movie but is in fact more real than life' because it takes the conventions of 'a genre movie and then . . . throw[s] real life [situations] smack against [them]'. The other is determinedly a movie-movie universe, one that is 'not about real life, [but] just about the movies'. *Kill Bill*, says Tarantino, is the first (Tarantino-directed) movie to be set in the latter universe.[19] With *Kill Bill*, the *wunderkind* sets out, then, to make the ultimate movie-movie – *stealing from everyone*, but now with the authority of a second-wave *auteur* and the annotations of a Miramax press kit. If we learn anything from the case of Quentin Tarantino it is that all films – originals and/as remakes – invest in the repetition effects that characterise all films, all of cinema itself.

Notes

1. See White's film on The Anti-Tarantino Page, http://www.impossiblefunky.com/qt/default.htm
2. Quoted in Clarkson, *Quentin Tarantino*, p. 246.
3. See Floyd, 'Quentin Tarantino'; Tarantino, 'Blood Lust'; and Indiana et al., 'Pulp the Hype'.
4. Biskind, 'An Auteur Is Born', p. 95.

5. Clarkson, *Quentin Tarantino*, p. xvi.
6. Ibid., p. 128.
7. Willis, 'The Fathers Watch the Boys' Room', p. 47.
8. Clarkson, *Quentin Tarantino*, p. 105.
9. Ibid., p. 39.
10. Ibid., p. 193.
11. Roger Avary, quoted in ibid., p. 217.
12. Bernard, *Quentin Tarantino*, p. 14.
13. Quoted in ibid., p. 121.
14. Quoted in ibid., pp. 261–2.
15. Ibid., p. 48.
16. Quoted in ibid., pp. 240–1.
17. Tarantino (belatedly) recreates the famous open doorway shot from *The Searchers* in *Kill Bill, vol. 2* (2004).
18. Smith, 'When You Know You're in Good Hands', p. 40.
19. Tarantino, 'Turning on a Dime', p. 15.

References

Adair, Gilbert (1983) 'Rev. of *Breathless*', *Monthly Film Bulletin*, vol. 50, no. 596 (September), pp. 241–2.

Altman, Rick (1995) 'A Semantic/Syntactic Approach to Film Genre', in Barry Keith Grant (ed.), *Film Genre Reader II*. Austin, TX: University of Texas Press, pp. 26–40.

Altman, Rick (1999) *Film/Genre*. London: British Film Institute.

Anderson, Christopher (1994) *Hollywood TV: The Studio System in the Fifties*. Austin, TX: University of Texas Press.

Andrew, Dudley (1987) '*Breathless*: Old as New', in Dudley Andrew (ed.), Breathless*: Jean-Luc Godard, Director*. New Brunswick, NJ: Rutgers University Press, pp. 3–20.

Andrew, Dudley (1987) 'Notes on the Continuity Script', in Dudley Andrew (ed.), Breathless*: Jean-Luc Godard, Director*. New Brunswick, NJ: Rutgers University Press, pp. 147–52.

Andrew, Dudley (2000) 'Adaptation', in Naremore (ed.), *Film Adaptation*, pp. 28–37.

Anobile, Richard J. (ed.) (1974) *Alfred Hitchcock's* Psycho. London: Picador.

Aquin, Stéphane (2000) 'Hitchcock and Contemporary Art', in Dominique Païni and Guy Cogeval (eds), *Hitchcock and Art: Fatal Coincidences*. Montreal: Montreal Museum of Fine Arts, pp. 173–7.

Atkinson, Mike (1995) 'Delirious Inventions', *Sight and Sound*, vol. 5, no. 7 (July), pp. 12–16.

Atkinson, Michael (1995) 'Son of Apes', *Film Comment*, vol. 31, no. 5 (September–October), pp. 62–6.

Bahrenburg, Bruce (1976) *The Creation of Dino De Laurentiis'* King Kong. London: W. H. Allen.

Balio, Tino (1990) 'Introduction to Part II', in Tino Balio (ed.), *Hollywood in the Age of Television*. Boston: Unwin Hyman, pp. 259–96.

Balio, Tino (1993) *Grand Design: Hollywood as a Modern Business Enterprise 1930–1939*, History of the American Cinema vol. 5. New York: Charles Scribner's Sons.

Bellour, Raymond (2000) *The Analysis of Film*, (ed.) Constance Penley. Bloomington, IN: Indiana University Press.

Bernard, Jami (1995) *Quentin Tarantino: The Man and His Movies*. London: HarperCollins.

Bernstein, Matthew (2000) 'Perfecting the New Gangster: Writing *Bonnie and Clyde*', *Film Quarterly*, vol. 53, no. 4, pp. 16–31.

Biesen, Sheri Chinen (2000) 'Raising Cain with the Censors, Again: *The Postman Always Rings Twice* (1946)', *Literature/Film Quarterly*, vol. 28, no. 1, pp. 41–8.

Biguenet, John (1998) 'Double Takes: The Role of Allusion in Cinema', in Horton and McDougal (eds), *Play it Again, Sam*, pp. 131–43.

Biskind, Peter (1994) 'An Auteur Is Born', *Premiere*, November, pp. 94–102.

Bloom, Harold (1973) *The Anxiety of Influence: A Theory of Poetry*. New York: Oxford University Press.

Bordwell, David (1985) *Narration in the Fiction Film*. London: Methuen.

Bordwell, David (1989) *Making Meaning: Inference and Rhetoric in the Interpretation of Cinema*. Cambridge, MA: Harvard University Press.

Boulle, Pierre (1963) *Planet of the Apes*, trans. Xan Fielding. New York: Vanguard Press.

Brooks, Tim and Earle Marsh (1995) *The Complete Directory to Prime Time Network and Cable TV Shows, 1946–Present*, 6th edn. New York: Ballantine.

Brooks, Xan (2001) 'Rev. of *Planet of the Apes*', *Sight and Sound*, vol. 11, no. 10 (October), pp. 54–6.

Broyles, William (2001) 'Time and Destiny', interview by Daniel Argent, *Creative Screenwriting*, vol. 8, no. 4, pp. 39–43.

Brunette, Peter and David Wills (1989) *Screen/Play: Derrida and Film Theory*. Princeton, NJ: Princeton University Press.

Bruno, Giuliana (2001) 'Driven', *2wice*, vol. 5, no. 2, pp. 56–64.

Cain, James M. [1934] (1981) *The Postman Always Rings Twice*. London: Pan.

Calabrese, Omar (1992) *Neo-Baroque: A Sign of the Times*, trans. Charles Lambert. Princeton, NJ: Princeton University Press.

Carroll, Noël (1982) 'The Future of Allusion: Hollywood in the Seventies (and Beyond)', *October*, no. 20, pp. 51–81.

Carson, Diane (2000) ' "It's Never the Way I Knew Them": Searching for Bonnie and Clyde', in Lester D. Friedman (ed.), *Arthur Penn's* Bonnie and Clyde. New York: Cambridge University Press, pp. 42–69.

Carson, L. M. Kit (1983) '*Breathless* Diary', *Film Comment*, vol. 19, no. 3 (May–June), pp. 33–8.

Carter, Bill (2004) 'Marooned Again with Gilligan', *The Age*, 9 December, Green Guide, p. 19.

Cawelti, John G. (ed.) (1973) *Focus on* Bonnie and Clyde. Englewood Cliffs, NJ: Prentice-Hall.

Cazdyn, Eric (2002) *The Flash of Capital: Film and Geopolitics in Japan*. Durham, NC: Duke University Press.

Christie, Ian (2002) 'The Rules of the Game', *Sight and Sound*, vol. 12, no. 9 (September), pp. 24–7.

Chute, David (1981) 'Tropic of Kasdan', *Film Comment*, vol. 17, no. 5 (September–October), pp. 49–56.

Clarkson, Wensley (1995) *Quentin Tarantino: Shooting from the Hip*. London: Piatkus.

Clover, Carol (1987) 'Her Body, Himself: Gender in the Slasher Film', *Representations*, no. 20, pp. 187–228.

Cockrell, Eddie (2002) '*Good Thief*'s Good Bet', *Variety*, 16–22 September, p. 28.

Cohen, Paula Marantz (2001–02) 'The Artist Pays Homage', *Hitchcock Annual*, pp. 127–32.

Combs, Richard (1980) 'Rev. of *Dressed to Kill*', *Monthly Film Bulletin*, vol. 47, no. 562 (November), p. 213.

Combs, Richard (1981) 'Rev. of *The Postman Always Rings Twice*', *Monthly Film Bulletin*, vol. 48, no. 568 (May), pp. 95–6.

Combs, Richard (1982) 'Rev. of *Detour*', *Monthly Film Bulletin*, vol. 49, no. 582 (July), pp. 145–6.

Combs, Richard (1990) 'Rev. of *Dick Tracy*', *Monthly Film Bulletin*, vol. 57, no. 679 (August), pp. 215–17.

Condon, Paul and Jim Sangster (1999) *The Complete Hitchcock*. London: Virgin.

Corrigan, Timothy (1991) *A Cinema Without Walls: Movies and Culture After Vietnam*. New Brunswick, NJ: Rutgers University Press.

Corrigan, Timothy (1998) 'Auteurs and the New Hollywood', in Jon Lewis (ed.), *The New American Cinema*. Durham, NC: Duke University Press, pp. 38–63.

Corrigan, Timothy (2002) 'Which Shakespeare to Love? Film, Fidelity, and the Performance of Literature', in Jim Collins (ed.), *High-Pop: Making Culture into Popular Entertainment*. Oxford: Blackwell, pp. 155–81.

Culler, Jonathan (1975) 'Defining Narrative Units', in Roger Fowler (ed.), *Style and Structure in Literature: Essays in the New Stylistics*. Oxford: Basil Blackwell, pp. 123–42.

Culler, Jonathan (1981) *The Pursuit of Signs: Semiotics, Literature, Deconstruction*. London: Routledge & Kegan Paul.

Cumbow, Robert C. (1987) *Once Upon a Time: The Films of Sergio Leone*. Metuchen, NJ: Scarecrow Press.

Deleuze, Gilles (1989) *Cinema 2: The Time-Image*, trans. Hugh Tomlinson and Robert Galeta. Minneapolis, MN: University of Minnesota Press.

Desowitz, Bill (2001) 'New Apes, New Planet, Old Story: Simians Still Rule', *New York Times*, 13 May, p. 2A.3.

Dika, Vera (2003) *Recycled Culture in Contemporary Art and Film: The Uses of Nostalgia*. Cambridge: Cambridge University Press.

Diski, Jenny (1992) 'The Shadow Within', *Sight and Sound*, vol. 1, no. 10 (February), pp. 12–13.

Dowell, Pat (1992) 'Rev. of *Unforgiven*', *Cineaste*, vol. 19, nos. 2–3, pp. 72–3.

Druxman, Michael B. (1975) *Make It Again, Sam: A Survey of Movie Remakes.* Cranbury, NJ: A. S. Barnes.

Durham, Carolyn A. (1998) *Double Takes: Culture and Gender in French Films and Their American Remakes.* Hanover, NH: University Press of New England.

Eaton, Michael (1991) 'Condemned to Repeats', *Sight and Sound*, vol. 1, no. 8 (December), p. 4.

Eaton, Michael (1998) 'Cinema and Television: From Eden to the Land of Nod?', in Elsaesser and Hoffmann (eds), *Cinema Futures*, pp. 137–42.

Ebert, Roger (1998) 'Rev. of *Psycho*', *Chicago Sun Times*, http://www.suntimes.com.

Ebert, Roger (2004) 'Rev. of *Dawn of the Dead*', *Chicago Sun Times*, http://www.suntimes.com.

Eberwein, Robert (1998) 'Remakes and Cultural Studies', in Horton and McDougal (eds), *Play It Again, Sam*, pp. 15–33.

Eco, Umberto (1985) 'Innovation and Repetition: Between Modern and Post-Modern Aesthetics', *Daedalus*, vol. 114, no. 4, pp. 161–84.

Eco, Umberto (1990) *The Limits of Interpretation*. Bloomington, IN: Indiana University Press.

Eisner, Joel and David Krinsky (1984) *Television Comedy Series: An Episode Guide to 153 TV Sitcoms in Syndication*. Jefferson, NC: McFarland.

Eisner, Ken (2001) 'Rev. of *Tortilla Soup*', *Variety*, 23–29 July, p. 19.

Elley, Derek (2001–02) 'Rev. of *Mean Machine*', *Variety*, 24 December–6 January, p. 22.

Ellis, John (1992) *Visible Fictions: Cinema, Television, Video*, rev. edn. London: Routledge.

Ellis, John (1998) 'Cinema and Television: Laios and Oedipus', in Elsaesser and Hoffmann (eds), *Cinema Futures*, pp. 127–35.

Elsaesser, Thomas (1990) 'The Institution Cinema: Industry, Commodity, Audiences', in Thomas Elsaesser with Adam Barker (eds), *Early Cinema: Space, Frame, Narrative*. London: British Film Institute, pp. 153–73.

Elsaesser, Thomas (1998) 'Fantasy Island: Dream Logic as Production Logic', in Elsaesser and Hoffmann (eds), *Cinema Futures*, pp. 143–58.

Elsaesser, Thomas and Kay Hoffmann (eds) (1998) *Cinema Futures: Cain, Abel or Cable?* Amsterdam: Amsterdam University Press.

Elsasser [*sic*], Thomas (1975) 'Two Decades in Another Country: Hollywood and the Cinéphiles', in C. W. E. Bigsby (ed.), *Superculture: American Popular Culture and Europe*. London: Paul Elek, pp. 199–225.

Erickson, Todd (1996) 'Kill Me Again: Movement becomes Genre', in Alain Silver and James Ursini (eds), *Film Noir Reader*. New York: Limelight, pp. 307–29.

Falcon, Richard (2003) 'Magnificent Obsession', *Sight and Sound*, vol. 13, no. 3 (March), pp. 12–15.

Falkenberg, Pamela (1985) ' "Hollywood" and the "Art Cinema" as a Bipolar Modeling System: *A bout de souffle* and *Breathless*', *Wide Angle*, vol. 7, no. 3, pp. 44–53.

Fassbinder, Rainer Werner (1992) 'Imitation of Life: On the Films of Douglas Sirk', in Michael Töteberg and Leo A. Lensing (eds), *Rainer Werner Fassbinder: The Anarchy of the Imagination*, trans. Krishna Winston. Baltimore, MD: Johns Hopkins University Press, pp. 77–89.

Fish, Stanley (1980) *Is There a Text in This Class? The Authority of Interpretive Communities*. Cambridge, MA: Harvard University Press.

Floyd, Nigel (1994) 'Quentin Tarantino: Blood Brother', *The Face*, October, pp. 92–9.

Forrest, Jennifer (2002) 'The "Personal" Touch: The Original, the Remake, and the Dupe in Early Cinema', in Forrest and Koos (eds), *Dead Ringers*, pp. 89–126.

Forrest, Jennifer and Leonard R. Koos (eds) (2002) *Dead Ringers: The Remake in Theory and Practice*. Albany, NY: State University of New York Press.

Foundas, Scott (2003) 'Rev. of *The Texas Chainsaw Massacre*', *Variety*, 20–26 October, p. 41.

Foundas, Scott (2004) 'Rev. of *Dawn of the Dead*', *Variety*, 22–28 March, p. 39.

Frayling, Christopher (2000) *Sergio Leone: Something to Do with Death*. London: Faber & Faber.

Free, Erin and Peter Galvin (2001) 'The Big Remake: Out of Time, Out of Place, Out of Ideas', *Independent Filmmaker*, no. 36, pp. 36–40.

Friedberg, Anne (1993) *Window Shopping: Cinema and the Postmodern*. Berkeley, CA: University of California Press.

Friedman, Lester D. (ed.) (2000) *Arthur Penn's* Bonnie and Clyde. New York: Cambridge University Press.

Friedman, Lester D. (2000) *Bonnie and Clyde*. London: British Film Institute.

Friend, Tad (1998) 'Copy Cats', *The New Yorker*, 14 September, pp. 51–7.

Frow, John (1986) *Marxism and Literary History*. Oxford: Basil Blackwell.

Frow, John (1990) 'Intertextuality and Ontology', in Michael Worton and Judith Still (eds), *Intertextuality: Theories and Practices*. Manchester: Manchester University Press, pp. 45–55.

Frow, John (1999) 'Rev. of *Play It Again, Sam*', *Screening the Past*, no. 7, http://www.latrobe.edu.au/screeningthepast/shorts/reviews/rev0799/jfbr7a.htm.

Gabbard, Krin (1998) 'The Ethnic Oedipus: *The Jazz Singer* and Its Remakes', in Horton and McDougal (eds), *Play It Again, Sam*, pp. 95–114.

Galbraith, Stuart (2002) *The Emperor and the Wolf: The Lives and Films of Akira Kurosawa and Toshiro Mifune*. London: Faber & Faber.

Gaudreault, André (1985) 'The Infringement of Copyright Laws and Its Effects (1900–1906)', *Framework*, no. 29, pp. 2–14.

Georgakas, Dan (1998) 'Robin Hood: From Roosevelt to Reagan', in Horton and McDougal (eds), *Play It Again, Sam*, pp. 70–9.

Grant, Catherine (2002) 'Recognising *Billy Budd* in *Beau Travail*: Epistemology and Hermeneutics of an Auteurist "Free" Adaptation', *Screen*, vol. 43, no. 1, pp. 57–73.

Greenberg, Harvey Roy (1991) 'Raiders of the Lost Text: Remaking as Contested Homage in *Always*', *Journal of Popular Film and Television*, vol. 18, no. 4, pp. 164–71; rpt. in Horton and McDougal (eds), *Play It Again, Sam*, pp. 115–30.

Greene, Eric (1996) *Planet of the Apes as American Myth: Race, Politics, and Popular Culture*. Hanover, NH: University Press of New England.

Grindstaff, Laura (2001) 'A Pygmalion Tale Retold: Remaking *La Femme Nikita*', *Camera Obscura*, vol. 16, no. 2, pp. 133–75; revised and rpt. as 'Pretty Woman with a Gun: *La Femme Nikita* and the Textual Politics of "The Remake"', in Forrest and Koos (eds), *Dead Ringers*, pp. 273–308.

Gunning, Tom (1981) 'Weaving a Narrative: Style and Economic Background in Griffith's Biograph Films', *Quarterly Review of Film Studies*, vol. 6, no. 1, pp. 11–25.

'Gus Van Sant vs. Alfred Hitchcock: A *Psycho* Dossier' (2001–02), *Hitchcock Annual*, pp. 125–58.

Halliday, Jon (1971) *Sirk on Sirk*. London: Secker & Warburg.

Hammett, Dashiell [1929] (1982) *Red Harvest*, in *Dashiell Hammett: The Four Great Novels*. London: Picador, pp. 5–192.

Har. (1981) 'Rev. of *The Postman Always Rings Twice*', *Variety*, 18 March, p. 133.

Har. (1984) 'Rev. of *Against All Odds*', *Variety*, 15 February, p. 24.

Hark, Ina Rae (1999) 'The Wrath of the Original Cast: Translating Embodied Television Characters to Other Media', in Deborah Cartmell and Imelda Whelehan (eds), *Adaptations: From Text to Screen, Screen to Text*. London: Routledge, pp. 172–84.

Harkness, John (1999) 'Psycho Path', http://www.now.com.

Harries, Dan (2000) *Film Parody*, London: British Film Institute.

Harris, Sue (2003) 'Rev. of *The Truth About Charlie*', *Sight and Sound*, vol. 13, no. 8 (August), pp. 60–2.

Harvey, Stephen (1980) 'Can't Stop the Remakes', *Film Comment*, vol. 16, no. 5 (September–October), pp. 50–3.

Hawker, Philippa (2000) 'Rev. of *Mission: Impossible 2*', *The Age*, 1 June, Today, p. 5.

Hillier, Jim (1992) *The New Hollywood*. New York: Continuum.

Hirsch, Foster (1999) *Detours and Lost Highways: A Map of Neo-Noir*. New York: Limelight.

Hoberman, J. (1980) 'Rev. of *Dressed to Kill*', *Village Voice*, 22–29 July, pp. 42 and 44.

Hoberman, J. (1985) 'Ten Years That Shook the World', *American Film*, June, pp. 34–59.

Hoberman, J. (1991) 'Facing the Nineties', in *Vulgar Modernism: Writing on Movies and Other Media*. Philadelphia: Temple University Press, pp. 1–10.

Hoberman, J. (1992) 'Sacred and Profane', *Sight and Sound*, vol. 1, no. 10 (February), pp. 8–11.

Hoberman, J. (2002) 'Sign of the Times', *Village Voice*, 6–12 November, http://www.villagevoice.com/issues/0245/hoberman.php.

Hoberman, J. (2003) 'They're Back', *Village Voice*, 30 June, http://www.villagevoice.com/issues/0327/hoberman.php.

Horton, Andrew and Stuart Y. McDougal (eds) (1998) *Play It Again, Sam: Retakes on Remakes*. Berkeley, CA: University of California Press.

Hughes, Simon (2001) 'Apocalypse now. Please!', *The Age*, 26 January, Today, p. 1.

Iampolski, Mikhail (1998) *The Memory of Tiresias: Intertextuality and Film*, trans. Harsha Ram. Berkeley, CA: University of California Press.

Indiana, Gary et al. (1995) 'Pulp the Hype: On the Q.T.', *Artforum* March, pp. 62–7 and 108–10.

Jameson, Fredric (1984) 'Postmodernism, or The Cultural Logic of Late Capitalism', *New Left Review*, no. 146, pp. 53–92.

Jameson, Fredric (1985) 'Postmodernism and Consumer Society', in Hal Foster (ed.), *Postmodern Culture*. London: Pluto, pp. 111–25.

Javna, John and Gordon Javna (1983) *60s!* New York: St. Martin's Press.

Jenkins, Henry (2000) 'Reception Theory and Audience Research: The Mystery of the Vampire's Kiss', in Christine Gledhill and Linda Williams (eds), *Reinventing Film Studies*. London: Arnold, pp. 165–82.

Jenkins, Steve (1982) 'Rev. of *Body Heat*', *Monthly Film Bulletin*, vol. 49, no. 576 (January), pp. 3–4.

Johnson, Vida T. and Graham Petrie (1994) *The Films of Andrei Tarkovsky: A Visual Fugue*. Bloomington, IN: Indiana University Press.

Johnson, Vida and Graham Petrie (2003) 'Ethical Exploration', *Sight and Sound*, vol. 13, no. 2 (February), pp. 17–18.

Jordan, Neil (2003) 'Double Down', Interview by Jamie Russell, *Sight and Sound*, vol. 13, no. 10 (October), p. 78.

Jowett, Garth (1976) *Film: The Democratic Art*. Boston: Little, Brown.

Kael, Pauline (1980) 'Master Spy, Master Seducer', *The New Yorker*, August 4, pp. 68–71.

Kael, Pauline (1987) *Taking It All In*. London: Arena.

Kapsis, Robert E. (1992) *Hitchcock: The Making of a Reputation*. Chicago: University of Chicago Press.

Kehr, Dave (1984) 'Hitch's Riddle', *Film Comment*, vol. 20, no. 3 (May–June), pp. 9–18.

Keller, Alexandra (1999) ' "Size Does Matter": Notes on *Titanic* and James Cameron as Blockbuster Auteur', in Kevin S. Sandler and Gaylyn Studlar (eds), *Titanic: Anatomy of a Blockbuster*. New Brunswick, NJ: Rutgers University Press, pp. 132–54.

Kermode, Mark (2003) 'What a Carve Up!', *Sight and Sound*, vol. 13, no. 12 (December), pp. 12–16.

Kerr, Paul (1983) 'My Name Is Joseph H. Lewis', *Screen*, vol. 24, no. 4–5 (July–October), pp. 48–66.

Kinder, Marsha (1974) 'The Return of the Outlaw Couple', *Film Quarterly*, vol. 27, no. 4, pp. 2–10.

Kitses, Jim (1996) *Gun Crazy*. London: British Film Institute.

Kline, T. Jefferson (1992) *Screening the Text: Intertextuality in New Wave French Cinema*. Baltimore, MD: Johns Hopkins University Press.

Klinger, Barbara (1989) 'Digressions at the Cinema: Reception and Mass Culture', *Cinema Journal*, vol. 28, no. 4, pp. 3–19.

Koehler, Robert (2002) 'Rev. of *Rollerball*', *Variety*, 11–17 February, p. 41.

Koehler, Robert (2003) 'Jazzy *Job* Works as Classy Caper', *Variety*, 2–8 June, p. 42.

Kolker, Robert P. (1998) 'Algebraic Figures: Recalculating the Hitchcock Formula', in Horton and McDougal (eds), *Play It Again, Sam*, pp. 34–51.

Krohn, Bill (2000) *Hitchcock at Work*. London: Phaidon.

Krutnik, Frank (1982) 'Desire, Transgression and James M. Cain', *Screen*, vol. 23, no. 1 (May–June), pp. 31–44.

Lafferty, William (1990) 'Feature Films on Prime-Time Television', in Tino Balio (ed.), *Hollywood in the Age of Television*. Boston: Unwin Hyman, pp. 235–56.

Leitch, Thomas M. (1990) 'Twice-Told Tales: The Rhetoric of the Remake', *Literature/Film Quarterly*, vol. 18, no. 3, pp. 138–49; revised and rpt. as 'Twice-Told Tales: Disavowal and the Rhetoric of the Remake', in Forrest and Koos (eds), *Dead Ringers*, pp. 37–62.

Levy, Shawn (2002) 'Nice'n'Easy', *Sight and Sound*, vol. 12, no. 2 (February), pp. 14–16.

Lor. (1987) 'Rev. of *No Way Out*', *Variety*, 12 August, p. 12.

Lor. (1988) 'Rev. of *D.O.A.*', *Variety*, 16 March, p. 14.

Lowenstein, Adam (2004) 'The Master, The Maniac, and *Frenzy*', in Richard Allen and Sam Ishii-Gonzàles (eds), *Hitchcock: Past and Future*. London: Routledge, pp. 179–92.

Lubin, David M. (1999) *Titanic*. London: British Film Institute.

McCarthy, Phillip (2000) 'Where Angels Don't Fear to Tread', *The Sunday Age*, 19 November, Review, p. 7.

McCarthy, Todd (2001) 'Breezy *Ocean's* Could Make Splash in B.O. Pool', *Variety*, 3–9 December, p. 33.

McCarthy, Todd (2001) 'Fox Wages Gorilla Warfare on B.O. with *Apes* Redo', *Variety*, 30 July–5 August, p. 17.

McCarthy, Todd (2001) 'Rev. of *Vanilla Sky*', *Variety*, 10–16 December, p. 32.

McCarthy, Todd (2002) 'Clooney's Star Shines in Soderbergh *Solaris*', *Variety*, 25 November–1 December, p. 22.

McCarthy, Todd (2002) 'Lyne's Cool *Unfaithful* May Warm Up Fox's B.O.', *Variety*, 6–12 May, p. 41.

McCarthy, Todd (2002) 'Remake of Japan Horror Pic Sounds a Tinny *Ring*', *Variety*, 7–13 October, p. 21.

McCarthy, Todd (2002) 'Stylish *Charade* Redo Pushes the *Truth*', *Variety*, 23 October–3 November, p. 31.

McCarthy, Todd (2002) '*Time Machine* Hits Snag in Distant Future', *Variety* 11–17 March, p. 31.

McDougal, Stuart Y. (1998) 'The Director Who Knew Too Much: Hitchcock Remakes Himself', in Horton and McDougal (eds), *Play It Again, Sam*, pp. 52–69.

McElwee, John P. (1989) 'Theatrical Re-issues, part 1', *Films in Review*, December, pp. 593–6.

McElwee, John P. (1990) 'Theatrical Re-issues, part 2', *Films in Review*, January–February, pp. 21–5.

McHoul, Alec and Tom O'Regan (1992) 'Towards a Paralogics of Textual Technologies: Batman, Glasnost and Relativism in Cultural Studies', *Southern Review*, vol. 25, no. 1, pp. 5–26.

Macksey, Richard (1997) 'Foreword', in Gérard Genette, *Paratexts: Thresholds of Interpretation*, trans. Jane E. Lewin. Cambridge: Cambridge University Press, pp. xi–xxii.

McNeil, Alex (1996) *Total Television: The Comprehensive Guide to Programming from 1948 to the Present*, 4th edn. Harmondsworth: Penguin.

Maddox, Garry (2003) 'Television a Tomb with a View for Lazy Hollywood Producers', *The Age*, 25 October, n.p.

'Make Mine a Double' (1990) *National Film Theatre Programme*, February, pp. 26–7.

'Make Mine a Double' (1990) *National Film Theatre Programme*, March, pp. 30–1.

Marc, David (1989) *Comic Visions: Television Comedy and American Culture*. Boston: Unwin Hyman.

Marc, David (1994) 'Sibling Rivalry', *Sight and Sound*, vol. 4, no. 7 (July), pp. 6–9.

Marc, David (1996) *Demographic Vistas: Television in American Culture*, rev. edn. Philadelphia: University of Pennsylvania Press.

Marc, David and Robert J. Thompson (1992) *Prime Time, Prime Movers*. Boston: Little, Brown.

Marie, Michel (2000) ' "It Really Makes You Sick!": Jean-Luc Godard's *A bout de souffle*', in Susan Hayward and Ginette Vincendeau (eds), *French Film: Texts and Contexts*. London: Routledge, pp. 158–73.

Marie, Michel (2003) *The French New Wave: An Artistic School*, trans. Richard Neupert. London: Blackwell.

Martin, Adrian (1997) 'Violently Happy: *Gun Crazy*', *Metro*, no. 109, pp. 57–8.

Martin, Adrian (1999) 'Norman's not Stormin', *The Age*, 28 January, Living Arts, p. 20.

Martin, Adrian (2003) 'Soderbergh's Planet Casts Psychic Spell', *The Age*, 27 February, p. 5.

Martin, Richard (1997) *Mean Streets and Raging Bulls: The Legacy of Film Noir in Contemporary American Cinema*. Lanham, MD: Scarecrow.

Maslin, Janet (1998) 'hanks&ryan@romance.com', *New York Times*, 18 December, p. E.1:1.

Mazdon, Lucy (2000) *Encore Hollywood: Remaking French Cinema*. London: British Film Institute.

Medhurst, Andy (2001) 'Rev. of *Charlie's Angels*', *Sight and Sound*, vol. 11, no. 1 (January), pp. 43–4.

Meehan, Eileen R. (1991) ' "Holy Commodity Fetish, Batman!": The Political Economy of a Commercial Intertext', in Roberta E. Pearson and William

Uricchio (eds), *The Many Lives of Batman: Critical Approaches to a Superhero and his Media*. London: British Film Institute, pp. 47–65.

Meisel, Myron (1975) 'Joseph H. Lewis: Tourist in the Asylum', in Todd McCarthy and Charles Flynn (eds), *Kings of the Bs: Working Within the Hollywood System*. New York: E. P. Dutton, pp. 80–103.

Michaels, Lloyd (1998) '*Nosferatu*, or the Phantom of the Cinema', in Horton and McDougal (eds), *Play It Again, Sam*, pp. 238–49.

Miller, Mark Crispin (1990) 'Hollywood: The Ad', *Atlantic Monthly*, April, pp. 59–62.

Milne, Tom (1981) 'Rev. of *The Postman Always Rings Twice* [1946]', *Monthly Film Bulletin*, vol. 48, no. 568 (May), pp. 100–1.

Milne, Tom (1983) 'Rev. of *Psycho II*', *Monthly Film Bulletin*, vol. 50, no. 596 (September), pp. 245–6.

Milne, Tom (1989) 'Rev. of *D.O.A.*', *Monthly Film Bulletin*, vol. 56, no. 662 (March), pp. 77–8.

Milne, Tom and Jean Narboni (eds) (1972) *Godard on Godard*, trans. Tom Milne. London: Secker & Warburg.

Mitchell, Elvis (2001) 'For the New Rat Pack. It's a Ring-a-Ding Thing', *New York Times*, 7 December, p. E.1:1.

Mogilevich, Mariana (2002) 'Charlie's Pussycats', *Film Quarterly*, vol. 55, no. 3, pp. 38–44.

Morris, Meaghan (1988) 'Indigestion: A Rhetoric of Reviewing', in *The Pirate's Fiancée: Feminism, Reading, Postmodernism*. London: Verso, pp. 105–21.

Mulvey, Laura (1977–78) 'Notes on Sirk and Melodrama', *Movie*, no. 25 (Winter), pp. 53–6.

Mulvey, Laura (2001) '*All That Heaven Allows*', Criterion Collection DVD Liner Notes, http://www.criterionco.com/asp/release.asp?id=95&eid=103&section=essay.

Mulvey, Laura (2003) 'Rev. of *Far From Heaven*', *Sight and Sound*, vol. 13, no. 3 (March), pp. 40–1.

Mulvey, Laura (2004) 'Death Drives', in Richard Allen and Sam Ishii-Gonzàles (eds), *Hitchcock: Past and Future*. London: Routledge, pp. 231–42.

Murray, Chris (2001) 'Let's Do It Again', *Empire*, January–February, pp. 64–8.

Musser, Charles (1990) *The Emergence of Cinema: The American Screen to 1907*, History of the American Cinema vol. 1. Berkeley, CA: University of California Press.

Musser, Charles (1991) *Before the Nickelodeon: Edwin S. Porter and the Edison Manufacturing Company*. Berkeley, CA: University of California Press.

Naremore, James (1973) *Filmguide to Psycho*. Bloomington, IN: Indiana University Press.

Naremore, James (1990) 'Authorship and the Cultural Politics of Film Criticism', *Film Quarterly*, vol. 44, no. 1, pp. 14–23.

Naremore, James (1998) *More Than Night: Film Noir in Its Contexts*. Berkeley, CA: University of California Press.

Naremore, James (1999–2000) 'Remaking *Psycho*', *Hitchcock Annual*, pp. 3–12.

Naremore, James (ed.) (2000) *Film Adaptation*. London: Athlone.

Naremore, James (2000) 'Introduction: Film and the Reign of Adaptation', in Naremore (ed.), *Film Adaptation*, pp. 1–16.

Neale, Steve (1990) 'Questions of Genre', *Screen*, vol. 31, no. 1, pp. 45–66.

Neale, Steve (2000) *Genre and Hollywood*. London: Routledge.

Nelson, Jenny L. (1990) 'The Dislocation of Time: A Phenomenology of Television Reruns', *Quarterly Review of Film and Video*, vol. 12, no. 3, pp. 79–92.

Newman, David and Robert Benton (1972) 'Lightning in a Bottle', in Sandra Wake and Nicola Hayden (eds), *The Bonnie & Clyde Book*. New York: Simon & Schuster, pp. 13–30.

Newman, Kim (1984) 'Rev. of *The Big Chill*', *Monthly Film Bulletin*, vol. 51, no. 601 (February), pp. 41–2.

Newman, Kim (1992) 'Rev. of *The Addams Family*', *Sight and Sound*, vol. 1, no. 9 (January), pp. 36–7.

Newman, Kim (1996) 'Rev. of *Flipper*', *Sight and Sound*, vol. 6, no. 9 (September), pp. 43–4.

Newman, Kim (1996) 'Rev. of *Last Man Standing*', *Sight and Sound*, vol. 6, no. 11 (November), pp. 52–3.

Newman, Kim (1998) 'Rev. of *The Avengers*', *Sight and Sound*, vol. 8, no. 10 (October), pp. 38–9.

Newman, Kim (2002) 'Rev. of *Just Visiting*', *Sight and Sound*, vol. 12, no. 3 (March), pp. 46–7.

Nogueira, Rui (ed.) (1971) *Melville*. London: Secker & Warburg.

Nowlan, Robert A. and Gwendoline Wright Nowlan (1989) *Cinema Sequels and Remakes, 1903–1987*. Jefferson, NC: McFarland.

O'Hehir, Andrew (1998) 'Gleaning the Tube', *Sight and Sound*, vol. 8, no. 8 (August), pp. 16–19.

O'Hehir, Andrew (2001) 'Gorilla Warfare', *Sight and Sound*, vol. 11, no. 9 (September), pp. 12–15.

O'Hehir, Andrew (2002) 'Rev. of *The Truth About Charlie*', *Salon.com*, http://www.salon.com/ent/movies/review/2002/10/25/truth_charlie/.

O'Regan, Tom (1996) 'Negotiating Cultural Transfers', in *Australian National Cinema*. London: Routledge, pp. 213–31.

O'Sullivan, Charlotte (1998) 'Rev. of *Dr. Dolittle*', *Sight and Sound*, vol. 8, no. 8 (August), pp. 37–8.

Paatsch, Leigh (2001) 'A-Grade Apes', *Herald Sun*, 9 August, p. 38.

Patterson, John (2003) 'Second Time Lucky', *The Age*, 24 February, The Culture, p. 6.

Penn, Arthur (1999) 'Song of the Open Road', *Sight and Sound*, vol. 9, no. 8 (August), pp. 58–9.

Perkin, Corrie (2000) 'Charlie Who?', *The Sunday Age*, 24 December, Review, p. 18.

Phillips, Mark and Frank Garcia (2001) 'The Original Series', *Cinefantastique*, vol. 33, no. 4 (August), pp. 34–7.

Plesset, Ross (2001) 'Unfilmed Scripts', *Cinefantastique*, vol. 33, no. 4 (August), pp. 26–7.

Porfirio, Robert G. (1985) 'Whatever Happened to the *Film Noir*?: *The Postman Always Rings Twice* (1946–1981)', *Literature/Film Quarterly*, vol. 13, no. 2, pp. 102–11.

Propp, Vladimir [1928] (1968) *Morphology of the Folktale*. Austin, TX: University of Texas Press.

'*Psycho* Boycott, The' (1998) *24 frames per second*, http://www.24framesper second.com/reactions/films_p/psychoboycott.html.

'*Psycho*, Official Universal Pictures web-site' (1998) http://www.psychomovie. com/.

'*Psycho*: Saving a Classic' (1998) http://members.aol.com/montag17/ psycho. html.

Pulleine, Tom (1980) 'Rev. of *Friday the 13th*', *Monthly Film Bulletin*, vol. 47, no. 558 (July), p. 132.

Pulleine, Tom (1981) 'Rev. of *Friday the 13th part 2*', *Monthly Film Bulletin*, vol. 48, no. 570 (July), p. 138.

Pulleine, Tom (1981) 'Stahl into Sirk', *Monthly Film Bulletin*, vol. 48, no. 574 (November), p. 236.

Pulleine, Tom (1984) 'Rev. of *Against All Odds*', *Monthly Film Bulletin*, vol. 51, no. 605 (June), p. 171.

'Puppet Love' (1998) *Sight and Sound*, vol. 8, no. 1 (January), p. 32.

Ray, Robert B. (1985) *A Certain Tendency of the Hollywood Cinema, 1930–1980*. Princeton, NJ: Princeton University Press.

Ray, Robert B. (2001) 'Film and Literature', in *How a Film Theory Got Lost and Other Mysteries in Cultural Studies*. Bloomington, IN: Indiana University Press, pp. 120–31.

Rebello, Stephen (1990) *Alfred Hitchcock and the Making of* Psycho. New York: Dembner.

Reimer, Robert C. (1996) 'Comparison of *All That Heaven Allows* and *Ali: Fear Eats the Soul*; Or, How Hollywood's New England Dropouts Became Germany's Marginalised Other', *Literature/Film Quarterly*, vol. 24, no. 3, pp. 281–7.

Remembrance Cinema Program (2003) Australian Centre for the Moving Image, 11 April–20 July.

Romney, Jonathan (2003) 'Future Soul', *Sight and Sound*, vol. 13, no. 2 (February), pp. 14–17.

Rosenbaum, Jonathan (1976) 'Rev. of *Obsession*', *Monthly Film Bulletin*, vol. 43, no. 513 (October), p. 217.

Rosenbaum, Jonathan (1998) 'Hack Job', *Chicago Reader*, http:// www. chireader.com/movies/archives/1998/1298/12258.html.

Rosenbaum, Jonathan (2000) 'International Sampler', *Chicago Reader*, http:// www.chireader.com/movies/archives/2000/0300/000317.html.

Ross, Kristin (1995) *Fast Cars, Clean Bodies: Decolonization and the Reordering of French Culture*. Cambridge, MA: MIT Press.

Roth, Marty (2000) 'Twice Two: *The Fly* and *Invasion of the Body Snatchers*', *Discourse*, vol. 22, no. 1, pp. 103–16; rpt. in Forrest and Koos (eds), *Dead Ringers*, pp. 224–41.

Rothman, William (1982) *Hitchcock – The Murderous Gaze*. Cambridge, MA: Harvard University Press.

Rothman, William (1999) 'Some Thoughts on Hitchcock's Authorship', in Richard Allen and Sam Ishii-Gonzalès (eds), *Alfred Hitchcock: Centenary Essays*. London: British Film Institute, pp. 29–42.

Royoux, Jean-Christophe (1999) 'Remaking Cinema', in Marente Bloemheuvel and Jaap Guldemond (eds), *Cinéma, Cinéma: Contemporary Art and the Cinematic Experience*, Rotterdam: Stedelijk Van Abbemuseum, Eindhoven, and Nai Publishers, pp. 21–7.

Russo, Joe and Larry Landsman (1986) '*Planet of the Apes* Revisited', *Starlog*, no. 105 (April), pp. 42–7.

Sarris, Andrew (1980) 'Rev. of *Dressed to Kill*', *Village Voice*, 22–29 July, pp. 42 and 44.

Sayles, John (1996) 'Walking Alone', Interview by Leslie Felperin, *Sight and Sound*, vol. 6, no. 9 (September), pp. 22–4.

Sayles, John and Gavin Smith (1998) *Sayles on Sayles*, London: Faber & Faber.

Schatz, Thomas (1993) 'The New Hollywood', in Jim Collins, Hilary Radner and Ava Preacher Collins (eds), *Film Theory Goes to the Movies*. London: Routledge, pp. 8–36.

Schatz, Thomas (1997) *Boom and Bust: The American Cinema in the 1940s*, History of the American Cinema Vol. 6. New York: Charles Scribner's Sons.

Schatz, Thomas (1997) 'The Return of the Hollywood Studio System', in Patricia Aufderheide et al., *Conglomerates and the Media*. New York: New Press, pp. 73–106.

Schembri, Jim (2001) 'Embrace the Big, Bad, Dopey Ape', *The Age*, 10 August, EG, p. 9.

Schickel, Richard (1992) *Double Indemnity*. London: British Film Institute.

'*The Searchers*: A Family Tree' (1981) *National Film Theatre Programme*, November–December, pp. 2–6.

Schneider, Steven Jay (2000) 'A Tale of Two *Psychos*', *Senses of Cinema*, no. 10, http://www.sensesofcinema.com/contents/00/10/psychos.html.

Sconce, Jeffrey (1995) ' "Trashing" the Academy: Taste, Excess, and an Emerging Politics of Cinematic Style', *Screen*, vol. 36, no. 4, pp. 371–93.

Sennett, Ted (1971) *Warner Brothers Presents*. New York: Castle.

Sesonske, Alexander (1999) '*Yojimbo*', Criterion Collection DVD Liner Notes, http://www.criterionco.com/asp/release.asp?id=52&eid=68&section=essay.

Silberg, Jon (2002) 'A Scandal in Suburbia', *American Cinematographer*, vol. 83, no. 12, (December), pp. 54–65.

Silver, Alain and Elizabeth Ward (eds) (1992) *Film Noir: An Encyclopaedic Reference to the American Style*, 3rd edn. Woodstock, NY: Overlook.

Silverman, Stephen M. (1978) 'Hollywood Cloning: Sequels, Prequels, Remakes, and Spin-Offs', *American Film*, vol. 3, no. 9 (July–August), pp. 24–30.

Simon, Ronald (1986) 'The Eternal Rerun: Oldies but Goodies', *Television Quarterly*, vol. 22, no. 1, pp. 51–8.

Simonet, Thomas (1987) 'Conglomerates and Content: Remakes, Sequels, and Series in The New Hollywood', in Bruce A. Austin (ed.), *Current Research in Film: Audiences, Economics, and Law*, Vol. 3. Norwood, NJ: Ablex, pp. 154–62.

Smith, Gavin (1994) ' "When You Know You're in Good Hands" ', *Film Comment*, vol. 30, no. 4 (July–August), pp. 32–43.

Smith, Gavin (2002) 'Dream Project', *Film Comment*, vol. 38, no. 6 (November–December), pp. 28–31.

Smith, Jack (1962–63) 'The Perfect Filmic Appositeness of Maria Montez', *Film Culture*, no. 27 (Winter), pp. 28–36.

Smith, Jim and J. Clive Matthews (2002) *Tim Burton*. London: Virgin.

Somigli, Luca (1998) 'The Superhero with a Thousand Faces: Visual Narrative on Paper and Film', in Horton and McDougal (eds), *Play It Again, Sam*, pp. 279–94.

Squiers, Carol (1985) 'Over Brian De Palma's Dead *Body Double*', *Art and Text*, no. 17, pp. 96–101.

Staiger, Janet (1983) 'Combination and Litigation: Structures of US Film Distribution, 1896–1917', *Cinema Journal*, vol. 23, no. 2, pp. 41–72.

Staiger, Janet (1985) 'The Hollywood Mode of Production to 1930', in David Bordwell, Janet Staiger and Kristin Thompson (eds), *The Classical Hollywood Cinema: Film Style and Mode of Production to 1960*. London: Routledge & Kegan Paul, pp. 85–153.

Staiger, Janet (1985) 'The Politics of Film Canons', *Cinema Journal*, vol. 24, no. 3, pp. 4–23.

Staiger, Janet (1986) 'Mass-produced Photoplays: Economic and Signifying Practices in the First Years of Hollywood', in Paul Kerr (ed.), *The Hollywood Film Industry: A Reader*. London: Routledge & Kegan Paul, pp. 97–117.

Staiger, Janet (1992) 'Rethinking "Primitive" Cinema: Intertextuality, the Middle-Class Audience, and Reception Studies', in *Interpreting Films: Studies in the Historical Reception of American Cinema*. Princeton, NJ: Princeton University Press, pp. 101–23.

Stam, Robert (1999) *Film Theory: An Introduction*. Oxford: Blackwell.

Stam, Robert (2000) 'Beyond Fidelity: The Dialogics of Adaptation', in Naremore (ed.), *Film Adaptation*, pp. 54–76.

Stern, Lesley (1995) *The Scorsese Connection*. London: British Film Institute.

Stern, Lesley (2000) '*Emma* in Los Angeles: Remaking the Book and the City', in Naremore (ed.), *Film Adaptation*, pp. 221–38.

Stern, Lesley (2000) 'Rev. of *Play It Again, Sam*', *Modernism/Modernity*, vol. 7, no. 1, http://muse.jhu.edu/ journals/modernism-modernity/v007/ 7.1stern. html.

Strick, Philip (1991) 'Rev. of *A Kiss Before Dying*', *Sight and Sound*, vol. 1, no. 2 (June), p. 50.

Strick, Philip (2003) 'Rev. of *Solaris*', *Sight and Sound*, vol. 13, no. 3 (March), pp. 54–5.

Sutton, Paul (1999) 'Remaking the Remake: *Irma Vep* (Assayas, 1996)', in Phil Powrie (ed.), *French Cinema in the 1990s: Continuity and Difference*. Oxford: Oxford University Press, pp. 69–80.

Tarantino, Michael (1999) ' "How He Does It" (1976) Or "The Case of the Missing Gloves" (1999)', in Kerry Brougher et al. (eds), *Notorious: Alfred Hitchcock and Contemporary Art*. Oxford: Museum of Modern Art, pp. 21–33.

Tarantino, Quentin (1994) 'Blood Lust, Snicker Snicker in Wide Screen', Interview by Dennis Hopper, *Grand Street*, no. 49, pp. 10–22.

Tarantino, Quentin (2003) 'Turning on a Dime', Interview by Mark Olsen, *Sight and Sound*, vol. 13, no. 10 (October), pp. 12–15.

Taubin, Amy (1996) 'Douglas Gordon', in Philip Dodd with Ian Christie (eds), *Spellbound: Art and Film*. London: Hayward Gallery and British Film Institute, pp. 68–75.

Taubin, Amy (2002) 'In Every Dream Home', *Film Comment*, vol. 38, no. 5 (September–October), pp. 22–6.

Taubin, Amy (2002) 'Steven Soderbergh Follows Andrei Tarkovsky into Space for a Walk with Love and Death', *Film Comment*, vol. 38, no. 6 (November–December), p. 22.

Thompson, Frank (1998) 'Songe de Titanic', *Film Comment*, vol. 34, no. 1, pp. 64–7.

Thomson, David (1981) 'Raising Cain', *Film Comment*, vol. 17, no. 2 (March–April), pp. 25–32.

Treherne, John (1984) *The Strange History of Bonnie and Clyde*. London: Jonathan Cape.

Tulloch, Lee (2000) 'Flipping Out Over Angels Remake', *The Age*, 17 May, Today, p. 1.

Ungari, Enzo (1987) *Bertolucci by Bertolucci*, trans. Donald Ranvaud. London: Plexus.

Variety Movie Guide (1998) ed. Derek Elley. London: Hamlyn.

Vieira, João Luiz and Robert Stam (1990) 'Parody and Marginality: The Case of Brazilian Cinema', in Manuel Alvarado and John O. Thompson (eds), *The Media Reader*. London: British Film Institute, pp. 82–104.

Vincendeau, Ginette (1993) 'Hijacked', *Sight and Sound*, vol. 3, no. 7 (July), pp. 23–5.

Vincendeau, Ginette (2003) 'Gamblers Anonymous', *Sight and Sound*, vol. 13, no. 3 (March), pp. 22–4.

Vincendeau, Ginette (2003) *Jean-Pierre Melville: 'An American in Paris'*. London: British Film Institute.

Wees, William C. (1993) *Recycled Images: The Art and Politics of Found Footage Films*. New York: Anthology Film Archives.

Whelehan, Imelda (1999) 'Adaptations: The Contemporary Dilemmas', in Deborah Cartmell and Imelda Whelehan (eds), *Adaptations: From Text to Screen, Screen to Text*. London: Routledge, pp. 3–19.

Willemen, Paul (1994) 'Through the Glass Darkly: Cinephilia Reconsidered [interview by Noel King]', in Paul Willemen, *Looks and Frictions: Essays in Cultural Studies and Film Theory*. London: British Film Institute, pp. 223–57.

Williams, Alan (2000) '*Pierrot* in Context', in David Wills (ed.), *Jean-Luc Godard's* Pierrot le fou. Cambridge: Cambridge University Press, pp. 43–63.

Williams, Phil (1994) 'The Evolution of the Television Rerun', *Journal of Popular Film and Television*, vol. 24, no. 4 (Winter), pp. 162–75.

Willis, Sharon (1993–94) 'The Fathers Watch the Boys' Room', *Camera Obscura*, no. 32, pp. 40–73.

Willis, Sharon (2003) 'The Politics of Disappointment: Todd Haynes Rewrites Douglas Sirk', *Camera Obscura*, vol. 18, no. 2, pp. 130–75.

Wills, David (1998) 'The French Remark: *Breathless* and Cinematic Citationality', in Horton and McDougal (eds), *Play It Again, Sam*, pp. 147–61.

Winogura, Dale (1972) 'Dialogues on Apes, Apes, and More Apes', *Cinefantastique*, vol. 2, no. 2 (Summer), pp. 16–37.

Wollen, Peter (2002) 'The Canon', in *Paris Hollywood: Writings on Film*. London: Verso, pp. 216–32.

Woods, Paul A. (2001) 'Origins of the Species', in Paul A. Woods (ed.), *The Planet of the Apes Chronicles*. London: Plexus, pp. 15–20.

Woods, Paul A. (2001) 'The Planet Goes Ape', in Paul A. Woods (ed.), *The Planet of the Apes Chronicles*. London: Plexus, pp. 123–36.

Worton, Michael and Judith Still (1990) 'Introduction', in Michael Worton and Judith Still (eds), *Intertextuality: Theories and Practices*. Manchester: Manchester University Press, pp. 1–44.

Wrathall, John (2002) 'Rev. of *Insomnia*', *Sight and Sound*, vol. 12, no. 9 (September), pp. 62–4.

Wyatt, Justin (1994) *High Concept: Movies and Marketing in Hollywood*. Austin, TX: University of Texas Press.

Wyatt, Justin and Katherine Vlesmas (1999) 'The Drama of Recoupment: On the Mass Media Negotiation of *Titanic*', in Kevin S. Sandler and Gaylyn Studlar (eds), *Titanic: Anatomy of a Blockbuster*. New Brunswick, NJ: Rutgers University Press, pp. 29–45.

Yakir, Dan (1981) ' "The Postman" Rings Six Times', *Film Comment*, vol. 17, no. 2 (March–April), pp. 18–20.

Yakir, Dan (1981) 'The Postman's Words', *Film Comment*, vol. 17, no. 2 (March–April), pp. 21–4.

Index